# CHRIST'S VICTORY
# OVER EVIL

# CHRIST'S VICTORY OVER EVIL

## Biblical theology and pastoral ministry

### Edited by Peter G. Bolt

APOLLOS (an imprint of Inter-Varsity Press)
*Norton Street, Nottingham NG7 3HR, England*
*Email: ivp@ivpbooks.com*
*Website: www.ivpbooks.com*

*First published 2009*

**British Library Cataloguing in Publication Data**
A catalogue record for this book is available from the British Library.

UK ISBN: 978-1-84474-379-7

Set in Monotype Garamond 11/13pt
Typeset in Great Britain by Servis Filmsetting Ltd, Stockport, Cheshire
Printed and bound in Great Britain by Ashford Colour Press Ltd, Gosport,
Hampshire

# CONTENTS

# CONTRIBUTORS

**Greg Anderson** is the Head of the Department of Mission at Moore College. He previously worked at Nungalinya College, Darwin, and in the Diocese of The Northern Territory in Aboriginal church leader training.

**Peter G. Bolt** is the Head of New Testament and Greek, Moore College, Sydney. He has recently published *Living with the Underworld* (2007). His previous publications include *Jesus' Defeat of Death: Persuading Mark's Early Readers* (2003) and *The Cross from a Distance: Atonement in Mark's Gospel* (2005). He has also edited (with Mark Thompson) *The Gospel to the Nations* (2000) and *The Selected Works of Donald Robinson* (2008), and (with Mark Thompson and Robert Tong) *The Faith Once for All Delivered* (2005) and *The Lord's Supper in Human Hands* (2008).

**Constantine R. Campbell** teaches Greek and New Testament at Moore College, Sydney. He is the author of *Verbal Aspect, the Indicative Mood, and Narrative: Soundings in the Greek of the New Testament* (2007); *Verbal Aspect and Non-Indicative Moods: Further Soundings in the Greek of the New Testament* (2008); *Not Ashamed: 2 Timothy* (2008); *Basics of Verbal Aspect in Biblical Greek* (2008). He is currently researching the theme of union with Christ in the theology of Paul.

**Matthew Jensen** is researching the First Epistle of John towards a PhD at the University of Sydney. He serves as the Secretary

of the United Evangelistic Council of NSW and attends Christ
Church St George.

**Jonathan Lilley**, his wife Melissa and three children live in Nowra,
where he is the assistant minister at All Saints Anglican Church
Nowra. Jonathan heads the ministry to indigenous people in the area.
He is a descendant of the Worim people of the Port Stephens area.

**Tony Payne** has been in charge of publishing at Matthias Media
since its inception in 1988. He is the editor of *The Briefing* and the
author or co-author of numerous Bible studies and books, including *Guidance and the Voice of God* (2nd ed., 1997), *Islam in our Backyard*
(2002) and *Fatherhood: What it Is and what it's for* (2004). Tony lives
with his wife Alison and their five children in Randwick, NSW.

**Willis (Bill) H. Salier** teaches in the New Testament Department
at Moore College, where he also serves as Vice Principal. He has
published *The Rhetorical Impact of the* semeia *in the Gospel of John*
(2004). His research interests continue in the Johannine corpus of
the New Testament, and also include teaching and learning in the
theological context.

**Mark D. Thompson** lectures in Theology at Moore College,
Sydney, where he also heads the Theology Department and serves
as Academic Dean. He has published *Saving the Heart: What Is an
Evangelical?* (1995); *A Sure Ground on which to Stand: The Relation of
Authority and Interpretative Method in Luther's Approach to Scripture*
(2004); *A Clear and Present Word: The Clarity of Scripture in a Confused
World* (2006). He has also edited (with Peter Bolt) *The Gospel to the
Nations* (2000) and *The Selected Works of Donald Robinson* (2008), and
(with Peter Bolt and Robert Tong) *The Faith Once for All Delivered*
(2005) and *The Lord's Supper in Human Hands* (2008).

**Donald S. West** is the Principal of Trinity Theological College,
Perth, where he teaches Biblical Theology, New and Old Testament
exegesis, and Christian Leadership. He has recently completed a
PhD on New Testament petitionary prayer.

# INTRODUCTION

**Peter G. Bolt**

> The world in which we live is the place where Jesus Christ rose from the dead.
>
> (Karl Barth, *A Letter to Great Britain from Switzerland*)

The Lord Jesus Christ has already won the victory. This is the objective reality that needs to inform our thought about every aspect of human life in this world. Especially as we contemplate the abiding presence of demonic evil in our world (whether in the language of 'evil' that has re-emerged into our public discourse, or in the threat of evil we feel in our personal experience), there is another word that constantly whispers in our ears the greatest victory this world has ever seen and will ever see: 'Christ is risen!'

It is not easy to hear that word. The presence of evil itself, or our fear of the demonic, can stifle the gospel whisper. From the beginning of the gospel mission this quiet word has seemed weak and powerless to a world confronted by evil powers, which raise both fear and fascination. And yet it is through this word of weakness (which speaks of the greatest victory of all time) that God works his mighty power to save.

The relationship between Christians and the forces of evil has been discussed from a variety of perspectives within the history of Christian thought, and recent influential mission studies and pastoral practices have proved to be a stimulus to further discussion. In September 2008 the Moore College School of Theology provided a multi-disciplined approach to 'Christ's Victory over the Powers', and the various contributions made at that time are now published in this volume.

The chapters in this volume seek to listen below the present clamour drawing attention to the demonic, in order to hear the whisper of the gospel message more clearly, and to explore the power it promises – even in the face of the demonic.

Tony Payne sets the scene for this exploration by outlining the history of the present fascination with demons found among contemporary 'expansive charismatic' circles. The very presence of the devil and demons in this world already presents people with enough clamour to distract from hearing the gospel word, but the rhetoric emanating from these circles has substantially increased its volume.

Peter Bolt then turns to the Scriptures. What does God's Word say about demons, and what does God's Word *refrain* from saying? A truly biblical theology will not only uphold what is clearly taught in God's Word, but will also be instructed by the Bible's own restraint. We can know the truth about the demonic only from what the Bible says, but what happens if it does not seem to say enough? And, more importantly, even when it does touch on the evil powers, how does this teaching serve the central message of the Scriptures, namely that Christ came to destroy the works of the devil by dealing decisively with our sin when he died on the cross?

Much discussion about the demonic draws upon the material found in the first three Gospels, recounting Jesus' encounters with the demonized. But it is instructive to notice that the fourth Gospel has no 'exorcisms' at all. Bill Salier examines this interesting 'absence', and shows how John nevertheless has a strong interest in the defeat of the devil, and that this centres around the climactic events of Jesus' life. Matthew Jensen takes this discussion further into the epistle of John, where this theme continues. Jesus' glorification accomplished the victory over the devil's works.

Jesus' death accomplished the justification of the ungodly. Mark Thompson exposes this central truth of the gospel, and shows how the assurance of being justified also includes the assurance that Christ has already defeated the evil powers and removed the devil's hold over Christ's people. Con Campbell continues this note of assurance by meditating upon the believer's present position 'in Christ', where the victory of Christ is already experienced. Even if there is a present struggle in which we are engaged, this does not diminish the safe place in which we stand.

Many Westerners may give little thought to the evil powers, but other cultures live with a greater awareness of the presence of evil. Greg Anderson and Jonathan Lilley share the fruit of their research conducted among indigenous Australians. What comfort does the quiet word of Christ's victory have, when the evil powers are much more a part of a person's culture?

The victory of Christ has already been accomplished, but the world in which we live is still given over to the devil, and the evil powers still threaten human existence. Don West urges Christians to pray, especially in response to the promises attached to prayer. As we struggle to live for Christ in this world, Christ's victory is there to be grasped – if only we would ask.

Christian ministry is gospel ministry: the quiet word of Jesus' cross, the confession that Christ is risen, applied to real human beings in the context of a disordered, suffering world. In the final chapter Peter Bolt and Don West draw out some implications of Christ's finished work in order to yield some principles of gospel ministry. The evil powers are operative, but there is no need to increase the clamour about them, nor is there any reason to fear. This is still the world in which Jesus Christ rose from the dead. That is the whisper that still needs to be heard.

# 1. A SHORT HISTORY OF DELIVERANCE

Tony Payne

## What is wrong with us?

### A perennial question

I want to begin to set the scene for this volume by briefly asking one of the oldest questions of all, *What is wrong with us?* Why do humans do evil? Why do we hurt and maim each other? Why do we embrace selfish and immoral behaviour, even when we know deep within ourselves that it is not good, and will only lead to harm? Why do we splinter into factions and squabble? Why do we engage in lewd and degrading acts that lead only to public disgrace? Why do our societies so easily disintegrate into dysfunction and terror?

The question could be posed a hundred ways, or by using a thousand examples. That there is something rotten lurking within humanity is almost universally acknowledged – but what is it? What is wrong with us and what is wrong with our world?

### The Christian answer

Christians have always answered this question by pointing to the multifaceted rebellion of this creation against its Creator. The

Christian view is that from the debacle of Genesis 3 onwards, humanity is deeply and individually culpable for its own evil, and yet is not alone in that culpability. We ourselves choose evil, and yet are tempted and led into evil by the serpent, and lead each other into evil as well. And so we have the classic formulation of the world, the flesh and the devil as that which directs, leads and nourishes the evil we find in ourselves and the world.

The gospel message, of course, is that Jesus has come to overthrow this evil troika – he has overcome the world, defeated the devil and his works, and died so that our flesh with all its desires may be crucified. Putting it this way, there seems little room for disagreement. But alas, this is not the only way to put it! When we press further to ask precisely how this victory of Jesus is won, what its effects are in the world now and to what extent and by what methods we may have freedom and victory over evil, we have lots of scope for difference of opinion, especially over the subject of how we account for the sin, wrongdoing and evil that continue to haunt Christians themselves.

But how are we as humanity to be delivered from evil? And how are Christians today delivered from evil?

### The expansives

In the past half century or so a version of the Christian answer to evil has arisen which gives a greatly expanded role to the devil and his demonic host.

Here is a brief extract that represents this answer:

> With all of us gathered around Stella, I touched her lightly on the head and said, 'In the name of Jesus Christ I take authority over any evil spirit tormenting this woman . . .'
>
> And that's as far as I got, for suddenly a harsh sardonic laugh came from her throat. I glanced at her face. She was glaring up at me through eyes narrowed to hate-filled slits, her lips curled in a mocking sneer.
>
> My heart began to hammer in my throat. I felt as if the evil thing staring at me out of Stella's eyes was measuring me in some way. Behind the sulfurous gaze I sensed a crafty intelligence. The lips parted.
>
> 'You're all a bunch of fools!'

My skin crawled. That was not Stella's voice. The smoldering eyes never left my face as it spoke again.

'This woman belongs to me.'

I was dumb with shock, hypnotized by those eyes.

'This is my house. I live here and none of you can cast me out.'

Summoning all my courage I tried to speak with assurance and authority.

'Demon, I command you to give me your name.'

Stella's face twisted even more grotesquely than before. 'Hate!'

Involuntarily I jumped backward. I knew what I should do. I should command that spirit to come out. But before I could collect myself the voice came again, sly, dripping with sarcasm.

'She says she loves him.'

'Loves who?' I asked the question automatically.

'You know who!' The voice was angry and petulant now. 'Him . . . Jesus!'

The word was spat out like a curse. 'But he can't have her, she's mine! She's always been mine!'

Suddenly I felt a tremendous indignation at the evil thing flaunting itself in Stella.

'You demon of hate,' I said, 'I charge you in the name of Jesus Christ to come out of this woman!'

To my astonishment both her arms shot straight up, the fingers of each hand curled like a claw, while a sound like the roar of a maddened animal came from her mouth. Just as suddenly she relaxed.[1]

This is not the script from a gothic horror film, nor even a scene from Frank Peretti's novel *This Present Darkness*. It is presented as a true story, taken from a book that shares the name of our school, *Deliver Us From Evil*, written by Don Basham and published in 1972.

This extract represents a major stream within charismatic Christianity that ascribes much of what is wrong with our world, and with Christians, to the work of the devil and his demonic host. Charismatic scholar Nigel Scotland has labelled this stream 'the expansives' – as having an expansive demonology – and briefly summarizes their world view like this:

---

1. Basham, *Deliver us from Evil*, 115–117.

the expansives live in a world which is ruled by an exceptionally big and powerful devil, who at times appears almost as an evil opposite equivalent to Jesus. The nations are believed to be ruled over by the prince of demons, and the skies and just about every human activity and relationship are infested by Satan's evil minions [. . .] Demons not only have unbelievers in their clutches, but cling to Christians and in many instances dwell within them. In some expansive circles, there is almost paranoia as believers have a strong foreboding that Satan is constantly attacking them and their situations. In order to protect themselves, therefore, such Christian people must constantly be on their guard and engage in 'spiritual warfare' by covering themselves with the blood, donning the whole armour of God, and utilizing a whole range of binding, rebuking and casting-out strategies.[2]

This stream within charismatic Christianity has become prominent only since the 1970s or so, and features well-known names like Derek Prince, Peter Wagner, Cindy Jacobs, John Wimber and Peter Horrobin (names we will return to in due course).

The expansive view of the place of Satan and demons is not the only stream within charismatic Christianity, nor was it much in evidence during the first seventy years or so of mainstream Pentecostalism. But it is now (as Scotland points out) very widespread, and the majority position within Pentecostal and charismatic Christianity. And as charismatic Christianity continues to grow, the deliverance ministry of 'the expansives' remains a source of challenge and perplexity for evangelical Christians as well.

The scene I wish to set is not so much a detailed description or analysis of the current state of 'expansive demonology', but an enquiry into its history and background. How did this historically novel answer to the problem of evil arise? What were its theological sources and antecedents? What was it in the background and development of Pentecostalism that eventually spawned this very expansive demonology, now so widespread?

Below will be a brief investigation that will wander down some historical byways that may not at first seem directly relevant. But

2. Scotland, 'Charismatic Devil', 88–89.

I hope that we will find in this short history of deliverance some reasons why evangelical Christians continue to find deliverance ministries both perplexing and attractive.

## The recovery of the full gospel

### *Sanctification*
#### *Wesley*

To understand modern Pentecostalism, and the rise of an expansive demonology, we need to tell the story of the recovery of the full gospel.

It begins in seventeenth-century Germany with the birth of the warm, inward heart religion known as Pietism. In reaction to the sterile Protestant scholasticism of the day, early Pietists like Spener and Francke emphasized the importance of personal conversion and regeneration, and the necessity of the Spirit's work in the life of the individual. The focus was on a personal 'experimental' religion. As Francke put it:

> To have a true sense of the gracious operations of the Holy Spirit in
> our souls, and know experimentally, that God of a Truth has erected his
> Kingdom in our Souls, which consists of Righteousness, Peace and Joy
> in the Holy Ghost.[3]

The pietists hit upon the then novel idea of holding small home groups for Bible discussion, and sought to promote among their followers an inward religion of the heart.

When a young Englishman named John Wesley had his heart strangely warmed at a pietist meeting in London in 1738, it was an experience that set the scene for generations of evangelical experience and teaching in Britain, America and Australia.

In the rationalist orthodoxy of his own time, Wesley saw an unengaged gentlemanly religion, lacking gospel reality, and any power for holiness and godliness. In its place Wesley promoted

---

3. Francke, *Faith in Christ*, 13, cited in D. Brown, *Understanding Pietism*, 102.

an experimental religion of the heart, a religion of regeneration and sanctification. He preached the freedom that guilty sinners could have from the devil's power through justification by faith alone. And he preached the changed life that unholy sinners could experience through the sanctifying work of the Spirit.

Wesley's view of sanctification is complex, and we do not have time to examine it in detail. However, in his *Plain Account of Christian Perfection* (1765) he reasserts his position that sanctification was not only a matter of striving for holiness, but a definitive crisis experience in which the believer claimed the sanctification that was rightfully his by faith. This 'entire sanctification' meant the doing away of the old nature, and a new experience of peace, joy and love for God, which made victory over sin in this life a reality.[4]

Rather like his Arminianism, Wesley's Christian perfectionism was nuanced. It involved process as well as the moment of crisis. And Wesley never linked his perfectionism with the baptism in the Spirit. His followers, however, were not so careful.

### Fletcher

Wesley's close colleague and designated successor, John Fletcher, identified the moment of entire sanctification with the biblical notion of the baptism in the Holy Spirit. This stemmed from his basically dispensational view of theological history – that there was a dispensation of the Father that looked forward to the manifestation of the Son; and then a dispensation of the Son opened by John the Baptist that looked forward to the time of the Spirit; and finally a dispensation of the Spirit (since Pentecost) that looked forward to the return of Christ.[5] Fletcher saw this biblical drama as being re-enacted in the Christian life, culminating in a baptism in the Spirit that brought true and entire sanctification and power for Christian living.

---

4. For a detailed discussion of the complexities of Wesley's view, see Lindstrom, *Wesley and Sanctification*.

5. Vol. 5 of Fletcher's *Five Checks to Antinomianism* contains the essence of Fletcher's position. Also see Knight, 'John Fletcher's Influence', 13–33.

As Melvin Dieter puts it:

> Since Pentecost, [Fletcher] taught, every believer has received the Holy
> Spirit in measure when born of God, but the full potential of salvation
> from sin inherent in the promise of the Spirit is not realized until, in a
> subsequent moment of complete faith and obedience to the will of God,
> one becomes so filled with the Spirit that holiness and love become the
> habitual pattern of one's life. There could come the moment of entire
> sanctification in which God, because of the sanctification won for us by
> Christ on the cross, cleanses those who believe from every inclination
> contrary to the love of God and fills their hearts with the pure love of
> God and neighbour by the 'baptism in the Holy Ghost', as promised by
> John the Baptist.[6]

For Fletcher this was a recovery of the true and full New
Testament (NT) gospel, a gospel of full salvation, not only from
the guilt of sin but from its influence in our lives.

There is no evidence that Wesley disagreed with Fletcher on
any of this – to the contrary, Wesley explicitly endorsed Fletcher's
writings and regarded him as having done the careful and thought-
ful systematic work that he as an itinerant preacher had never had
the time to do. And it was Fletcher's bestselling writings on the
subject that turned out to be influential in the next stage of our
short history.

### American Methodism

It is difficult for us to appreciate just how large Methodism was in
the United States during the first half of the nineteenth century.
There were more Methodists than Baptists by a ratio of ten to
six, and more Methodists by the same ratio than all the other
Protestant groups combined.

It was a dominant movement, and through it Wesleyan holiness teaching, mediated via Fletcher, became massively influential.
Flowing out of the holiness revivals in the 1830s, Phoebe Palmer
rose to prominence in Methodism as editor of the popular

---

6. Dieter, 'Wesleyan Perspective', 43.

magazine *Guide to Christian Perfection* and author of the bestselling book *The Way of Holiness*. The gathering she founded in her home, the 'Tuesday Meeting for the Promotion of Holiness', ran for sixty years and was widely imitated.

In the sanctification teaching of Mrs Palmer, and of American Methodism generally, whatever tension there may have been in Wesley's thought between process and crisis was resolved decisively in favour of crisis. True holiness and sanctification were achieved not through lifelong effort but through what she called the 'shorter way'. Christian believers prepared to offer themselves completely and unreservedly as a living sacrifice upon the altar of Christ would be entirely sanctified and attain victory over all known sin.

Following Mrs Palmer, this language of 'altar' and 'consecration' became characteristic of the holiness movement that swept American evangelicalism in the middle of the nineteenth century. Charles Finney and the Oberlin school taught much the same, although more from a lapsed Calvinist perspective than a Wesleyan one. The great revival of 1857 was a holiness revival, with William Boardman's *Higher Christian Life* the bestselling book of the period.[7]

The rhetoric of the entire sanctification movement was for a return to the full NT gospel of holiness. There was variegation and disagreement of course. Many identified the crisis experience of sanctification with the 'baptism in the Spirit'. Others were reluctant to, and preferred to see Spirit-baptism as a further and different endowment for service and witness.

### The Smiths and Keswick

The name of William Boardman is also important in our short history because it was Boardman, along with Robert Pearsall Smith and his wife, Hannah Whittall Smith, who came to England in the early 1870s, and ran meetings for the promotion of holiness

---

7. For this account of the development of American Wesleyan holiness teaching, see Dayton, *Theological Roots*, 64–65, and Hardesty, *Faith Cure*, 26–30.

in London and Brighton. These meetings were instrumental in the formation of the Keswick Convention, that extraordinary re-entry of Methodist piety and entire-sanctification holiness into the Church of England.

The goal of Keswick was to pursue 'the Scriptural possibilities of faith in the life of the Christian in the daily walk (a) as to maintained communion with God; and (b) as to victory over all known sin'.[8] Keswick addressed those who were restless, cast down, powerless and almost doubting the reality of the faith they possessed. In the words of Charles Harford:

> To such the message of the Keswick Convention is addressed: it sets before them a life of faith and victory, of peace and rest as the rightful heritage of the child of God, into which he may step not by laborious ascent [. . .] not by long prayers and laborious effort, but by a deliberate and decisive act of faith.[9]

To be sure, especially as time went on, the entire sanctification emphasis at Keswick was more subtle than its American counterpart, and never linked as definitively to the baptism in the Spirit. But its emphasis on entire sanctification was a central and defining feature of its platform, an emphasis it passed on to offshoot conventions and holiness ministries across the British Empire, most notably for us in Australia the Katoomba Convention (started in 1903) and the Belgrave Heights Convention in Melbourne (started in 1918).

### What is happening theologically?

It is worth pausing here and reflecting on what was happening theologically in the rise of the holiness movement, with its teaching of entire sanctification and victory over sin in this life.

Originally, it was an understandable and mostly biblical reaction to the dry, antinomian rationalism of the Deists and the hyper-Calvinists. Wesley was quite right to insist that justification won by

---

8. Harford, *Keswick Convention*, 5.
9. Ibid., 6.

Christ was not so we might rest complacently in our sins, but that we might strive for the holiness without which no one will see the Lord (Heb. 12:14). He was right to assert, as Paul does in Romans 6, that we are no longer slaves of 'Sin', but now belong to a different master called 'Righteousness'. There has been a decisive and definitive break from the dominion of sin, which leads to change and growth in holiness by the enabling of the Spirit.

However, following Wesley's lead, and taking it further, the entire sanctificationists held that freedom from the power of sin was as decisive and claimable now as was freedom from the guilt of sin. The victory over sin in our lives was not just for the next age, when there would be no more sin – it was for now! And walking in that victory required only the yielding of faith.

This was the problem with ordinary carnal Christians. They kept back something from God. They retained a degree of control, a degree of will and action, rather than ceding to God complete control of their lives.

The Wesleyan desire to see every part of life consecrated and yielded to the Lord, with him alone on the throne, is perhaps most poetically summarized in Frances Havergal's famous hymn, which was something of a Keswick theme song: 'Take my Life and Let it Be Consecrated Lord to Thee':

> Take my will and make it Thine;
> It shall be no longer mine;
> Take my heart, it is Thine own,
> It shall be Thy royal throne [. . .]

> Take my love, my Lord, I pour
> At Thy feet its treasure store;
> Take myself and I will be
> Ever, only, all for Thee.

We can see the appeal of all this to the godly mind that believes in entire justification by faith alone – why not entire sanctification by faith alone? And in the midst of the struggle with sin, and the failings and disappointments of Christian living, who could not but be attracted by the offer of a 'shorter way' to end the struggle now?

It was sufficiently appealing and powerful to worry the likes of J. C. Ryle, who wrote a critique of what he called 'Pearsall Smithism' that has come down to us as his famous book *Holiness*. (Ryle asks what we are to make of all the Pauline exhortations to godliness and effort and striving, if all is to be achieved by yielding in faith, and by resting in a victory given from outside?)

The theological problem here is not the abhorrence of sin or the passion for holiness; nor is it the expectation that the cross of Christ would do away with sin. The problem is twofold.

It is first a miscalculation as to timing. The entire sanctification-ists were right to see the new age as the home of righteousness, and to see Christ as the one who saves us completely from sin and makes us fit for his eternal kingdom. But they were mistaken in drawing forward the perfection of that age into this age.

Seen from another angle, the fault lies in a reduction of the significance of the last days, that period of eschatological tension between the inaugurating work of Christ and its culmination when he returns. In the developing theology of the holiness movement, the last days is squeezed from both sides.

On the one hand, the daily Christian life is viewed as a subjective re-enactment of the NT era, in which we walk in the Pentecostal power of the apostles. For Fletcher more than Wesley, and for the nineteenth-century holiness movement more than both, there was a primitivist or restorationist impulse. It was not only a desire to return to the NT emphasis on holy living, but an expectation that the supernatural power of the NT age would again invade the life of everyday Christians. The drama of the NT would once again become the drama of the Christian walk.

The last days were of course under pressure from the other direction as well, from an over-realized eschatology – whereby the blessings of the future age, such as complete victory of sin, were being claimed for the present. The theological space we call the last days – the time of tension, of the overlap of the ages – was drastically reduced as they gathered to themselves both the powers of the NT era, and the perfection of the age to come.

The second theological problem stems from the holiness move-ment's underlying Arminianism – its struggle to hold together God's sovereignty and man's responsibility. Whereas Calvin, and

Ryle for that matter, saw no inconsistency in our trusting in God's sanctifying work and yet toiling to work out our salvation in fear and trembling, for the Arminian holiness movement it was more a case of either/or. It must either be God's work or ours. And since it transparently could not be ours, then logically it must be his. Or, perhaps more accurately, his *following* ours. For we do have to yield and trust, to let go and let God, if we are to receive the divine blessing of entire sanctification and victory over sin in this life.

This logical rigidity is something Arminianism shares with its mortal enemy hyper-Calvinism. Rather than affirming on the basis of Scripture that both things are true in salvation compatibly and simultaneously – both divine sovereignty *and* human responsibility – the attempt is made to resolve the tension logically. The biblical data are squeezed to fit the conclusions, and the result is a distortion of what the Bible teaches about the Christian life.

### Healing
*Healing and the cross*
Entire sanctification is not all that William Boardman brought to London in 1870. He also brought with him the rising interest in faith healing that was sweeping American holiness circles.[10]

The progression was natural enough. Because of the victory of Christ on the cross, we are justified by faith; now we have discovered that we can also be completely sanctified by faith. Why also not be healed of our bodily infirmities by faith?

The historical context here is, of course, nineteenth-century medicine – which is to say, not much medicine at all. The epidemic of the time, somewhat akin to depression in the twenty-first century, was neurasthenia or 'nervous exhaustion', for which the 'rest cure' was the preferred treatment. Retreats or rest homes were common.

The famous healing of Carrie Judd in 1879 gave enormous impetus to the healing movement. She wrote an influential book, *The Prayer of Faith*, and set up a healing home, to which people could come for rest, prayer and divine healing. This became a model for many others.

---

10. Hardesty, *Faith Cure*, provides a useful account of the progression.

When William Boardman brought the healing message to London, he found a ready recipient in Elizabeth Baxter, who followed the American model by setting up a healing home called Bethshan.

Baxter, like Otto Stockmayer and Andrew Murray, other leading figures in the healing movement, were regular speakers at Keswick, although it is unclear how much divine healing by faith became part of the Keswick message.

As with entire sanctification, the new emphasis on healing was seen as a recovery of a lost aspect of the NT gospel, and a return to the powers of the apostolic age. James 5 was a key passage, but so too was Isaiah 53:4, particularly in its quotation by Matthew:

> That evening they brought to him many who were oppressed by demons, and he cast out the spirits with a word and healed all who were sick. This was to fulfil what was spoken by the prophet Isaiah: 'He took our illnesses and bore our diseases.' (8:16–17)

At one level, this is uncontroversial. The victory of Christ is indeed the decisive moment of defeat for disease and death, the moment when the renewal of the creation is achieved and assured.

But, as with entire sanctification, the healing movement was inclined to claim the benefits of the new creation now. They saw no reason why the disease-free world of Revelation 22 could not be enacted within our world by a return to the Pentecostal power of the NT age.

## The rise of science

This too, we must remember, was the century of Darwin and of Nietzsche. Science was rising, biblical-historical criticism was booming and God was being increasingly consigned to a small corner of reality – a corner not truly knowable, which could be accessed only by feeling (as in Schleiermacher) or via morality (as in Kant) or not at all (as in Deism).

I am unsure how one ever proves these connections and influences, but was there a reaction to all this on the part of evangelical Christianity? Was there a desire to counter the deistic banishment of God with a supernaturalist revival of God? Was there an increased hunger for his direct, observable power and influence through giving divine miraculous healing of the body?

There is one final piece of nineteenth-century background to complete the picture.

### Premillennial expectation

This was also the time of J. N. Darby and the rise of intense millenarian hope. There was an expectation that the end was near, and that the final phase of history was upon us.

This gave rise to one of the characteristic apologetics of the holiness and healing movements, which also became important for Pentecostalism in the early twentieth century: that God was restoring the full gospel, and pouring out a fresh Pentecost of the Spirit upon his people in preparation for the imminent return of Christ.

D. Wesley Myland's book *The Latter Rain Covenant*, published in 1910, is perhaps the clearest expression of the widespread idea that just as God had sent his Spirit at Pentecost at the beginning of the Spirit age, so he would pour him out again before the end. The key passage quoted was from Deuteronomy:

> And it shall come to pass, if ye shall hearken diligently unto my commandments which I command you this day, to love the LORD your God, and to serve him with all your heart and with all your soul, That I will give you the rain of your land in his due season, the first rain and the latter rain, that thou mayest gather in thy corn, and thy wine, and thine oil. (11:13–14 Authorized Version)

The wonderful new things happening in the church – the recovery of entire sanctification, the baptism in the Holy Spirit and the re-emergence of divine healing – was evidence that the latter rain had begun to fall.

### And so the kindling is gathered
#### The five themes

As we come to the close of the nineteenth century, the following five themes were swirling around within American holiness churches:

1. The classic evangelical doctrine of free justification by faith alone through the cross of Christ.
2. A second blessing of entire sanctification by faith leading to a life of holiness and victory over sin.
3. The baptism in the Holy Spirit, identified by some with the crisis of entire sanctification and by others with a special endowment of power for witness and service.
4. Divine faith healing.
5. An expectation of the imminent return of Christ (often thought of premillennially).

A. B. Simpson, for example, the founder of the Christian and Missionary Alliance, summarized his gospel as Christ the Saviour, Sanctifier, Healer and Coming Lord.[11]

As Donald Dayton points out, these five themes were like dry kindling that needed only a small spark to ignite the wildfire that was to become twentieth-century Pentecostalism.[12]

### Azusa Street, Pentecostalism and the full gospel

That spark came through a holiness preacher and healer named Charles Parham, who began to teach that God may have more to do through the baptism in the Holy Ghost than had previously been experienced. At one of his meetings in 1901 in Topeka, Kansas, a woman named Agnes Ozman began to speak in a strange language, and the idea began to gain currency that tongues-speaking, as at Pentecost, was the authentic evidence of baptism in the Holy Ghost. Five years later, when Parham's student William Seymour took these teachings to Azusa Street in Los Angeles, a tongues-speaking revival broke out, and modern Pentecostalism was born.

In one sense, all that was added was tongues. Seymour himself wanted to emphasize his continuity with what had come before:

> We preach old-time repentance, old-time conversion, old-time
> sanctification, and old-time baptism with the Holy Ghost, which is

---

11. According to Dayton, *Theological Roots*, 176.
12. Ibid., 164–165.

the gift of power upon the sanctified life, and God throws in the gift of tongues.[13]

H. S. Maltby, writing in 1913, put it even more sharply:

During the Reformation God used Martin Luther and others to restore to the world the doctrine of justification by faith (Rom. 5:1). Later on the Lord used the Wesleys and others in the great holiness movement to restore the gospel of sanctification by faith (Acts 26:18). Later still he used various ones to restore the gospel of divine healing by faith (Jas. 5:14, 15) and the gospel of Jesus's second coming (Acts 1:11). Now the Lord is using many witnesses in the great Pentecostal movement to restore the gospel of the baptism with the Holy Ghost and fire (Luke 3:16; Acts 1:5) with signs following (Mark 16:17, 18; Acts 2:4; 10:44–46; 19:56; 1:1 – 28:31). Thank God, we now have preachers of the whole gospel.[14]

God was restoring the full gospel to his church, including not just sanctification and healing, but miraculous gifts including tongues.

Of course, the Azusa Street outbreak and the birth of a tongues-speaking Pentecostalism gave rise to bitter controversy and division within the holiness movement. Some made the transition to full Pentecostalism smoothly. Others vigorously objected, including A. B. Simpson and The Christian and Missionary Alliance.

There was disagreement over how many key works of grace God gave in the Christian life. Was it three: conversion, then sanctification, then baptism in the Spirit with tongues? Or was it just two, with the sanctification being merged with the baptism in the Spirit, at which time tongues may or may not be added as well?

In mainstream Pentecostalism it settled into four main themes, which were regarded as the 'full or fourfold gospel'. Aimee Semple McPherson's International Four-square Gospel Church summarized it neatly:

---

13. Cited in Hardesty, *Faith Cure*, 105.

14. Maltby, *Reasonableness of Hell*, 82–83, cited in Dayton, *Theological Roots*, 19–20.

Jesus saves us according to John 3:16. He baptizes us with the Holy
Spirit according to Acts 2:4. He heals our bodies according to Jas.
5:14–15; and Jesus is coming again to receive us unto Himself according
to 1 Thess. 4:16–17.[15]


## The rise of expansive demonology

Given the short history I have sketched, the eventual emergence
of an expansive demonology does not seem at all strange. The
expectation was for a life of victory and peace and joy now, a life
that re-enacted the power of Christ and the apostles in the NT
age, and that drew the blessings and benefits of the new creation forward into this one. It was never going to be long before
someone began to focus on the work of the devil and his demons
as an unaddressed impediment to the life of victory, wholeness
and peace that is the Christian's birthright.

Interestingly, an expansive demonology took some time to
emerge. There was no particular interest in demons and Satan
in early Pentecostalism – the notable exception being Welsh
Revivalist Jessie Penn-Lewis's turn of the century book *War on
the Saints*, which paints an alarming picture of legions of deceiving spirits ready to counterfeit and destroy God's work of revival.
Indeed, according to Mrs Penn-Lewis, when one yields to God's
Spirit, receives his baptism, and enters upon a whole new vista
of spiritual experience, one is particularly open to the attack of
demonic, deceiving spirits.[16]

### *Branham and Roberts*
There is general agreement that the pioneer of modern demonology
was William Marion Branham, who along with A. A. Allen and Oral
Roberts conducted massive healing revival rallies across America
during the 1940s and 1950s.[17] Branham was a controversial figure,

---

15. Cox, *Four-Square Gospel*, 21.

16. Penn-Lewis, *War on the Saints*, 279–280.

17. See e.g. Walker, 'Devil you Think you Know', 86–108.

a Oneness Pentecostal who made bold claims about words of knowledge, visions and prophecies, and who claimed God's power to heal. In the latter stages of his career he made the casting out of demons and the loosening of demonic power in people's lives a key part of his ministry, as did Allen and, to a lesser extent, Roberts.

It is a little difficult to isolate exactly what Branham taught on the subject, due to lack of evidence, or indeed to draw the family tree of influence accurately. But two within Branham's circle, Derek Prince and Don Basham, proved important in systematizing and popularizing the new demonology in the late 1960s and early 1970s.

### Prince and Basham

Cambridge-educated Englishman Derek Prince was a key figure in the development of late twentieth-century deliverance ministries. To justify the new-found emphasis on demonic deliverance, he simply pointed to one of Pentecostalism's key texts, Mark 16:17: 'And these signs shall follow them that believe; In my name shall they cast out devils; they shall speak with new tongues' (Authorized Version).

We know all about speaking with new tongues, said Prince, but whatever happened to the casting out of devils, especially given that it is mentioned first? In fact, the order is significant according to Prince: first cast out the devils, then receive the baptism of the Spirit evidenced by tongues. If the casting out is not done, then people can enter the Christian life with demons still inside them.[18]

This becomes a key teaching of the 'expansives': that while Christians are not under the complete power of Satan, and not possessed or owned by Satan, they nevertheless can suffer from demonic influences, oppressions and strongholds, in the form of demons of particular kinds who cling to their souls, thus preventing them from entering into the victorious life that should be theirs.

Prince writes that salvation is not just forgiveness of sins, but the whole package of what God has done for us, his

---

18. See e.g. his undated pamphlet *Expelling Demons*.

all-inclusive provision for man [. . .] It includes the forgiveness of sins,
the gift of eternal life, the provision of physical healing, the power to live
a life that is different, every provision for this life and the assurance of
eternity in the presence of Almighty God.[19]

This is a statement that would have sat comfortably on the lips of
any of the late nineteenth-century American Methodists, and most
of the Keswick people in England as well. It was merely the end-
time recovery of a Spirit-empowered full gospel taken to its next
logical step.

### Wimber and Horrobin

Following the teaching of Prince, and further popularized by Don
Basham, the 'expansive' view of demonic activity and the need for
deliverance ministry spread across the English-speaking world.
Frank and Ida Hammond further popularized the teaching in
the US, and passed it on to New Zealanders Graham and Shirely
Powell, and Bill Subritzky. Subritzky in turn influenced Peter
Horrobin in the UK.

Frank Peretti's novels, beginning with *This Present Darkness*
in 1986, also played an important role in helping an expansive
demonology gain widespread interest and currency among mainstream Pentecostal and evangelical Christians.

There are other names whose story and influence we could
trace if time permitted. Another of Branham's disciples was Paul
Cain, who went on to achieve notoriety as one of the Kansas City
Prophets in the late 1980s. Cain was very influential in the developing ministry of John Wimber, and it was through Wimber's Third
Wave charismatic renewal that deliverance ministries began to be
seriously considered by evangelicals. We could also examine Peter
Wagner's writings about territorial spirits or Neil T. Anderson's
bestselling books on spiritual warfare.[20]

---

19. Prince, *Complete Salvation*, 8.
20. E.g., among others, for Wagner, *Engaging the Enemy; Prayer Shield;*
    *Confronting the Powers;* (ed.), *Territorial Spirits* and *Breaking Strongholds;* and,
    for N. T. Anderson, *Bondage Breaker;* (with Warner), *Beginner's Guide.*

As this expansive demonology spread, it also developed in sophistication. A detailed body of knowledge has been assembled, based partly on scriptural hints but largely through practical experience, as to how demons are organized and operate, and how Christians, churches and cities are to be delivered from their malign influence. There are now quite well-developed theories about how the hierarchy of the demonic army functions, about 'entry points' (how a demon initially gains access to someone's body), about how demons can be recognized, about what prerequisites there are to cast them out (both in the person affected and in the one doing the deliverance), about how different physical manifestations demonstrate that the demon has in fact been cast out, and about how a believer can stay demon-free.

Bill Subritzky, for example, teaches that there are three demonic 'strong men' or generals who lead Satan's army in the world: Jezebel, Antichrist and Death-and-Hell. Their demonic minions can enter people through means as diverse as parental rejection, occult dabbling and rock music. I personally like Subritzky's suggestion that the rise of feminism was masterminded by the Spirit of Jezebel.[21]

Frank and Ida Hammond claim that Satan has deployed prince spirits over each local church to oppress and ruin it where possible, and (like Peter Wagner) assert that there are ruling demonic potentates set over nations and territories that need to be opposed in spiritual battle if the gospel is to make progress. Like many among the expansives, the Hammonds also attribute mental illness to the activity of demonic spirits.[22]

Derek Prince suggests that one needs to get the demon to give his name before he can be cast out, and goes on to catalogue some of the names he has heard: fear, hatred, lies, doubt, envy, jealousy, confusion, perversity, schizophrenia, death, suicide, adultery, mockery, blasphemy, witchcraft, and some others (he says) unfit to print.

---

21. See Nigel Wright's summary of various teachings by the 'expansives', including Subritzky, in *Theology of the Dark Side*.
22. Hammond, *Pigs*.

Prince goes on to argue that since 'spirit' is the same word in Greek and Hebrew as breath, evil spirits usually leave the body via the mouth or nose, always giving a definite manifestation, depending on what sort of demon they are. Sexual demons come out with spitting or vomiting, often with large amounts of mucous. The demon of fear comes out with sobbing, and lying with a loud roar. The demon of nicotine with a cough or a gasp.[23]

Peter Horrobin likewise investigates how it is that demon-oppressed people sometimes have surprising, almost supernatural, strength. He theorizes that the demon must be operating directly on the adrenal glands to pump adrenaline to the muscles, and this suggestion is made only the more likely because the adrenal glands sit on top of the kidneys, and in Hebrew thought this is the location of the human heart.[24]

Examples of this level of detailed speculative demonology are, as it were, legion.

## Deliverance and the full gospel

How does this expansive stream of Pentecostal demonology relate to the short history I have painted above?

The elaborate, almost fantastical, demonology of a Derek Prince or a Peter Horrobin may seem quite a distance from the earnest evangelical perfectionism of John Wesley. And yet the trajectory that began with Wesley's entire sanctification led inexorably via American Methodism and the holiness revivals to full gospel Pentecostalism and eventually to an expansive view of demons and deliverance ministry.

The theological themes or impulses developed over time, but the common threads are identifiable.

There is the trend towards what we might call subjective primitivism: the desire to see the supernatural power, dynamism and holiness of Jesus and the apostolic age restored and re-enacted in

23. Prince, *Expelling Demons.*
24. Horrobin, *Healing through Deliverance*, 1: 94.

the daily lives of Christians. This impulse is seen first in the blessing of complete sanctification and holiness, and then progressively in the emergence of healing, tongues-speaking, the miraculous charismata and finally in an expansive demonology and deliverance ministry. In each case the Gospels and Acts are viewed not so much as foundational documents, but as normative descriptions and prescriptions for daily Christian experience.

There is also a certain Arminian logic running as a thread through our story. We must do certain things (such as yield by faith, or have faith for healing, or perform the requisite actions for demonic deliverance) that will then prompt God to do his part (to bring complete sanctification or complete healing or casting out of the demon). There is discomfort with holding the different strands of the Bible's teaching together simultaneously – on the one hand, that God has crucified the flesh in us, and is at work in us by his Spirit, leading and enabling us to live a new life of godliness; and on the other hand that we have an obligation to mortify the misdeeds of the body, to put to death what is earthly in us and to walk in a manner worthy of our calling.

There is a similar unwillingness to maintain the now–not-yet tension that runs through the NT's description of our lives now in the last days. The history we have been tracing is marked by an over-realized eschatology that collapses the cross and the eschaton together, shrinking the theological space of the last days, and dragging the glories of the new creation back into this age – whether in respect of perfect holiness or perfect health.

Against this backdrop the emergence of a focus on the demonic is almost inevitable. Demonic activity is another obstacle to living in the victory, power and wholeness of body and mind that is regarded as the normal Christian experience, following the pattern of the Gospels. If one is exercising faith to live a life of abundant victory – whether in the spiritual, physical, emotional or even financial realm – and yet is experiencing struggle and failure, then something (such as a demon) must be interfering.

Historically, the focus on demonic activity developed as an offshoot of the healing ministry. Peter Horrobin, who has written the most recent and detailed work supporting demonic deliverance, locates this ministry as a subset of a more holistically viewed commitment to divine healing. For Horrobin, healing has three dimensions: physical healing, inner (or emotional) healing and deliverance. Real health – physical, emotional and spiritual – will be attained only if deliverance ministry is given its proper place.[25]

Interestingly, too, Horrobin's ministry also partakes of the tradition of the 'healing home' – the Ellel residential centres where the Christian can go for healing and deliverance, a branch of which now occupies what used to be the Gilbulla Conference Centre on Sydney's outskirts.

In closing, we note that although the elaborate demonology of the 'expansives' may sound strange to many of us, it nevertheless retains a real attractiveness to evangelical believers. For which of us does not long for the tensions and struggles of this present evil age to be resolved? Which of us is not eager to find rest and release from the evil within our own hearts, and the struggles and failings of our Christian lives? And which of us is not guilty of minimizing or ignoring the wiles of the devil, or downplaying the spiritual nature of our battle to remain strong in the Lord?

The promise of deliverance from evil is beguiling in the same way that Wesleyan perfectionism is, whether in its more extreme manifestations or in its slightly gentler Keswick garb. In its historical and theological origins we may end up finding the demonic deliverance ministries a closer relative than we might at first imagine.

---

25. Ibid., 21.

# 2. TOWARDS A BIBLICAL THEOLOGY OF THE DEFEAT OF THE EVIL POWERS

**Peter G. Bolt**

## The cry for deliverance

'Wretched man that I am! Who will deliver me from this body of death?' (Rom. 7:24). The apostle Paul's cry for deliverance springs out of the depths of his soul. This is a cry provoked from an acute awareness of the deep scars left upon him by his sin. It is wrenched out of the experience of a struggle between knowing the right, but doing the wrong. It wells up and bursts out of his desperate realization that, if left to his own devices, this is a battle he can never win.

The cry for deliverance screams out from almost every page of human history. People, such as ourselves, crying out, wanting to be free from the oppression of evil powers, evil powers outside and evil powers deep within. But notice that the apostle's cry is for a particular kind of deliverance: 'from this body of death'. This immediately gets to the heart of our problem when it comes to the evil powers, and hints towards the real solution Christ has won.

Any discussion of the evil powers, especially in our current environment, raises questions about the proper reading of the

Bible. The basic hermeneutical assumption of this chapter is that the evil powers are properly understood only within the framework of biblical theology. But is this even possible? Is it even possible to discover a 'biblical theology of evil powers'? The answer depends upon what we mean by 'biblical theology'.

## Towards a biblical theology of evil powers?

### Yes, if 'biblical' = 'not unbiblical'

In Christian circles, the adjective 'biblical' is sometimes no more than a 'hooray-word' of affirmation and acceptance. Since God's people are those who 'tremble at his word' (Isa. 66:5), it is important to ensure that our understanding about any topic is informed by biblical truth, perhaps especially when the given topic is fraught with as much potential error as this one.[1] A 'biblical theology of evil powers' must mean, at a minimum, that we want to ensure our teaching on evil powers is *not unbiblical*.

But there is also more to a 'biblical theology' than this.

### Yes, if 'biblical theology' = a Bible summary

It is certainly possible to have 'a biblical theology of evil powers' in the sense of a 'Bible summary' about evil powers, such as might be found, for example, in a Bible dictionary. Summarizing the Bible's evidence is certainly an essential step in understanding this topic, as it is in understanding any topic, but it must also be said that to assemble, classify and articulate the Bible's teaching on demons still falls far short of 'a biblical theology' when that term is more exactly understood.[2]

---

1. If Barth was correct in relation to the discussion of angels, that 'a good deal of hampering rubbish has accumulated in this field in both ancient and more modern times [. . .] so much so that it was, and is, therefore very difficult even to pose correctly the correct questions' (*CD* III.3, xi), how much more is this so in relation to the discussion of demons in our present environment?

2. Unfortunately, even some definitions of 'biblical theology' do not include

### But what about 'biblical theology', carefully defined?

According to Geerhardus Vos, 'Biblical Theology is that branch
of Exegetical Theology which deals with the process of the self-
revelation of God deposited in the Bible.'[3] Biblical theology,
strictly speaking, is the study of God's self-revelation, within
human history, over time. God's self-revelation also has implications for us poor humans. This is brought out in Graeme
Goldsworthy's further elaboration:

> Biblical Theology is a way of understanding the Bible as a whole, so
> that we can see the plan of salvation as it unfolds step by step. It is
> concerned with God's message to us in the form that it actually takes
> in Scripture.[4]

With this definition of biblical theology, it becomes clear that 'a
biblical theology of evil powers', when carefully defined, is actually
impossible.[5] If biblical theology is the articulation of what God
has done in history for the sake of our salvation, then to talk of
'a biblical theology of evil powers' is already to grant the devil a
significance which he no doubt well appreciates, but which is far
more than he deserves.[6]

---

much beyond 'Bible summary'. Thus the definition given by Yarborough,
'Biblical Theology', 61, fails to capture the sense of biblical theology
being the study of God's self-revelation: 'Study of the Bible that seeks
to discover what the biblical writers, under divine guidance, believed,
described, and taught in the context of their own times.'

3. Vos, *Biblical Theology*, 5.

4. Goldsworthy, *According to Plan*, 33.

5. Moreau, 'Demon', 163: 'When demons were created, how they came to
be demonic, and their organizational structure are not given significant
attention in Scripture because the focus throughout the Bible is on God
and his work in Christ rather than on the demonic attempts to demean
that work.' Unfortunately, after this fine beginning, Moreau concludes
with a little more confidence about what can be known than is warranted.

6. Cf. K. Barth's introductory remarks to *CD* III.3, xii: 'I love angels, but
have no taste for demons, not out of any desire for demythologisation

In addition, simply to provide a summary of what the Bible says about evil powers also becomes problematic, for if the material about the evil powers is extracted from the main storyline of the Bible, then it is automatically a distorted picture, warped out of perspective by being taken out of the proper context of being just another subordinate item in the record of God's self-revelation.

This chapter will first address a 'not unbiblical' view of evil powers, then provide a Bible summary, but all of this is heading towards explaining the evil powers in relation to the Bible's Christocentric message.

Immediately, several proof-texts that provide the proper perspective spring to mind:

> Now is the judgment of this world; now will the ruler of this world be cast out. (John 12:31)

> The reason the Son of God appeared was to destroy the works of the devil. (1 John 3:8)

And an important text that takes us back to the cry for deliverance 'from this body of death':

> Since therefore the children share in flesh and blood, he himself likewise partook of the same things, that through death he might destroy the one who has the power of death, that is, the devil, and deliver all those who through fear of death were subject to lifelong slavery. (Heb. 2:14–15)

In other words, when we address the evil powers in relation to the central message of the Scriptures, it becomes clear that we must

---

Footnote 6 (*cont.*)

    but because they are not worth it.' Perhaps there is a warning, in his comment, for any dabbler in the demonic that those who might skip the earlier sections in the volume, to 'begin right at the end, namely, with the demons, [. . .] should be told that I regard them as lacking in seriousness' (xi). The demonic has no dignity of its own; cf. K. Barth, *The Christian Life*, 127.

only ever deal with them from the perspective of their defeat. So, even if we cannot properly construct a 'biblical theology of the evil powers', this chapter will be moving 'towards a biblical theology of (the defeat of) the evil powers' – or, perhaps even better, 'towards a biblical theology of Christ's victory (over the evil powers)'.

But let us begin by seeking to be 'not unbiblical'.

## Towards a not unbiblical theology of evil powers

### The problem: paucity of evidence

There is a particular danger of falling into unbiblical thinking about evil powers, simply because of the paucity of the biblical evidence. Despite increasingly shrill calls for Christian churches to take evil powers more seriously, it is extremely well recognized that the Bible itself does not really say much about them.[7] The Old Testament (OT) is practically silent about demons, then an explosion of references appear as Jesus arrives in the biblical story – at least according to Matthew, Mark and Luke; then there is a tiny demonic dribble into the period of history recorded by the Acts, and only an occasional drip elsewhere in the New Testament (NT).[8]

Now, of course, the number of verses dedicated to a topic does not really say much about its significance, or otherwise, but it does clearly affect how much we can say. This well-recognized situation is usually treated as a problem to be solved, and several strategies are employed to supplement the biblical evidence.

---

7. E.g. Lyonnet, 'Satan', 522: 'In contrast to later Judaism and to the majority of the literatures of the ancient Near East, the Bible makes use of an extreme restraint, limiting itself to informing us of the existence of [Satan], and of his wiles, and of the means to fortify ourselves against them'; J. H. Walton, 'Serpent', 738: 'Israel had little knowledge of a being named Satan or of a chief of demons, the devil, during the OT period.'

8. Moreau, 'Demon', 164, notes that NT references are 'relatively rare' outside the [Synoptic] Gospels.

### Supplementation 1: comparative material

There is certainly no shortage of ancient sources of relevance to understanding demonological views in the ancient world, whether for the OT period, or the NT period. 'Epigraphic, papyrological and literary sources for the study of demonology are widespread,'[9] and, in fact, it is only recently that the comparative value of some of this material has begun to be more widely appreciated. The recent renaissance in the study of magic, for example, has led to a much greater understanding of the magical world view, in which evil powers had a very high profile.[10]

This new lease of life notwithstanding, it has for a long time been common practice among those seeking to articulate the demonology of the Bible to turn to the demonology of surrounding cultures to supplement the paucity of biblical evidence. Probably due to the usual assumption that the intertestamental literature acts as a bridge between the Old and New Testaments,[11] this material, in particular, has exerted a profound influence, especially upon theories of the origins of evil powers (see below).

### Supplementation 2: 'ministry experience'

More recently, a second source of supplementation has been proposed with increasing frequency.

The 'expansive charismatics' are quite clear that it is not only possible to supplement the biblical material, but, in fact, it is *necessary* to do so. Their proposal is that the gap in the biblical presentation must be filled from knowledge gained about

---

9. Kotansky, 'Demonology', 269, who points out that 'amulets and magical texts have been undervalued as a source of comparative material'.

10. Bolt, *Jesus' Defeat of Death*, 34–39.

11. Stuhlmacher, *How to Do Biblical Theology*, 7, 75–78, argues that the usage of intertestamental literature is usually based upon 'an inadmissible abstraction' of two independent groups of writings (OT/NT) later brought together into a canon, which therefore creates a long (so-called) intertestamental period. More careful attention to the actual canonical process, and especially to the influence of the Septuagint (LXX), makes it 'no longer possible' to speak this way.

demons by the 'ministry experience' of those involved in 'deliverance ministries'. A few examples of such urgings will suffice (emphasis added):

> To understand and further equip ourselves for this cosmic-earthly struggle, we must explore the realms of theology, biblical exegesis, and the experience of the people of God. (Murphy)

> *Where Scripture is silent or not clear*, there is need for guidelines and humility on all sides in areas of experimentation and *ministry concerning the demonic*. (Woodberry)

> All churches need a renewed study of the biblical worldview and *the practice of spiritual conflict*. They also need to draw on *the experience of people ministering in this area*. (Engelsviken)[12]

Within these circles there is an urgent pastoral requirement to draw upon this ministry experience, for it is insisted that Christians need to know the schemes of the devil (2 Cor. 2:11, *ta noēmata*, 'thoughts'; ESV: 'designs') so as to prevent him from gaining a foothold (Eph. 4:27; ESV: 'opportunity') – whether this is understood in terms of full 'possession', or in terms of a temporary control or possession.[13] The consequential fear aroused by this 'logic' causes a strong drive towards gaining more information. Given the paucity of information in the Scriptures, this must therefore be derived from 'ministry experience'.

As a natural consequence, a situation is introduced in which the practitioner becomes privileged, over against those without experience:

> Since the need for healing can be the result of physical, emotional, and spiritual problems such as sin, or the demonic, there will need to be more collaboration between practitioners, biblical scholars and theologians, medical doctors, and psychologists. All must be open

---

12. Murphy, *Handbook for Spiritual Warfare*, 13; Woodberry, 'Power and Blessing', 105; Engelsviken, 'Spiritual Conflict', 125.

13. E.g. Moreau, 'Demon', 165.

to the insights from the other fields, *with special attention to practitioners, since so much has been written by those without experience with the phenomena of the demonic.*[14]

Once ministry experience is privileged like this, it becomes incorporated into the expansive charismatic's hermeneutic, so that it often forms a crucial plank in an 'argument', instead of using standard exegetical procedures.[15]

However, before leaving this point, it is worth noting that this kind of procedure is not found only among the expansive charismatics. For a long time it has been quite common in discussions of demonology to assume that those who live or work in non-Western cultures may be closer to the truth about evil powers, simply because in such cultures the demonic is said to be more familiar. Even if in a different guise, this is exactly the same appeal to supplement the biblical evidence by experience.

### Supplementation 3: implicit cultural presuppositions
The third way of supplementation is more subtle. Interpreters of the Bible can bring their own implicit cultural presuppositions to this study, as they can to any study.

Now, at this point we could lapse into that terribly unsightly kind of rhetoric where accusation and counter-accusation are flung around, about who is most enslaved to their presuppositions in regard to evil powers. Who is most enslaved to Enlightenment thought: the non-charismatics, with their apparently demon-free universe; or the charismatics, with their apparently deistic one?

---

14. Woodberry, 'Power and Blessing', 105 (emphasis added).

15. E.g. Travis and Travis, 'Deep-Level Healing Prayer', argue from examples (107) and 'case studies' (111–113). See also Moreau, 'Demon', 165, who adds to his survey of the biblical material, 'this parallels the experience of many people today. While experience is not the final arbiter of doctrinal formulations our experience should be in accord with our doctrine'; and Wright, 'Charismatic Interpretations', 151–152: 'Those who reflect upon the charismatic movement only at a distance are at a grave disadvantage at this point.'

Who is most enslaved to secularism: the non-charismatics, with their focus on ordinary life and their apparent overlooking of the devil's extraordinary workings, or the charismatics, with their focus upon the extraordinary, and their apparent inability to see anything demonic about the ordinary?[16]

But setting the mudslinging aside, we all need to be aware of the possible cultural influences we bring to this topic. For example, how much of our implicit demonology really comes from the Scriptures, or how much do we owe to the elaborate pictures of evil powers drawn from the pseudepigraphal material? How much do we owe to the pictures of the devil drawn so powerfully by the poets of Western literature, such as Dante, Milton and even C. S. Lewis?[17] To pick an even simpler illustration, why do we keep on talking about Jesus doing 'exorcisms', when the NT never once calls him an exorcist, nor is the exorcism language used for his driving out spirits?[18] How much of the magical world view do we import into our portrait of his ministry, simply by using this well-established magical label?

### Problems with supplementation
*A 'non-biblical' theology of evil powers*
Any kind of supplementation results in a non-biblical view of the evil powers, by definition. Even if partially based upon the limited

---

16. After several decades of such mudslinging, it should be patently clear that the only thing achieved is the inhibition of genuine conversations about what might be the truth, and what might be the true issues. So e.g. the frequent insinuation that non-charismatics either do not believe in the reality of evil powers or do not take them seriously enough is completely misguided. In my opinion the debate is not about their existence or influence (about both of which I, for one, have no doubt); it is about what we are supposed to do with them once we acknowledge their existence. It is a question not of metaphysics, but of *practice*.

17. Cunningham, 'Satan', 364.

18. This is not often observed, but, without buying into his final dichotomy, see e.g. Moreau, 'Demon', 164: 'Interestingly the term "exorcism" is not used of Jesus' ministry. An exorcism implies a particular ritual, and Jesus, as well as the early church, relied on authority rather than ritual.'

scriptural evidence, to whatever extent it is derived from sources other than the Bible it is non-biblical.

Now, for sure, sometimes 'supplementation' is actually necessary, and other times it is certainly helpful.[19] So, for example, we could perhaps argue that we engage in supplementing the Bible every time we look up a lexicon to understand its language. The language of the Bible automatically takes us into a culture wider than the Bible's, and it is of immense help to understand the way the biblical words were used elsewhere. This often illuminates the text and always exposes something about the original hearers of the text, plus this kind of study therefore enables something of the rhetoric of the ancient text to be recovered and refelt by contemporary hearers.[20]

But having acknowledged that it both can and should be done – and having added the confession that I myself have actually done it[21] and will do so again even before the end of this chapter – we must always be aware that, in whatever form it is done, supplementing the biblical material brings its own problems.

*Privileging experience over word*
The Scriptures have a strong focus upon the need to hear and be directed by God's word. This focus is particularly sharp in the context of other apparently more direct sources of information about the spirit world (e.g. Isa. 8:19–20). It therefore seems rather misguided to privilege experience over word.

It is particularly dangerous to do so when it comes to the dramatic experiences certainly possible in the world of magic and evil spirits, for it is difficult to shake yourself away from such experiences once they have happened. Simon Magus stands as a

---

19. In fact, such careful work often shows up the poverty of the slick generalizations that have often been imposed upon the text of Scripture; see e.g. the judicious analysis of 'the satan' by Day, 'Satan, I–III', or the work on Beelzeboul by Herrmann, 'Baal-Zebub'.
20. See my work on the healing and exorcism miracles in *Jesus' Defeat of Death*.
21. My own use of extra-biblical sources is apparent in Bolt, 'Jesus, Daimons and the Dead', *Jesus' Defeat of Death* and *Living with the Underworld*.

clear reminder to us of the danger of basing truth upon your own dramatic experiences (Acts 8:9–24).[22] Even those who engage in so-called 'deliverance ministry' have recognized the problem of such practices tending to monopolize people to such an extent that they lose balance in their Christian life.[23]

In this regard we should also remember that the devil himself is anti-word (see e.g. Mark 4:15; cf. Gen. 3:1a, 4–5) and that his natural home is the world of sensual experience and outward appearances (see Luke 4:6; Gen. 3:1–5). To trust in experiences that come from him is a dangerous exercise. The universal testimony – of both Scripture and ministry experience – is that demons cannot be trusted, but are deceptive to the core (see Gen. 3:1–5; John 8:44b; 1 Tim. 4:1).[24]

It is also worth taking into account Jesus' own 'ministry experience' at this point (e.g. Mark 1:24; 3:11–12).[25] Even when the demons spoke

---

22. This was not the last that Christian history would hear of this famous magician. Early Christian literature implies his conversion was not genuine, and reports that he continued to conflict with the Christian mission as the years went on. See Stoops, 'Simon [Magus]'; Fossum, 'Simon Magus'.

23. Woodberry, 'Power and Blessing', 101–102, refers to those whose 'involvement with the demons has so monopolized their time that they have lost balance in other areas of their Christian life'; Scotland, 'Charismatic Devil', 96, refers to those suffering 'demonophilia'. Non-charismatics have also pointed to the same problem, drawing attention to the distraction of such things from gospel work; see e.g. Tinker, 'Phantom Menace', 80–81, who is particularly thinking of 'Strategic Level Spiritual Warfare' (SLSW).

24. Note Wright, 'Charismatic Interpretations', 163: 'The demonic realm might well *masquerade* as ontological and structured; but if its essence is deception, such appearances should be treated with circumspection.'

25. And perhaps also that of the apostle Paul (Acts 16:17–18). Chrysostom connected Paul's rebuke of the Philippian slave girl with Christ's silencing of the demons. Like Christ before him (Mark 1:24), Paul 'didn't wish to have the witnessing coming from [the demon]. Why, then, did the demon do this? Because he wanted to overturn the balance

what was actually true, Jesus silenced them, refusing to let them speak. The suggestion that knowledge of the evil spirits is to be derived from 'ministry experience' seems to run completely against what we see in Jesus' ministry. Even if the devil is permitted to speak for himself, he cannot be permitted to speak as a spokesman for God.

With this kind of biblical evidence in mind, why should the devil be permitted to bear testimony to anything nowadays, and why should we countenance listening to him, let alone urging that this is what should be done? When he is foolishly permitted to become his own interpreter, it is really no surprise that the Bible, the Christian life and Christian ministry are all transformed so that he increasingly appears to play the central role in all of them, resulting in the loss of balance already noted above.

### When does non-biblical become unbiblical?

The basic caution is simple. When drawing upon non-biblical material, we need to be careful we do not spill over to become unbiblical.

We need to enquire carefully, not only about what the Bible *says* about evil powers, but also ask what it *does not say* – and then be governed by its restraints. Why Nigel Scotland applies the label 'expansive' to the majority of present-day charismatics is because of their tendency to provide expansive details about the evil powers. In these circles demons are precisely named, their relationships mapped, their functions precisely diagnosed, down to the precise points of entry into the human body.[26] Quite clearly the

---

Footnote 25 (*cont.*)

of things and to seize the title from the apostles so as to convince many to run close to them. If this were allowed to happen, since they would easily be believed by this witnessing, the demons would then easily be able to introduce their false teachings. In order, then, for this not to take place so that not even the beginning of a fraud should sprout, he seals up their mouths, even though they say the truth. He does this in order that no one would pay any attention to the demons' lies, but that they should tightly close their ears to all that is said by them' (Benedict, *Devil and Magic*, 121–122).

26. Scotland, 'Charismatic Devil', 91–92, who reports the rather illogical

reserve of the Scriptures about these things has been well and truly dispensed with, and the results sound more like ancient magical spells than the Bible.

It seems that this over-precision has moved from being non-biblical, to being unbiblical. This is clear in at least two areas.

*Reopening a gap that should stay closed* This over-precise mapping of evil powers has reopened a gap that should have been left closed, by reintroducing the sense of a huge distance between humanity and God, brimming over with beings.[27] Along with this distance comes an increased fear.[28]

---

claim that the baptism of the Holy Spirit gives a stronger awareness of evil (cf. Wright, 'Charismatic Interpretations', 150). Not everyone insists on the need to know the names, but for others it is required for proper dealing with the spirits (74); cf. Wagner, *Confronting the Powers*, 165. The need to name the manifold spirits was, of course, a feature of ancient magical spells; for examples, see Betz, *Greek Magical Papyri*.

27. Kay, 'Pentecostals and Angels', 79. This is amenable with the 'great chain of being', which had such an impact on Christian theology of earlier times, but is highly questionable as a description of the biblical presentation. See Lovejoy, *Great Chain of Being*, for the vast array of spiritual beings (80–81, 190–191) along the chain of being with its roots in Plato (24–61), its elaboration in Neoplatonism (61–66) and flowering in medieval thought (ch. 3) and beyond. See also Doyle, *Eschatology*, 97–101; cf. Russell, *Satan*, 65. Wright, 'Charismatic Interpretations', 151, speaks of the charismatic tendency towards 'remythologization'.

28. Anecdotally, this fear is apparent in the strategies used to commend the institution of 'deliverance ministries', as well as among the congregations who have succumbed to such appeals. It is also illustrated by the intense interest in the question of whether Christians can be possessed, or experience some other kind of demonization. It is difficult to see anything other than fear as a result of teaching that demons 'can influence, take hold of, or attach themselves to believers', especially if it is said, as do the Hammonds, that everyone is demonized at least to some extent, thus necessitating 'deliverance' as a regular part of parish ministry. Cf. Scotland, 'Charismatic Devil', 95–96, referring to Hammond, *Pigs*, 12.

This fear is already apparent in cultures where there is an intense awareness of the presence of manifold evil powers threatening human life. Even if Western secularism has spilled over into disbelief in the demonic world altogether, this should not cause us to forget that a healthy removal of fear from such demonic threats can actually be attributed to the deep impact of the gospel on Western society. It is also interesting to observe that, as Western society moves further away from its gospel roots, there is a corresponding return of fear and fascination at the threat of evil forces and powers.

It is clearly unbiblical to reinstate distance between humanity and God, to fill it with demons and therefore return people again to fear. For Christ's work has closed the gap between God and human beings; and his work is the 'perfect' love that 'casts out fear' (1 John 4:18; cf. Rom. 8:15). To be sure, the expansive charismatics are not the first, nor the only, ministry that operates by creating fear. However, the Christian life is sustained by the assurance of God's closeness, and any ministry that opens up or sustains a fear-filled distance has become profoundly unbiblical.

*Filling a gap that should stay open* The drive towards supplementation is also unbiblical at a far more basic level. It is problematic because it treats the paucity of biblical evidence as a gap that needs to be filled. Part of what it means to be 'biblical', however, is being prepared to live with the scriptural 'gaps' (cf. Deut. 29:29), or, better still, to embrace the gap as actually being instructive and useful.

If there is a gap in the biblical material, instead of rushing to fill it from elsewhere, it is important to ask how the Bible uses it in communicating its main message. The answer, most likely, will be that the gap draws the hearer in more tightly to the central message of the Scriptures.[29] And so, when it comes to the paucity of information about the evil powers, the biblical narrative 'fills the gap', not by supplying further information about demons, but

---

29. Narrative critics speak of narratives creating 'gaps' in order to draw readers into the narrative movement in order to maximize its impact.

by explaining what God has done about the disorder in the world, of which the demons are a part.

The willingness to live with the Bible's own restraint is an important step towards a truly biblical theology. As we head further in that direction, it is time to turn to a summary of what the Bible says about evil powers.

## Towards a Bible summary of evil powers

When it comes to the evil powers, the relevant language can be discussed in two categories, the *demonic* and the *devil*.

### The demonic

The English word 'demon' is a transliteration of the Greek word *daimōn* (only LXX Isa. 65:11; and Matt. 8:31),[30] or its diminutive form *daimonion*, the more usual term in the LXX (17×) and NT (63×).[31]

In both OT and NT demonic beings fall into two basic groups. There are those spoken about 'from below', which we can call 'the dirty demons', and those described 'from above', 'the pasty principalities'.[32]

---

30. *Daimōn* also occurs in textual variants at Mark 5:12; Luke 8:29; Rev. 16:14; 18:2.

31. Philo and Josephus, as with the NT, also prefer the diminutive, in each case probably following the usage found in the LXX. LXX: Deut. 32:17; Tobit 3.8, 17; 6.8, 15–17; 8.3; Pss 90:6; 95:5; 105:37; *Odes of Solomon* 2.17; Isa. 13:21; 34:14; 65:3; Baruch 4.7, 35; NT: Matt. 7:22; 9:33, 34; 10:8; 11:18; 12:24, 27–28; 17:18; Mark 1:34, 39; 3:15, 22; 6:13; 7:26, 29–30; 9:38 [16:9, 17]; Luke 4:35, 41; 7:33; 8:2, 27, 29–30, 33, 35, 38; 9:1, 42, 49; 10:17; 11:14–15, 18–20; 13:32; John 8:48–49, 52; 10:20–21; Acts 17:18; 1 Cor. 10:20–21; 1 Tim. 4:1; Jas 2:19; Rev. 9:20; 16:14; 18:2; cf. Luke 4:33.

32. These correspond to K. Barth's two categories of 'lordless powers', namely the 'chthonic' and the 'spiritual' (*Christian Life*, 213–232). World religions also distinguish lower and higher demons; cf. the uncouth lower demons in Hinduism (Gnanakan, 'Manthiravadi', 141–143).

## The dirty demons

There are two Hebrew words, both extremely rare in the OT, which act as generic terms for 'evil spirits'.[33] Although often obscured by our English translations, several other words may refer to particular evil spirits, such as Lilith (only Isa. 34:14) or Azazel (only Lev. 16:8, 10, 26) or the noon-time and night-time demons (Ps. 91:5–6) and the like.[34] The references in 1 Samuel to the 'evil spirit from the LORD' (1 Sam. 16:14–23; 18:10) that troubled Saul and apparently departed when David played his harp,[35] rather than referring to an evil being, may simply have been a way of speaking of Saul's troubled personality.[36] The OT references forbidding divination, wizardry and other magical practices also need to be taken into account here, since many magical practices operated by means of these 'dirty demons' from below.[37]

---

33. Namely, šēdîm ('demons', twice only: Deut. 32:17; Ps. 106:37) and śĕ'îrîm ('hairy demons' or 'satyrs', four times only: Lev. 17:7; 2 Chr. 11:15; Isa. 13:21; 34:14).

34. Kuemmerlin-McLean, 'Demons', 139; Kuemmerlin-McLean, 'Magic – Old Testament'; Scurlock, 'Magic – Ancient Near East'; Chavalas, 'Magic'; Kotansky, 'Demonology', 269, who points out that such beings 'although important, are rare in the OT and do not seem to have influenced later concepts'. For further beings that may have been recognized as evil spirits, see the various entries in Van der Toorn, Becking and Van der Horst, Dictionary of Deities and Demons.

35. This story has similarities to Greek enthusiasm and contributed to David's reputation in the Dead Sea Scrolls as an exorcist (Kotansky, 'Demonology', 270). Cf. Chajes, Between Worlds, 58: 'King David is the first recorded exorcist in Jewish – or at least Judean – history, and King Saul the first demoniac. When King Saul was tormented by an evil spirit, the young David was called upon to heal him with the sweet strains of his lyre.'

36. See the caution sounded by Woodhouse, 1 Samuel, 295, n. 14.

37. See e.g. O'Mathúna, 'Divination'; Hagan, 'Divination'; Kuemmerlin-McLean, 'Magic – Old Testament'; Scurlock, 'Magic – Ancient Near East'; Léon-Dufour, 'Magic'.

A study of the language of the demonic in the Greek OT shows that it clusters around three ideas.

*Affliction* First, demons can be associated with harm inflicted upon individuals. In the canonical books this occurs only once, in Psalm 91, which is a positive meditation upon the security of God's people, bringing the assurance that there is no need to fear any attacks from demons. In the apocryphal book of Tobit the *daimonion* language is used of the demon Asmodeus, who afflicted Sarah, daughter of Raguel, and caused the death of a succession of seven potential husbands on their wedding night (Tobit 3.17; 6.8, 15–17; 8.3).

*Idols* Secondly, demons are associated with idolatry. This thin strand can be traced from Deuteronomy 32:17, through the Psalms (96:5; 106:37), the prophets (Isa. 65:3, 11), on through the intertestamental period (Baruch 4.7), and into the NT (e.g. 1 Cor. 10:20; Rev. 9:20).[38] Since to worship idols was to worship demons,[39] identifying the role of idolatry in biblical theology is an

---

38. Cf. Wiéner, 'Idols', 252; Brunon and Grelot, 'Evil Spirits', 149, point out that the Greek translators 'systematized this demoniacal interpretation of idolatry, identifying the pagan gods with the evil spirits (Ps. 96:5; Baruch 4.7) and even introducing the demonic where it was not in the Hebrew (Ps. 91:6; Isa. 13:21; 65:3).' It should be noted, however, that the latter verses also refer to demons, even if the generic term is absent, so the LXX is not really introducing anything except a consistency of vocabulary.

39. We should note, however, that when idols are declared to be demons, not gods, this would have been by no means insulting to the idolater, whether the Greeks reading the LXX, or the Corinthians addressed by Paul. Since it was regarded as inappropriate for the gods to have direct dealings with humanity, it was a fairly standard view that the being which 'inhabited', or was associated with, an idol, was not actually the god itself, but an intermediary, a demon. For a late first- or early second-century exposition of this theory, see Plutarch, *De defectu oraculorum*. It is rather surprising to find discussions of idolatry that make no mention of the demonic connection; e.g. Spender, 'Idol, Idolatry'.

important step towards uncovering how evil powers are portrayed in order to highlight God's self-revelation over time. Similarly, if it is true that 'in one sense, the Bible is the story of God's people who are constantly turning themselves away from idols',[40] then this will bring the theme of the evil powers very close to the centre of the biblical account.

*Desolation* Thirdly, demons were associated with desolation arising from God's judgment. Demons lived in waste places, and so to be overrun with demons is a sign that the land has been wasted. And so Isaiah prophesied that when God judged Edom and Babylon, these enemies of Israel would be overrun with demons (Isa. 13:21; 34:14).

In the intertestamental period the prophet Baruch spoke of Israel's worshipping the demons and being desolated as a result (for the vocabulary, see Baruch 4.7, 35; but for the context, see vv. 7, 12, 19, 25, 30–35). He then promised that Israel's enemies would, in turn, experience exactly the same fate: they would be judged by God, and, as a result, would be a wasteland inhabited only by the demons. Much later, the book of Revelation alluded to this passage from Baruch, to refer to the doom of Babylon. God will judge the great city (now a symbol of the entire wayward sinful human race), and it will be inhabited only by dirty demons (Rev. 18:2).

If we drop back to the post-exilic period, it is important to observe that the prophet Zechariah apparently picked up this demons-of-the-wasteland theme and applied it to the land of Israel. Looking forward to the messianic age, Zechariah spoke of the day when 'there shall be a fountain opened for the house of David and the inhabitants of Jerusalem, to cleanse them from sin and uncleanness' (Zech. 13:1). And 'on that day', he says (v. 2), 'I will remove from the land the [false] prophets and the spirit of uncleanness', or, as the Greek OT puts it, 'the unclean spirit' (*to pneuma to akatharton*).

Here we have two of our three ideas combined. Because Israel's sin was idolatry, the nation had worshipped demons, and their punishment was consistent with the crime. Just like Edom, or

---

40. Wiéner, 'Idols', 251.

Babylon, Israel had been overrun with demons, but now Zechariah promises that one day this problem will at last be set right.

Since Zechariah 13:2 is the only place that the exact expression 'the unclean spirit' is found in the canonical OT,[41] it is clearly an important backdrop to the use of the phrase by the Synoptic Gospels, where the 'unclean spirits' are most frequently found.

The specific language of *evil* spirit is extremely rare in the Bible.[42] The two terms more regularly used in the Synoptics are *daimonion* and the Semitic-flavoured term we have already seen used in Zechariah 13:2, *pneuma akatharton*, 'unclean spirit'.[43]

However, despite the fact that these 'dirty demons' can be found as a thread that stretches from the Law, through the inter-testamental period, the Synoptic Gospels and on into the last book

---

41. See Bolt, 'Jesus, Daimons and the Dead', 77, n. 3, for the few occurrences elsewhere.

42. The actual expression 'evil spirit(s)', using the adjective *ponēros*, occurs only six times in the NT – only in the writings of Luke (Luke 7:21; 8:2; Acts 19:12–13, 15–16; cf. Matt. 12:45 = Luke 11:26, 'seven spirits more evil than itself'). It occurs only seven times in the LXX, where it is not even clear that it always refers to an actual being. When the Lord sent a *pneuma ponērōn* between Abimelech and Shechem, it appears to be simply a way of talking of hostility between the parties (Judg. 9:23); similar too is the 'evil spirit' from the Lord on Saul (1 Sam. 16:14–16; 19:9); the 'evil spirit' pursued by Ephraim is probably a reference to idolatry (Hos. 12:1 LXX – the Masoretic Text [MT] has 'the east wind'). The '*daimonion* or evil spirit' in the magical context of Tobit 6.8 is probably the only clear reference to a being. Cf. also the use of the term 'the evil one' for the devil.

43. The expression occurs twenty-two times in the NT: Matt. 10:1; 12:43; Mark 1:23, 26–27; 3:11, 30; 5:2, 8, 13; 6:7; 7:25; 9:25; Luke 4:36; 6:18; 8:29; 9:42; 11:24; Acts 5:16; 8:7; Rev. 16:13; 18:2. See also the unique combination 'spirit of an unclean demon' (Luke 4:33). Although not a term known to the Greek-speaking world, it would have been readily understandable by reference to the 'uncleanness' associated with the underworld (*miasma*) and the Pythagorean notion of the 'unclean souls' (Diogenes Laertius, *Lives* 8.31–32; Plutarch, *De genio Socratis* 591C); see Bolt, 'Jesus, Daimons and the Dead', 77, n. 3.

of the Bible, they have not attracted as much attention in demonologies as the second kind of demons, those that can be described
as 'from above'.[44] To give these powers the kind of respect they
deserve, let us call them the 'pasty principalities'.

### The pasty principalities
*From below to above* The dirty demons are disgusting and horrible,
since they are the ones so close to disease, suffering and death – and
the dirty world of magic seeking to manipulate them. They are dark,
forbidding, threatening, fearsome, and it is unsurprising that these
beings that can be described as 'from below' have not held as much
fascination in mainstream circles as those that can be described as
as 'from above', who seem cleaner and more respectable!

   To the Ephesians Paul spoke of 'the prince of the power of the
air' (Eph. 2:2).[45] The 'air' was an 'after-life' space; that is, a place souls
went after they died. Older views located the after-life below the
ground – it was, literally, the 'underworld'. Gradually, the after-life
was transposed into the heavens, with souls being released at death
into the air, with the impure souls remaining in the lower regions
because they were heavier, and the pure souls, being lighter, soaring
aloft to the regions among the stars. Thus the 'prince of the power of
the air', which refers to the regions above, is equivalent to the 'prince
of demons' (Mark 3:22), which refers to the regions below.[46]

---

44. For documentation and discussion, see Elgvin, 'Belial, Beliar,
    Devil, Satan'; Aune, 'Archai'; Caird, *Principalities and Powers*; O'Brien,
    'Principalities and Powers'; Dunnett, 'Powers'.

45. According to *2 Enoch* 29.4–5, after the devil fell from heaven 'he was
    flying in the air continuously'. According to Charles, *Apocrypha and
    Pseudepigrapha*, 2: 447, n., citing Eph. 2:2; 6:12, this tradition of Satan's
    location in the air appears to have been generally received among Jews;
    *Testament of Benjamin* 3.4; *Ascension of Isaiah* 4.2; 7.9; 10.29; Tuf. Haarez, f.9.2
    (as cited in Charles, *Apocrypha and Pseudepigrapha*, 2: 447). The latter shows
    the after-life status of this space: 'and there the souls of the demons are'.
    Cf. Athanasius, *De incarnatione* 25.

46. Cornford, 'Greek Views', 26–33; F. R. Walton, 'After-Life'; Bailey, *Some
    Greek and Roman Ideas*.

The point of this is that, just as views of the underworld pro-
gressed from speaking of an after-life below the ground to a
celestial after-life, in which the dead inhabited spaces in the air,
below the moon, and in the lofty places up in the stars, so, too, evil
powers were transformed from the dirty demons below to forces
found in the celestial realms.

*Evil powers in the heavens* Once again, there is not a lot of biblical
material on these beings[47] – despite the popularity of the thought
of the demonic world being organized so that each nation, or
city, or even each local church, is presided over by an evil power
of some kind, and of the consequent notions of 'Strategic Level
Spiritual Warfare' (SLSW), as popularized in dramatic Christian
novels, such as those of Frank Peretti.[48]

Views of evil powers existing in the heavenly places draw upon
material such as that referring to the 'sons of God' presenting themselves to God (Job 1 – 2), and the picture of the 'heavenly council',
from time to time arrayed like courtly advisers around God's
throne.[49]

---

47. Contra Wright, 'Charismatic Interpretations', 161: 'The Biblical material
    in support of the worldview we are describing is considerable and may not
    be dismissed or overlooked.'

48. Wagner, *Territorial Spirits; Engaging the Enemy; Prayer Shield; Breaking
    Strongholds; Confronting the Powers*. See also Dawson, *Taking Our Cities* and
    *Healing America's Wounds*. Silvoso, *That None Should Perish*, was the first
    to weave SLSW thinking into a strategy for urban evangelism. See also
    Peretti's novels: *This Present Darkness; Piercing the Darkness; Prophet*. For
    individual churches having their own local demons, see Hammond,
    *Pigs*, as reported by Wright, 'Charismatic Interpretations', 153. For some
    analysis and critique, see Kay, 'Pentecostals', 79; Wright, 'Charismatic
    Interpretations', 153–154, 159–162; Tinker, 'Phantom Menace'.

49. See Parker, 'Council', who points out there is abundant evidence for such
    a council of the gods outside Israel (205), and notes its transformation
    whenever it occurs in the OT to enable Yahweh to be the chief among the
    gods (1 Kgs 22:19b–22; Isa. 6:1–11; Job 1:6–12; 2:1–7a; Zech. 3:1–7; see also
    Isa. 40:1–8; Pss 25:14; 89:8; Jer. 23:18, 21–22; Job 15:8; Amos 3:7; Rev. 4–5).

The notion that different areas of the world are under the influence of their own 'territorial spirits' became very popular in later Jewish apocalyptic, but it can draw support from two texts only.[50] In the LXX version of Deuteronomy 32:8, supported by Qumran, we read that the nations were established 'according to the number of the angels of God'. The MT, however, reads, 'according to the number of the sons of Israel'.[51]

At the other end of the OT, when the people of God had been ejected from the Promised Land, the vision of Daniel refers to the Princes of Persia and of Greece (10:13, 20), who are fought by the archangel Michael (cf. 10:13, 21; 12:1). Elsewhere in Daniel's vision the same expression is used for human kings (10:1, 13b; 11:2), but, although these princes could be fought by God's angels and still be human (see 2 Kgs 6), the sense of the narrative suggests they are evil powers in the heavenly realms. Daniel 7 depicts the kings of the earth as bloodthirsty beasts, stripped of their power in a heavenly court scene, in which all authority in heaven and earth is given to one like a son of man. This appears to be an apocalyptic vision where the events on earth have their heavenly counterparts.

The NT also touches on these principalities and powers, without any elaboration beyond the use of the terms.[52] Although this lan-

---

Footnote 49 (*cont.*)

Ps. 82:1–7 is unique in that Yahweh addresses the other deities, 'announcing their demise as a consequence of their misrule of the world. His own assumption of world rule in their places is then acclaimed by the psalmist'.

50. See Tinker, 'Phantom Menace', 75–76. Despite the paucity of biblical material, 'in late Jewish and early Christian thought, the idea that each person and each nation had its own angel or angels was common' (Russell, *Satan*, 45).

51. Deut. 32:8, *hote diemerizen ho hypsistos ethnē hōs diespeiren huious Adam estēsen horia ethnōn kata arithmon angelōn theou*: 'When the most high divided (the) nations as he scattered the sons of Adam, he established boundaries of the nations according to the number of the angels of God.' The LXX is endorsed by Qumran.

52. A variety of terms are used (*angeloi*, Rom. 8:38; *archē*, Rom. 8:38, Col. 1:16, Eph. 6:12; *dynameis*, Rom. 8:38; *stoicheia*, Gal. 4:3, 9, Col. 2:8, Heb. 5:2,

guage is used of earthly rulers (Luke 12:11; Rom. 13:1; Titus 3:1), in other contexts it clearly refers to heavenly powers (Rom. 8:38; Eph. 3:10; 6:12; Col. 1:16; 2:15; 1 Pet. 3:22).[53] Significantly, Paul is clear that these principalities and powers have already been triumphed over in the cross of Jesus Christ. As the battle was fought between Jesus and the rulers of this earth resulting in the cross, a corresponding battle was fought in the heavens, and the pasty principalities were defeated (1 Cor. 2:6, 8; Col. 2:15).

## The devil

From various ancient texts that have survived, and the magical spells in particular, it is possible to glean a vast range of named evil powers.[54] In marked contrast, the devil is really the only one named by the Bible.

### The only named power

In the Hebrew OT the word 'satan' (*śāṭān*) is used for various adversaries – whether heavenly (Num. 22:22, 32; Job 1 – 2; Zech. 3; ?1 Chr. 21:1), or human (1 Sam. 29:4; 2 Sam. 19:22; 1 Kgs 5:4;

---

2 Pet. 3:10, 12; *thronos*, Col. 1:16; *kosmokratōr*, Eph. 6:12; *kyriotēs*, Col. 1:16, Eph. 1:21, 2 Pet. 2:10, Jude 8; *exousia*, Rom. 13:1–2, 1 Cor. 15:24, Eph. 3:10, 6:12, Col. 1:13, 16, 2:10, 15, 1 Pet. 3:22), but 'Paul is not interested in maintaining the individuality of the powers. He threw them all in one heap. He apparently recognised their existence, but was not interested in their hierarchy or relationships' (Van den Heuvel, *Rebellious Powers*, 23).

53. Aune, 'Archai', 79, lists three problems of interpretation of the NT evidence: (1) Are these figures human or angelic? (2) If they are spiritual, are they evil or good? (3) Does each word used for these beings represent a distinct category?

54. See e.g. Mastema 'hateful one', 'animosity' (*Jubilees* and Dead Sea Scrolls; Van Henten, 'Mastema'); Sammael, 'blind god', Melkira, 'king of evil', angel of iniquity (*Martyrdom of Isaiah*; Riley, 'Devil'); Asmodeus (Tobit; see Hutter, 'Asmodeus'), Beliar/Belial, 'useless' (OT, pseudepigrapha; Sperling, 'Belial'); Prince of error (*Testament of Solomon* 2.7; Riley, 'Devil'). For the use of multiple names in the magical spells, see the many examples scattered throughout the collection in Betz, *Greek Magical Papyri*.

11:14, 23, 25; Pss 38:20; 71:13; 109:4, 6, 20, 29; ?1 Chr. 21:1) – and
for adversaries, not of God, but of human beings. Some would
see only one clear instance of its being used as a proper name,
when an evil being by this name operating on earth incited David
to number Israel (1 Chr. 21:1).[55] Traditionally, however, this
same evil being has been identified as the one who operates as
an adversary in the heavenly places in Job and Zechariah (Job
1:6–9, 12; 2:1–4, 6–7; Zech. 3:1–2). The Job story also indicates
that this adversary appears to go between both places, appearing in the heavenly court after having come 'from going to and
fro on the earth, and from walking up and down on it' (Job 1:7).
More careful attention to the four contexts in which the word is
applied to a heavenly being, however, indicates that it refers to a
being who only temporarily has the role of accuser, never with
any sense of that being's acting independently from God, and is
clearly used of at least two different spiritual beings (see Num.
22:22–35; cf. Zech. 3).[56]

Turning to the Greek OT, we find that the transliteration *satan*
(1 Kgs 11:14, 2×) or *satanas* (Sirach 21.27),[57] occurs only three
times, and each time of a human adversary. Whenever it translates

---

55. So Elgvin, 'Belial, Beliar, Devil, Satan', 153. See to the contrary, however,
    the careful discussion in Day, 'Satan, I–III': If 'Satan' has been added
    by the chronicler (cf. 2 Sam. 24:1) to distance Yahweh from malevolent
    behaviour, and it is a proper name, then this passage contains 'the
    beginnings of a moral dichotomy in the celestial sphere'. The chronicler,
    however, has not removed Yahweh's 'malevolent intent' on other
    occasions (2 Chr. 10:15; 18:18–22), and the adjustment in 21:1 can be
    understood as part of his ideal portrait of David, to portray David's
    relationship with Yahweh favourably. Thus, even if *śāṭān* is a proper
    name here, 'the term is still a long way from connoting Satan, God's
    archenemy' (730).
56. See the discussion in Day, 'Satan, I–III'. Note the conclusion drawn by
    Dunnett, 'Satan', 714: 'In the Old Testament then, Satan is not an evil
    power opposed to God.' This development occurred at a later time,
    probably under the dualistic influences of Zoroastrianism.
57. This is possibly a reference to the celestial power; see Day, 'Satan, I–III', 730.

the MT's other uses of *śāṭān*, the Greek OT prefers *diabolos*, which literally means 'slanderer',[58] but which English speakers are used to hearing rendered as 'devil'.

In the NT, although it is still true that only one evil being is named, his names become many and various,[59] each focusing upon a particular aspect of his evil working. He is the Satan ('the adversary', 'the accuser'),[60] the devil ('the slanderer'),[61] the tempter,[62] the evil one,[63] Beelzeboul, 'the prince of the demons',[64] a murderer

---

58. The cognate *diabolē* was used for a 'slander spell' in the magical material; see e.g. *Papyri Graecae Magicae* 4.2570–2622; 2622–2707; Betz, *Greek Magical Papyri*, 83–84, 86–88. It is interesting to notice its use in LXX Num. 22:32.

59. Although the question 'whether [these terms] are all manifestations of one reality is a complex issue' (Cunningham, 'Satan', 359), it does seem that this is most likely.

60. For the OT use, see above. In Second Temple Judaism the word is rarely used in the Hebrew literature and, following the LXX translation of most references to Satan (see next note), *diabolos* is the commonest term in the Greek literature. For Satan in the NT, see Matt. 4:10; 12:26; 16:23; Mark 1:13; 3:23, 26; 4:15; 8:33; Luke 10:18; 11:18; 13:16; 22:3, 31; John 13:27; Acts 5:3; 26:18; Rom. 16:20; 1 Cor. 5:5; 7:5; 2 Cor. 2:11; 11:14; 12:7; 1 Thess. 2:18; 2 Thess. 2:9; 1 Tim. 1:20; 5:15; Rev. 2:9, 13, 24; 3:9; 12:9; 20:2, 7.

61. *Diabolos* in the LXX is used for 'an accuser' (Ps. 109:6; Esth. 7:4; 8:1) or 'adversary' (1 Maccabees 1.36), and as translation for Satan (1 Chr. 21:1; Job 1:6–7, 9, 12; 2:1–4, 6–7; Zech. 3:1–2; Wisdom 2.24). In the NT: Matt. 4:1, 5, 8, 11; 13:39; 25:41; Luke 4:2–3, 6, 13; 8:12; John 6:70; 8:44; 13:2; Acts 10:38; 13:10; Eph. 4:27; 6:11; 1 Tim. 3:6–7; 2 Tim. 2:26; Heb. 2:14; Jas 4:7; 1 Pet. 5:8; 1 John 3:8, 10; Jude 9; Rev. 2:10; 12:9, 12; 20:2, 10. *Diabolos* is also used for being 'slanderous' in 1 Tim. 3:11; 2 Tim. 3:3; Titus 2:3.

62. *Ho peirazōn*: Matt. 4:3; 1 Thess. 3:5; cf. Matt. 4:1–11 = Luke 4:1–13; Mark 1:13; 1 Cor. 7:1–5; Rev. 2:10.

63. Matt. 6:13; 13:19, 38; John 17:15; Eph. 6:16; 2 Thess. 3:3; 1 John 2:13–14; 3:12; 5:18–19.

64. This name has generated a great deal of discussion; see Gaston, 'Beelzeboul'; Herrmann, 'Baal-Zebub'; Penney and Wise, 'Beelzebub'. The

and a liar (John 8:44),[65] Beliar,[66] the one who holds the power
of death,[67] the great dragon, who is the serpent of old,[68] and the
deceiver of the whole world.[69]

---

Footnote 64 (*cont.*)

term is related to the god of Ekron mentioned in one passage in the OT,
where he is called Baal Zebub, 'the lord of the flies' (2 Kgs 1:2–3, 6, 16; LXX:
*baal muia*; cf. Josephus, *Jewish Antiquities* 9.2.1: *Akkarōn Theos Muia*). His
association with 'flies' gives him similarities to the Mesopotamian god Nintu
and the Greek god Zeus (Pausanias, *Description of Greece* 8.26.7). Symmachus
and the NT (and *Testament of Solomon* 6.1–2) use the form *beelzeboul*, which, by
comparison with Akkadian documents from Mari, has now been shown to
be a preservation of the original form of this name, 'Baal the prince [of the
underworld]', a chthonic god able to help in cases of illness. Baal Zebub is
probably to be explained as a contemptuous Jewish modification.

The attempt to explain Beelzeboul as a figure different from the devil,
in order to identify him as Israel's territorial spirit (cf. Parsons, 'Binding
the Strong Man', 111), does not fit the Gospel context well.

65. His 'murder' was by causing the downfall of humanity and, with the
introduction of their sin into the world, the arrival of death: Gen. 2:16–17;
3:1–19; Rom. 5:12–14.

66. Although a very common name for the devil in intertestamental literature
and other Jewish material, this term occurs only once in the Bible (2 Cor.
6:15). Sperling, 'Belial'.

67. *To kratos echonta thanatou*, Heb. 2:14–15.

68. *Ho ophis ho archaios*: Rev. 12:9; cf. Gen. 3 and 2 Cor. 11:3; *ho drakōn ho megas*:
Rev. 12:3–4, 7, 9, 13, 16–17; 13:2, 4, 11; 16:13; 20:2. See also Wisdom 2.24.

69. *Ho planōn tēn oikoumenēn holēn*: Rev. 12:9; 20:7–8. Cf. Gen. 3:1, 13; 1 Tim.
2:14, and perhaps Rom. 7:11. The devil has also received some traditional
names, evoked by biblical material – such as e.g. 'Lucifer'. This name
comes from Isa. 14:3–20, from the Latin for 'morning star', or 'day star'
(v. 12); cf. 2 Pet. 1:19, Rev. 2:28, 22:16. The Vulgate also uses 'Lucifer'
in Job 11:17; 38:32; Ps. 110:3. The Hebrew term refers to an astral
being, and, although it is difficult to identify any comparable myth, it
has similarities to the Ugaritic story of Athtar, who could not be king in
the heights of Saphon and therefore became king over all the earth, or
perhaps of the netherworld. See Watson, 'Helel'.

Before we leave the devil, two further questions need to be addressed: his *origin* and his *organization*.

### The origin of the evil powers

For centuries[70] Christian demonology has often included the view that Satan began life as an angel,[71] who, prior to the fall of Adam, organized a revolt among other angels,[72] with the result that they were all cast down from heaven to earth, where they continued to afflict human beings. Despite its popularity, however, the theory is derived from the pseudepigrapha, and not from the Bible itself.[73]

---

70. The theory that Satan began his baneful influence as an angel who fell, and who then led a revolt among other angels, has been deeply embedded in English culture, both expressed and reinforced by the powerful and influential poetry of William Shakespeare ('Angels are Bright still, though the brightest fell' [Shakespeare, *Macbeth*, Act 4, scene 3, lines 22–23]) and John Milton. It was enshrined in Roman Catholic teaching by the Fourth Lateran Council in 1215 (Eckhardt, 'Between the Angelic', 411–412), and is still part of the Catechism of the Roman Catholic Church; see nos. 391–395, Catholic Church, *Catechism*, 98–99, much to the dismay of some commentators; see Daly, 'Creation', 105–106. Working forward from the other end, however, Russell, *Satan*, reports no reference to Satan's fall in the earliest fathers until it turns up in those drawing on Enoch's Watchers, in the second century, Justin (65) and Irenaeus (80–81), and Tertullian (93–94) and Cyprian (105–106) in the third, to whom we can also add Athanasius, *De incarnatione* 25.

71. Despite the (typical) claim by Blocher, 'Evil', 467, that 'Scripture reveals that evil appeared in heaven before it entered the world', the texts cited (2 Cor. 11:3; John 8:44; Rev. 12:9; 20:3) need not be taken as delivering support to the claim.

72. The reasons that have been given for Satan's fall have varied from being a free choice gone bad, pride (cf. 1 Tim. 3:6), envy (of God and/or human beings) or lust (based on Gen. 6).

73. 'Unlike Christian theology, in Israel there was no inclination to embody all evil in a central figure or trace its cause to a single historical event, such

Its origins can most probably be traced to Zoroastrianism, whose literature contains a story in which the evil one declares to God, 'I shall destroy you and your creatures forever and ever. And I shall persuade all your creatures to hate you and to love me.'[74] Because Zoroastrian dualism was not amenable to the biblical world view, it was melded with the older 'combat myths' which had already come into the OT in the modified form of Yahweh's being the supreme being in the council of the gods.[75] In this setting, evil can be attributed to some failing in the lesser beings, and can also be opposed by various champions of righteousness, such as the Angel of the Lord (Zech. 3:1; *Jubilees* 17.15 – 18.16) or Michael (Dan. 10:13, 21; 12:1; Jude 9; Rev. 12:7) or, supremely, Jesus Christ. The post-exilic Jewish pseudepigraphal writings attach this idea of a heavenly rebellion on to two different OT texts, thus providing two versions of Satan's fall. In one version the enigmatic account of the sons of God coming in to the daughters of men (Gen. 6:1–4; perhaps cf. Jude 6 and 2 Pet. 2:4) is elaborated to say that these illicit unions gave birth to the giants, who were destroyed by the flood but whose disembodied souls became demons (*1 Enoch* 6 – 16), under the leadership of Azazel, identified as the messenger of Satan (*1 Enoch* 54.6), or the devil himself (*Jubilees* 10.1–11), as well as the Serpent (*Apocalypse of Abraham* 23) and Baal Zebub (*Testament of Solomon* 6.1–2). The second version was probably inspired by the mythological descriptions applied to the kings of Babylon and Tyre (Isa. 14:4–20; Ezek. 28:11–19), and pushes the angelic rebellion back to the second day of creation, when (as God himself explains)[76]

---

Footnote 73 (*cont.*)

    as Satan's fall,' J. H. Walton, 'Serpent', 737, who suggests that the Genesis account actually polemicizes against the ancient cosmological myths.

    Wright, 'Charismatic Interpretations', 151, notes how important 'the myth of the fall of angels' is to contemporary charismatics, and how it is extended by some to their notions of 'territorial spirits', 'hierarchically structured'.

74. Boyce, *Textual Sources*, 46.

75. Riley, 'Devil', 246.

76. Cf. Unger, *Biblical Demonology*, who places the angelic fall (given his eschatological position) to have taken place between Gen. 1:1 and 1:2.

one from out of the order of angels, having turned away with the order
that was under him, conceived an impossible thought, to place his
throne higher than the clouds above the earth, that he might become
equal in rank to my power. And I threw him out from the height
with his angels, and he was flying in the air continuously above the
bottomless. (*2 Enoch* 29.4–5)[77]

Once the intertestamental elaborations were in place, it became
almost impossible for later generations not to read their dramatic
accounts into the biblical stories. However, whatever the enigmatic
episode of the sons of God teaches, it does not seem to be a heavenly fall to account for the presence of evil powers in the world,[78]
and despite Isaiah 14 and Ezekiel 28 and 31 being favourite proof-
texts for 'the fall of Satan',[79] these passages are almost certainly not
teaching such a view.[80]

When it comes to the NT, when Jesus spoke of the devil's
beginnings, he was referring to the account in Genesis 3, and
goes back no further (John 8:44; cf. 1 John 3:8). In addition,
where the imagery of the fall of Satan is picked up by the NT
(Luke 10:17–20; John 12:31; Rev. 12 and even 20:3), it does
not refer to a primeval fall, but to his defeat by means of
the cross.[81]

---

77. *Book of Adam and Eve* 1.6 is derived from this account: 'The wicked Satan
[. . .] set me at naught and sought the Godhead, so that I hurled him down
from heaven' (Charles, *Apocrypha and Pseudepigrapha* 2: 447, who provides
a summary of the demonology of the book, which, as he admits, is not an
easy task to perform).

78. For discussion, see Clines, 'Significance'; Eslinger, 'Contextual
Identification'; D. L. Peterson, 'Genesis 6:1–4'.

79. See Noll, *Angels of Light*, 109–110, who refers to Forsyth, *Old Enemy*,
130–133, and Clifford, *Cosmic Mountain*, 160–173.

80. J. H. Walton, 'Serpent', 738; referring to Forsyth, *Old Enemy*, 232–238;
Ferguson, *Demonology*, 73; cf. 71–73.

81. Ferguson, *Demonology*, 17; cf. Dunnett, 'Satan', 715.

*The organization of the evil powers*

The later Jewish elaborations also provided a military-style organization to the evil powers,[82] that has also come over into later Christian demonologies – and which has become especially important in contemporary expansive charismatic circles.

Despite such elaborate schemes, the biblical evidence is, once again, too sparse to enable any confidence that evil powers operate within a highly complex organizational structure. In the OT no relationship can be demonstrated between Satan and the demons;[83] and in the NT the clearest evidence of such a relationship is in the title 'the prince of demons' (Mark 3:22), which most likely describes his role as the one who keeps departed spirits in the underworld,[84] rather than someone at the head of a heavenly army, and in two references to the devil having 'messengers' (angels; Matt. 25:41 and Rev. 12:9). This is not a lot of material to go on.

In addition, the claim that the devil has an ordered, hierarchical organization[85] is sometimes based upon Jesus' parable in the Beelzeboul controversy, in which he speaks of 'a kingdom [being] divided against itself' (Mark 3:24).[86] However, this too is a fairly

---

82. Brunon and Grelot, 'Evil Spirits', 149: 'Later Judaic thought organizes this world more systematically. Evil spirits are regarded as fallen angels.' Noting that *1 Enoch* 6.8 provides a militarily styled organization, with 20 named angels, each commanding 10 more, Aune, 'Archai', 79, is clear that, although such attempts to classify the powers may abound, they are not earlier than the first century. *Testament of Solomon* organizes the powers into 7 spirits, and then 36 more, each thwarted by an angel of God (Dunnett, 'Powers', 620).

83. Kuemmerlin-McLean, 'Demons', 140.

84. See Bolt, *Jesus' Defeat of Death*, 124–127.

85. Blocher, 'Evil', 467, speaks of 'an empire of evil'; Scotland, 'Charismatic Devil', mentions the expansive charismatics' notion of a 'hierarchy of wickedness' with which the evil powers rule the world (93), and a 'hierarchy of power' as the main means by which the devil works (89–90).

86. Cf. Engelsviken, 'Spiritual Conflict', 123: 'The answer first points out the improbability that Satan would drive out demons, since that would mean

slim base of evidence, especially when this is by no means the only, nor the best, way to understand this saying.

In fact, it is difficult to see why the evil powers should be granted a high degree of organization at all. Is this just imposed by the interpreter, because of familiarity with God's ways of working?[87] God is the god of order, but why wouldn't Satan's domain be totally chaotic, random and directionless?[88]

### The demons, the devil and the dead

With all the interest in the devil's origins, and his supposed organization, one of his most obvious features according to the Scriptures is regularly overlooked; that is, his link with death.[89] We

-----

that his kingdom would be divided against itself and therefore would be destroyed. This argument assumes that Satan has a kingdom and a deliberate strategy and that he holds people captive (Matt. 12:29).'

87. It is clearly possible for the interpreter to impose order when there is none (Cunningham, 'Satan', 389). As a close analogy, Cunningham suggests that it may have been the anti-satanists who actually created Satanism (386), as an elaborate conspiracy theory (386), and notes that the therapist subculture has enabled the building of a coherent picture of Multiple Personality Disorder since 1984 (the first international conference on MPD), but in fact the order may actually have been imposed upon the phenomena 'not so much saying the same things as being heard the same way'. Cf. Peters, 'Satanism'.

88. The use of the language of 'design' (*noēma*, 'thought'; 2 Cor. 2:11) or 'scheme' (*methodeia*, 'method'; Eph. 6:11) with respect to the devil need not be taken as describing the devil's ontology, for it is phenomenological, i.e. it is used of things originating with the devil at the point they confront a human being. As the soldier needs to be prepared for whatever 'method' might be presented to him by the enemy (without buying into the rationality that may or may not lie behind the assault), so too Christians must be prepared for whatever comes at them (e.g. false teaching; see Eph. 4:14).

89. However, Eckhardt, 'Between the Angelic', 412, notes that death and the devil are often associated, and Dunnett, 'Satan', 715, that 'Satan is regarded in the New Testament as "master of death and destruction".'

have already noted his connection with the realm of death, in that he is 'the prince of the power of the air' (Eph. 2:2), an after-life space, and the 'prince of demons', which speaks of his position in the underworld (Mark 3:22). He is known for being a liar and a tempter, but his lies and temptations are intermediate causes, which serve his major function: to kill. It was his temptation that led to Adam and Eve's fall and, with that sin, death entered the world (Rom. 5:12; Gen. 3:1–19; cf. Wisdom 2.23–24). With an eye on that primal event, Jesus spoke of him as being 'a murderer from the beginning' (John 8:44; cf. 1 John 3:12). When the writer to the Hebrews summarized the meaning of the Son of God's incarnation and death, he said it was in order to neutralize 'the one who has the power of death, that is, the devil' (Heb. 2:14–15).

The connections with death and the realm of the dead are reinforced when we turn to the pasty principalities and the dirty demons – especially when illuminated from other sources. If the principalities and powers are behind the beasts of Daniel, then they spread bloodshed and death. They are also exactly the kinds of beings a person might meet in the after-life, and this appears to be how they are understood in Romans 8:38–39. The demons are associated with idolatry, and idolatry with death.[90] The word 'demon' was used regularly for the spirits of the dead, and the expression 'the prince of demons' has many analogies in other cultures, all referring to a being who was like a gate-keeper of the underworld spirits.[91] The demons used by magic, necromancy, divination, sorcery and the like were spirits of the dead,[92] and on it goes.

---

90. Wiéner, 'Idols', 252, referring to Wisdom 13 – 14, esp. 14.12–21.
91. One such analogy is found in the name Beelzeboul; see Herrmann, 'Baal-Zebub'. For further analogies, see Bolt, *Jesus' Defeat of Death*, 124–127.
92. See Bolt, 'Jesus, Daimons and the Dead'; Kotansky, 'Demonology'. The connection between demons and ghosts has regularly been observed, even if it has not been fully appreciated; cf. Ferguson, *Demonology*, who notes the demons are ghosts in Plutarch (35), the Greek world (40–42), and in the Hellenistic Jews Philo and Josephus (81), noting that this is Josephus' most frequent use (85).

In other words, it is important to notice that the biblical teaching associates the evil powers very closely with death and the realm of the dead, and it clearly and specifically gives the power of death to the devil as his major function. The fact that so many views on demonology overlook, ignore or deny the connection between the evil powers and death is a serious distortion of the biblical picture. This mistake leads to interpreters' missing exactly how the presentation of the evil powers serves the main message of the Scriptures. But once the devil and the demons are connected with death and the underworld, this becomes clear; for by that connection they are drawn closer to the central, Christocentric message of the Scriptures.

Jesus defeated these evil powers, in order to liberate us from death, sin's curse, so that we might live again. 'Who shall deliver us from this body of death?' Only the one who has defeated the devil.

## Towards a biblical theology of (the defeat of) the evil powers

Now that we have completed a summary of the biblical material touching on the evil powers, we can begin to move more intentionally towards a biblical theology of the defeat of the evil powers.

### Features of 'a biblical theology'
#### Christocentricity
A biblical-theological approach will be Christocentric. The only way to understand the evil powers properly is in relation to the life, death and resurrection of the Lord Jesus Christ, for the sake of our salvation.

#### Development over time
Biblical theology is interested in the development of a theme over time. Although this can occasionally be found in discussions of evil powers,[93] a non-temporal approach is more usual, as if the

---

93. See e.g. Brunon and Grelot, 'Evil Spirits', 149: 'The portrait of the evil
    spirits, malevolent spiritual beings, comes to light only slowly in revelation.'

evil spirits have always and will always be a part of the way things are. In fact, there is no reason to think that the devil is interested in time at all,[94] but not so with the Lord God. He is the Alpha and Omega (Rev. 1:8), who determines both beginning and end. He is moving this world from creation to new creation, and by his word is carrying all things along to this appointed goal (Heb. 1:3). When the evil powers are understood in relation to God's time-line, it becomes the time-line of their defeat.

### From the margins to the middle

This thread of God's self-revelation forms the middle core of the Scriptures, and so the middle core of the history of this world. Since evil powers appear at the margins of the biblical story, how do we move from these marginal figures to understand God at the middle?

In part, this is done by picking up the various clusters of ideas we have already noted from our Bible summary, and watching for these as we travel along God's time-line. Recall that there are two kinds of demons (the dirty and the pasty), and there is the devil; that they afflict human beings, are associated with the idols of the nations, and so with magic, divination and the like; to be overrun with demons is a sign of God's judgment; and, finally, the demons and the devil are strongly associated with death.

Noticing these connections assists the movement from the margins to the middle. For now we can attempt to relate this cluster of ideas to the core business of the Bible, in order to find how the evil spirits at the biblical margins help to illuminate the glorious message of the Son of God at the middle.

-------

94. In the Garden of Eden the serpent denied the past and the future, in order to bring the focus solely on the present, on what could be seen to delight the eyes (Gen. 3:5–6). Satan told Jesus that all the kingdoms of the world *and their glory* (their outward appearance) had been given to him (Luke 4:5–6). The Bible shows the devil as only being interested in the 'now', in how things seem to the senses at the moment. Even in these last days, when he knows his own time is short (Rev. 12:12) and the form of this world is passing away (1 Cor. 7:31), it is fair to say that Satan offers human beings no time-line.

*Epochs in history*
The Bible opens with the period known as the 'primeval history' (Gen. 1 – 11), and then, as the Bible's main storyline unfolds, three epochs, or time periods, can be identified, shaped by God's promises, which, once given, then structure the course of historical events.[95] In what follows, we will seek to move through these epochs, with an eye on our cluster of ideas and upon the ultimate goal of Christ's defeat of the evil powers. What is there in the OT period that prepares us for the flurry of demonic activity when the Messiah arrives?[96]

### Primeval history: the lie told and felt

The Bible's first explicit mention of 'evil powers' comes with the crafty serpent who takes the initiative in leading Eve, then Adam, to fall (Gen. 3).[97] Despite the brevity of the paragraph, it contains a wealth of information on how the serpent operated, which can be taken as something of a paradigm for the way the devil has worked throughout the ages.[98]

---

95. Robinson, 'Gospel'; cf. Robinson, 'Origins'.

96. Noted by many; e.g. Moreau, 'Demon', 163.

97. Although, for those with eyes to see, even the creation account in Gen. 1, which depicts God's bringing order out of chaos, may also show God's victory over the evil powers which ever threaten his orderly world. Although the first time an evil power appears in the Bible it is in the form of the mythological figure of the serpent, Gen. 1 may, indeed, polemicize against the various 'combat myths' of the surrounding cultures. Cf. J. H. Walton, 'Serpent', 736: 'Though the Genesis creation account contained no serpentine sea monster to threaten God's establishment of cosmic order, here we find a serpent who begins to work against the order that exists in the human realm.'

98. Although the identification was made much later, from a biblical-theological point of view, this evil power is identified as the devil (Wisdom 2.23–24; Rev. 12:9; Rom. 16:20, cf. Gen. 3:15; and see also 2 Cor. 11:3). As for his strategies, he questions God's word, before denying it outright (Gen. 3:1, 4); he portrays God as a liar who is not generously caring for human interests (v. 5), withholding good things, especially wisdom. He

The consequences of the fall are devastating for the rest of human history. Despite the serpent's denying that Adam and Eve would die, God's promise prevails, and so death entered the world through their sin (2:17; 3:14–19; cf. Rom. 5:12; Wisdom 2.23–24). The following narrative reinforces this point, and thereby demonstrates that the advent of death into the world is the significant teaching of the fall account. As sin spreads further and further, so does human mortality. In the genealogy of Genesis 5, no matter how long the people of the past might have lived, or how many children they might have bred, the verdict over their lives was exactly the same: 'and they died'. This is the same verdict that hangs over the head of every human being, and gives rise to the terrible cry 'Who will deliver us from this body of death?'

However, God began to answer that cry at exactly the moment that death entered into the world. In what has traditionally been regarded as the first statement of the gospel, God promised that one day the seed of the woman would crush the serpent's head (Gen. 3:15). This promise generates an expectation and hope that one day the Lord would provide a man who would reverse the curse of the fall and finally bring rest to our painful toil (cf. Gen. 5:29). There will be a victor, and when he comes the serpent's legacy will be gone, death will be removed and Eden restored.

At the end of Genesis 4 – 11, after documenting the spread of sin and death further and further, the narrative arrives at the story of the tower of Babel (Gen. 11:1–8). This event depicts organized sinfulness, human society seeking to make a name for themselves in defiance of God, which resulted in the dividing of languages and the scattering of the nations (Gen. 10), thus laying the seed of tension and discord among the nations. From now on

---

Footnote 98 (*cont.*)

promises greater wisdom, insight and pleasure. He denies God's future and proposes an alternative. He causes a focus upon the present and upon the delightful appearance of things, rather than the dreadful consequences of disobeying God's word, and denies that the man and woman will die. In the whole process he disrupts the order God established in creation, and causes profound disharmony in the relationship between man and woman.

in the biblical story, 'Babel' – or more often, 'Babylon' – connotes humanity organized in rebellion against the Creator. It is also interesting to notice that Babylon is especially associated with the dirty demons (e.g. Isa. 13:21; cf. Isa. 34:14; 65:1–4; Baruch 4; Rev. 18).

The curse on Adam's fall and the pain it introduced into the world has an even nastier context now. It is bad enough for human beings to have to live 'in darkness and in the shadow of death' (Luke 1:79), but now the world in which they live is filled with anti-God forces much larger than themselves, which now threaten their already fragile mortal existence.

### Historical epoch: the promise given and threatened

As his answer to this organized rebellion, God calls one man to leave his home to go to a country God would show him. With this call of Abram, the historical epoch begins. We know from later in the Scriptures that in his former life Abraham was an idolater (Josh. 24:2; cf. Gen. 35:2–4), which, in biblical thought, makes him someone who worshipped demons. Despite this background, God promised to bless Abram and to make him the source of the world's blessing (Gen. 12:1–3), and he then sealed these promises with a covenant (Gen. 15). These promises then shape and structure the biblical story from this moment on.

The word of the promise often seems so small in the face of the larger hostile forces operative in this fallen world. Abraham certainly feels their threat, sometimes triumphing over them (Gen. 14), and other times apparently succumbing to fear of them (e.g. Gen. 20). His descendants continue to carry the promise, but, by the end of Genesis, the stage is set for a major clash with one of the superpowers of the nations.

The clash arrives in the book of Exodus, when Moses battles with Pharaoh, and so with Egypt's gods, and with Pharaoh's magicians, and so with Egypt's evil powers. The ten plagues document this conflict, with the result that Egypt lies in ruins (Exod. 10:7). In the Bible's first great act of deliverance the Israelites are saved by the Passover lamb, brought through the sea and sent towards the Promised Land.

Part of God's reasons for allowing his people to stay in Egypt for so long (430 years, according to Exod. 12:40–41) was because 'the iniquity of the Amorites is not yet complete' (Gen. 15:16). Here the Amorites probably do duty for the entire list of peoples who inhabited the land promised to Abram (see Gen. 15:18–21). These people had practices detestable to the Lord. As part of Israel's conquest of the land they were to be blotted out, along with their gods (Exod. 23:23–24; 33:2; 34:11–17). And there is no doubt that the 'dirty demons' were very much a part of the life of these nations. Even before Israel came into the Promised Land God warned them to destroy the Canaanite gods, for any covenant with the people of the land would become a snare to the Israelites (Exod. 34:12). The conquest of the land first involved battling the kings Sihon of Heshbon and Og of Bashan (Num. 21). Their defeat so filled the Moabites with fear of the Israelites that they turned to magical practices by asking Balaam, the diviner, to curse Israel (Num. 22). In God's humorous defeat of Balaam's curse through a talking donkey, the book of Numbers shows his effortless power in dealing with the demonic forces of Israel's neighbours.

As the conquest continues under Joshua and then the Judges, the various kings and nations are driven before Israel. Their gods are shown to be pitiful in comparison with Yahweh – and remember, with the gods of the nations fall the demons. David finally completes the process by the conquest of the Philistines, and at last Israel comes to a time of rest (2 Sam. 7). Whatever else this involves, it includes the clear display that Yahweh has been victorious over the surrounding nations, their gods and the detestable practices of their dirty demons. Indeed, even Saul had begun the process of ridding the land of such practices (1 Sam. 28, esp. v. 9), and in subsequent times good kings removed idols and their trappings, and bad kings became entangled once again in this murky world of divination and magic. The low point of such practices came with Manasseh (2 Kgs 21, esp. vv. 3, 6, 11), whose evil was so bad that, even despite Josiah's reforms (2 Kgs 23, esp. v. 24), his dealing with the demons (23:26–27) became the last straw that took Judah into exile.

At whatever stage of Israel's history, the dirty demons were part of their cultural environment, potentially threatening to ensnare the people. This is where the comparative material of other nations can illuminate the extent of this temptation, for whether we turn to Egypt,

Canaan, Assyria, Babylonia or, in the later period, Greece, the environment in which Israel existed was simply brimming over with demons.

It is against this cultural environment that we need to understand the strong condemnation of, and prohibition against, Israelites being involved with the idolatry of the surrounding nations, and all its associated features, such as magic and divination. And, of course, prohibiting these things also excluded Israel from any involvement with the demons. The many prohibitions of sorcery and the like would also have included what we call 'exorcism', for it was an integral part of these forbidden practices.[99] This helps to explain why there is no trace of exorcism in the OT – and it also raises interesting questions about how Jesus would have been viewed, if he was mistaken as a magician because he cast out demons.

This demon-filled cultural environment also makes the OT's relative silence about demons all the more remarkable.[100] It can be taken to indicate that Israel found in Yahweh a positive, satisfying alternative. Rather than consulting 'the mediums and the necromancers who chirp and mutter' (Isa. 8:19), Israel had the word of their God; and, even if troubled by the thought of demons, they could find their refuge in him (Ps. 91).

In Solomon's age this refuge in the arms of Yahweh was peculiarly symbolized by the building of the temple. No matter where the Israelites might be, they could turn to the temple and God would hear their prayer for deliverance (1 Kgs 8:30, 33–40,

---

99. Cf. Vriezen, *Outline*, 224: 'Whereas in Babylon and Assyria the literature of exorcism plays an important part there is no trace of these things in the Old Testament, and already at an early date it was forbidden officially to perform any exorcism, sorcery or interrogation of the spirits (Exod. 22:18; 1 Sam. 28; Deut. 18:9ff.; Lev. 19:31; 20:27).' See also Brunon and Grelot, 'Evil Spirits', 149.

100. For the Bible's paucity of evidence, see the discussion above. For particular comment on the OT, see e.g. Vriezen, *Outline*, 225; Von Rad, *Theology*, 1: 278; and Koehler, *Old Testament Theology*, 160, who comments on the various demons, *šēdîm*, *śĕʿîrîm*, Lilith and others, 'All these belong to a realm of uncertainty. We do not know what part angels, spirits and demons played in the life and faith of Old Testament man.'

44–53). And even the nations could turn to Israel's temple, and God would hear their prayer also, so that they too could find their refuge in him (vv. 41–43).[101] Now that Israel was at its glorious height, with the nations subdued, in fulfilment of his promise to Abraham, God's blessings began to overflow to the world. In this golden age, with Israel at the centre of the world, Solomon was peculiarly gifted with divine wisdom, and this wisdom began to flow outwards to the nations, the natural home of the demons.[102]

### Prophetic epoch: desolation and hope

But Solomon was also the beginning of the decline. Once again the various elements of our cluster of ideas need to be borne in mind as we consider Solomon's dark side. His many wives were probably politically motivated, a human attempt to secure peace in a world filled with many languages, cultures and hostile nations. His many wives brought with them their gods, and their gods brought their whole gamut of detestable practices, and so the demons were once again on Israelite soil. The downward slide began with Solomon and, with one or two exceptions among the kings, continued until first the northern kingdom of Israel and then the southern kingdom of Judah had been spewed out of the land.

As we have seen, if we follow the hint in Zechariah 13:2, the desolation of the land of Israel as God's judgment on their idolatry could also be pictured as the land being overrun with unclean spirits.

As Israel's sin grew worse and the judgment of the exile fell, the prophets also brought a message of hope. Restoration would come, through forgiveness hard won by the Servant of the Lord.

---

101. Naaman the Syrian provides one concrete example of a Gentile who finds refuge in Yahweh, and then subsequently renounces any other gods (2 Kgs 5, esp. v. 17; cf. Luke 4:27).

102. For the development of Solomon's reputation as a magician, see Torijano, *Solomon*; cf. Duling, 'Solomon'. In contrast to the wisdom supposed to yield the secrets of the universe, as in magic, it is interesting that the wisdom given by God to Solomon yields the kind of practical common sense about ordinary, everyday living found in the book of Proverbs.

The Servant was pictured as a warrior who would deliver those held captive by the strong man (Isa. 49:24–26; cf. Mark 3:27); having buckled on his armour (Isa. 59:17–20; cf. Eph. 6:10–20), he would bring an enormous deliverance. The deliverance God would bring would be so vast it would flow out beyond Israel to the nations (Isa. 49:6). Isaiah spoke of the time that the shroud of death would be taken away from the nations (Isa. 25:6–9). When Ezekiel spoke of the restoration, he used the image of a valley of dry bones being restored to life (Ezek. 37). By the time of Daniel the resurrection from the dead had become attached to the kingdom of God (Dan. 2:44; 12:1–2), which would one day be given to one like a Son of Man (Dan. 7:13–14).

It is also in Daniel's visions that the ungodly kingdoms of this earth are pictured as beasts, raging across the earth, killing and devouring as they go (Dan. 7). And, as we have seen, the earthly rulers and dominions and all their battles upon the earth are given counterparts in the heavenly places. It is as if the answer to the death and destruction inflicted upon humanity by these principalities and powers is found only in the hope of resurrection. It is as if Israel's long history of battling with the nations, which at this stage had already been lost on earth, was now projected into the heavens. Daniel's visions speak of a great and future day when the battle will be decided in Israel's favour, and the only kingdom left alive will be the kingdom of God, with people from all tongues and nations ruled over by the one like a Son of Man. And that will be the day of resurrection.

These grand hopes of the major prophets are sustained by the post-exilic prophets. And among them little Zechariah looks forward to the time when the fountain of cleansing will be opened in David (13:1), and, as it is opened, the unclean spirit will be cast out of Israel's land (Zech. 13:2).

## Epoch of fulfilment: cleansing of land, nations and cosmos
### Messiah in the midst
When the Messiah finally arrived, he brought the epoch of fulfilment. As we have already noted, it is in this period of biblical history that the references to the demonic are most frequent. However, even here we need to keep things in proportion. Even at this moment it is

important to understand how the evil powers serve the good news of Jesus Christ. When Jesus dealt with the unclean spirits, it was only one aspect of his ministry, and therefore needs to be understood within the total package of what he came to do.

As soon as Jesus was baptized by John, and declared to be the Son of God and Servant of the Lord by the voice from heaven (Mark 1:11), he was tested by Satan in the famous wilderness encounter (Mark 1:13; Matt. 4:1–11; Luke 4:1–13). The devil announced that all the kingdoms of the world and their glory had been given to him. He then offered to give it all to Jesus, if only Jesus would fall down and worship him. Here, at the beginning of Jesus' ministry, we have an apocalyptic perspective on everything that will take place. As the Messiah comes into Israel's midst, the great battle in the heavens will be fought on earth. By the end of his ministry Jesus will declare himself to be the glorious Son of Man of Daniel 7:13–14, to whom all authority in heaven and earth has been given (Matt. 28:18). So, here in the temptation scene, the devil offers Jesus what properly belongs to the Messiah and what will one day be properly awarded to the Son of Man. But the devil's offer is from the wrong person and with the wrong timing. The Son of God will worship only the Father, and will not short-circuit the job he has come to do. He will only come to his glory by first going to the cross. The great apocalyptic battle will be fought on God's terms and in God's way.

As he began his public ministry, Jesus proclaimed that the kingdom of God had drawn near (Mark 1:15). As the Messiah in the midst of Israel, he healed their diseases as a concrete demonstration that the era of forgiveness of sins had arrived.[103] And since the fountain had now been opened in the house of David for the cleansing of Jerusalem, as Zechariah had predicted, it is no surprise that he set about cleansing the land from the unclean spirit (Zech. 13:2; cf. Matt. 12:43–45).

As Jesus did so he focused not on the devil himself but on the victims of the devil's destructive actions. He came to deliver people, and that is what he did. Sometimes this resulted in fairly dramatic expulsions of unclean spirits, symbolizing the grand deliverance the

---

103. See Bolt, 'Forgiveness of Sins'.

Messiah was bringing to Israel, which would later flow out to the rest of the world. At other times the deliverance was less 'dramatic', but just as real nevertheless. For, as Satan told Jesus in the temptation scene, all the kingdoms of this world still belonged to Satan. The 'ordinary' structures of human life are also the way that Satan's influence is exerted. Peter was on Satan's side merely by thinking like a human being (Mark 8:33). As Jesus called upon people to seek first the kingdom of God and his righteousness (Matt. 6:33), he was calling them to shift their thinking, their allegiance and their lifestyle towards God and his kingdom. This repentance towards God entailed leaving behind all the things that human beings naturally find their security in: work, family, possessions, homes, culture, status in society, sense of achievement and so on. These are part of 'ordinary life' and are just as much instruments of the devil as the more dramatic afflictions seen in some of the Synoptic scenes.

When Jesus' ministry brought him into conflict with the Jewish religious leaders, he told them that he cast out demons to bind the strong man, in preparation for the ultimate deliverance of the captives (Mark 3:22–30). If the prince of demons was bound, the underworld would then give up its dead! The Spirit of the Lord was upon him as the Suffering Servant, promised by the prophet Isaiah. In Matthew and Luke's version of this incident Jesus then declared that if he was in the disciples' midst, casting out demons as the Spirit-equipped Servant of the Lord, the kingdom of God had come upon them – and its arrival was just around the corner. The long-awaited resurrection of the dead was almost upon them.

Isaiah had spoken of the Servant's bringing forgiveness to the land of Israel, and Jesus' healing and casting out demons was part of this restoration. But the main event was yet to come. For the Servant had come to die, giving his life as a ransom for many (Mark 10:45). Sin had brought death into the world and, no matter how wealthy a person might be, none could afford the ransom from the grave (Ps. 49). But now, at last, the Servant of the Lord had come in order to give his life as a ransom for many. The time had come for the greatest act of deliverance ever.

## The crushing cross

Fufilling the Servant's role, Jesus went to the cross. According to the NT portrayals, his death was the result of a wicked collaboration between the rulers and authorities of this world, on the one hand, and the principalities and powers in the heavenlies, on the other.

From the beginning Israel's Messiah was opposed by Israel's rulers, who by the end of the Gospel accounts had joined forces with Pilate, the representative of the nations. According to Acts 4:23–28, in this coalition arrayed against Jesus, Psalm 2 was fulfilled. As both Jewish and Gentile rulers put the Messiah to death, this was the nations of the world gathering together, as they did at Babel, but this time they were engaging in a great cosmic battle in an attempt to overthrow the Lord and his anointed.

But the Gospels have added another dimension to this cosmic battle. From the beginning the devil and the unclean spirits rose up against Jesus, and the human opposition appears to be caught up in this demonic opposition. In the Beelzeboul controversy it is clear to the reader that Jesus is not the one in league with Satan, which implies that the Jewish religious leaders are. By the end of the Gospels Satan has specifically used the treachery of one of Jesus' closest friends to ensure that the Messiah is destroyed. When Jesus died on the cross, that was the great heavenly battle being fought out on the earth, and apparently the devil won.

But from Jesus' perspective earlier in the Gospels account this was a war the devil would lose. Casting out unclean spirits was the minor skirmish that anticipated this great moment when the prince of this world would be cast out (Luke 10:18; John 12:31; Rev. 12). The casting out of demons was binding the strong man; the death of Jesus would be his defeat. Jesus would die as the ransom for many, to liberate the strong man's captives. The death of the Servant would be the moment when the serpent's head was finally crushed, and the judgment and pain of the fall would at last be overturned. The captives could now go free, because someone had come to deal with their sin, and so ransom them from the grave.

## The resurrection lift-up

On the third day Jesus rose from the dead, confirming that his version of his death was the true one. Death had no hold on him, because the devil had no ground for accusation against him (John 14:30; Rom. 8:31–34). He was raised up to heaven as the mighty Son of Man and granted all authority in heaven and earth (Matt. 28:18). He was declared to be both Lord and Christ, and seated at the right hand of God, far above every rule, authority, principality and power. From here he poured out the Spirit, promised for the last days, the down payment of the inheritance to come.

And so his exaltation to this position was all for the sake of the church (Eph. 1:22). His resurrection from the dead declared his great victory over the evil powers. The end of the dirty demons, the pasty principalities and the devil himself had come at last. The one who held the power of death, and wielded it to hold humanity in lifelong slavery, had finally been neutralized (Heb. 2:14–15).

*Light to the nations*
The immediate consequence of Jesus' being raised from the dead with all authority in heaven and earth was the launch of the mission to the nations. His apostles were specially commissioned as his witnesses, this unrepeatable function establishing their ministry as foundational for the Christian movement. As his apostles took the gospel out to the nations of the world, they entered the territory which had always been the natural home of the demons. The risen Christ specially commissioned the apostle Paul for this task, telling him that he would be sent among the nations, 'to open their eyes, so that they may turn from darkness to light and from the power of Satan to God, that they may receive forgiveness of sins and a place among those who are sanctified by faith in me' (Acts 26:18).

The book of Acts has been a happy hunting ground for many hermeneutically suspect interpretations. It must not be read moralistically, as if it provides examples for future generations to follow. It is the record of the spread of the gospel through the ministry of Christ's specially appointed witnesses. It is descriptive, rather than prescriptive; that is, it does not provide illustrations of what will be normative experience for all time, but reports what actually happened in the foundational period of the early Christian mission. If anything in Acts is to be regarded as normative experience, then we should expect to have teaching on that experience in the epistles.

When it comes to the evil powers, once again, these appear on the periphery of the account, with reports of only five encounters with the demonic by representatives of the Twelve, the seven deacons or the apostle Paul (5:15–16; 8:6–7; 16:16–18; 19:11–17). The magical context of the first-century world is apparent in these encounters, with a fair degree of supersitious/magical behaviour apparently overlooked as God brings transformation to human lives. The function of these scenes is not to provide a pattern to follow, but to show the remarkable effects of the gospel as it spread from Jerusalem to Samaria and then to the ends of the earth.

The only people labelled as exorcists are those outside the Christian ambit, and it is clear that as people are converted to Christ their magical practices (13:8–10; 19:18), divination (16:16) and idolatry (15:20) are dispensed with fairly dramatically. In the place of such dramatic practices (so detestable to God since the early days of the OT), these converts from the nations turned to the ordinary Christian practices of meeting together to be fed on the Word of God and to pray. And what they found was that this Word continued to run across the face of the earth to work its powerful work of salvation.[104]

*Then comes the end*
According to Revelation 12's apocalyptic picture of Jesus' work on the cross, the devil is defeated because he no longer has any grounds for accusation in the courts of heaven, since Christ's death has dealt with human sinfulness once and for all:

> And I heard a loud voice in heaven, saying, 'Now the salvation and the power and the kingdom of our God and the authority of his Christ have come, for the accuser of our brothers has been thrown down, who accuses them day and night before our God. And they have conquered him by the blood of the Lamb and by the word of their testimony, for they loved not their lives even unto death.' (Rev. 12:10–11)

As a result of his defeat, he knows his time is short and so he turns on Christ's people 'in great wrath' (cf. Rev. 12:12, 17).

---

104. See Rosner, 'Progress'.

The 'spiritual warfare' in which the Christian is engaged is not a particular aspect of the Christian life, but is the Christian life itself. This explains the need for Christians to be alert and to resist the devil, knowing that he is a defeated enemy and will quickly flee. But there is no call to engage the devil directly, by turning back to the ancient magical practice known as exorcism. Resisting the devil is done through submitting to God (Jas 4:7). The spiritual warfare of the Christian life is 'fought' by faith, hope and love, through believing the Word of God and praying to our heavenly Father.

For, in this continued conflict situation, the battle is fought through exactly the same means as it began, namely through the proclamation of the Word of God and through prayer that God might open blind eyes. There is no call in the NT for anyone to engage directly with the devil, and neither is this necessary. He may be enraged, but Christians must fix their eyes upon Jesus, and calmly get on with their Christian service in the midst of ordinary life, confident that as the gospel progresses further into the nations, so the devil's domain will continue to recede.

First through his apostles, and then through the apostolic gospel, the risen Son continues to place his enemies under his feet. He will continue to apply his great victory to the nations of this world until the end finally comes. In his great chapter on the future resurrection of the dead, Paul shows the divine programme that governs these last days. Christ must reign until he has put all his enemies under his feet (1 Cor. 15:25), and then the end will come, when he delivers 'the kingdom to God the Father after destroying every rule and every authority and power' (15:24). Since the last enemy to be destroyed is death (15:26), the end will mean the great day of resurrection, when, at last, Christ's victory will be fully realized and our deliverance will be complete. Christ has already neutralized the devil by dying for our sins, thus removing the grounds of the devil's accusation. Once the believer is justified by faith the Spirit is received as the down payment of the good things to come, and, being the Spirit of resurrection, begins to bring life to our dead bodies, straining ahead to the day of resurrection (Rom. 8:11). Then the victory of Christ will be known to us, not (as now) simply by faith, but then in glorious reality.

Who will deliver us from this body of death? Thanks be to God, through Christ Jesus our Lord.

## 3. DELIVERANCE WITHOUT EXORCISM? JESUS AND SATAN IN JOHN'S GOSPEL

**Willis H. Salier**

### Introduction

The aim of this chapter is to assess the contribution the Fourth Gospel makes to an understanding of Christ's victory over the powers. The Fourth Gospel is of interest in this discussion, especially in the modern age where there appears to be a resurgence in interest in the demonic, and the resultant deliverance ministries developed to deal with it.[1] It is of interest because at first glance its contribution would appear to be negligible, or at least problematic. The evidence from the Synoptics is that the casting out of demons was an integral element of Jesus' ministry. However, such incidents are noticeably absent from the Fourth Gospel, for no exorcisms are recorded in John's Gospel.[2] This is one of numerous outstanding differences between John and the

---

1. So e.g. Sandford and Sandford, *Comprehensive Guide*; Horrobin, *Healing through Deliverance*.

2. The language of exorcism will be used throughout this chapter to refer to

Synoptics and clearly raises the broader issue of their relationship. Absences can be significant. Occasionally this theme is reprised on the many police procedurals that proliferate in our television schedules: it is the absence of a noise or a particular clue that provides the key to the mystery. This investigation will begin with a brief exploration of this 'absence' and canvass a number of suggested solutions. Following this, John's Gospel will be surveyed, especially examining a number of references to the character of the devil or Satan. It will be seen that, between the absence of any references to the casting out of demons and the presence of the devil as a character in the narrative, the Johannine perspective emerges to contribute to an understanding of Christ's victory over the powers.

## Explaining an absence

The absence of exorcisms usually draws comment from commentators in passing, but there have been few extended studies until relatively recently.[3] Generally speaking, attempts to account for the absence of exorcisms fall into two broad categories: *accidental* and *deliberate* omission.

### Accidental omission

As Twelftree notes, the simplest solution is that John did not know of Jesus as an exorcist.[4] This may be due to either his own lack of experience with the ministry of Jesus or the absence of exorcism stories in the sources he was using.[5] This is highly unlikely for a number of reasons. First, there is strong evidence that Jesus was

---

the phenomenon of casting out demons, noting Peter Bolt's reservation as to its usage (chapter 2 in this volume).

3. The three main studies that stand out are Plumer, 'Absence of Exorcisms'; R. Piper, 'Satan, Demons'; Twelftree, *Jesus the Exorcist*, and, more recently, *In the Name*.

4. Twelftree, *In the Name*, 184.

5. Plumer, 'Absence of Exorcisms', 350–354.

widely known as a 'powerful and popular exorcist'.[6] Unless the Fourth Gospel was written by a hermetically sealed apostle to a hermetically sealed Christian community, such a lack of knowledge is most unlikely, regardless of the absence or otherwise of such accounts in a putative signs source.[7] The second reason for doubt in this respect is that there are hints that John was aware of the Synoptic tradition generally and possibly some of the exorcism stories in particular. While begging the question of the precise relationship between John and the Synoptics, an emerging consensus in Johannine scholarship suggests John represents an independent but aware tradition with respect to the Synoptics.[8] In short, it looks as if the omission is deliberate.

### Deliberate omission

Most who offer any comment on the matter suggest that the omission is part of a deliberate strategy, but there is considerable divergence in the possible reasons given. The three most prominent studies on the question come from Plumer, Piper and Twelftree.

#### Eric Plumer

Plumer suggests that John's interests are primarily apologetic and pastoral. First, his interest is apologetic in that Plumer suggests the exorcisms were 'omitted in part because of their magical connotations'; that is, the 'Evangelist was deliberately trying to obviate any possible misinterpretation of Jesus as a magician or wonderworker'.[9] Secondly, the interests are pastoral in view of the ongoing dispute between the Johannine community and Judaism. The charges that Jesus was in league with the devil were a

---

6. Twelftree, *In the Name*, 184. See also Plumer, 'Absence of Exorcisms', 353–354; R. Piper, 'Satan, Demons', 252–257.

7. With respect to this point, see the important chapter by Bauckham, 'For Whom?' For a useful overview of the case against a signs source for the Fourth Gospel, see Van Belle, *Signs Source*.

8. Paul Anderson uses the term 'interfluential' to describe the relationship; see 'Why This Study Is Needed', 13–67, esp. 61–62.

9. Plumer, 'Absence of Exorcisms', 358.

particular point of sensitivity for the Johannine Christians in their dispute with Judaism, such that 'the icon of Christ the Exorcist was irreparably damaged'.[10] Embarrassment of one sort or another is therefore a primary motive.

Plumer's first point is unlikely, in that John happily reports a variety of healing stories, some using contemporary techniques that could appear to be 'magical' (John 9).[11] His second point relies on a reconstruction of the dispute between the Johannine community and Judaism that is increasingly under reconsideration and a speculative reading of passages such as John 7:20, 8:48, 52 and 10:20 that suggests they reflect the Beelzebul controversy recorded in the Synoptics (Mark 3:22–23). While Plumer suggests that ultimately the omission of the exorcism stories is a theological treatment of the charge, he admits that this controversy is seen 'through a glass, darkly'.[12] A closer reading of the relevant passages in the Fourth Gospel suggests another explanation is to hand.[13]

### Ronald Piper

A more sociologically oriented view comes from Piper, who notes that the language of demons and possession comes in the heat of conflict between Jesus and his opponents and is on at least two occasions aligned with the charge that Jesus is a Samaritan. Piper's suggestion is that the language of demonic possession in the Fourth Gospel is reserved for the demonizing of opponents and is a function of conflict between the Johannine community and its opponents in the synagogue.[14] Furthermore he discusses the references to the devil/Satan in the context of the Johannine

---

10. Ibid., 362.

11. Inclusions like this count against many other explanations that have recourse to embarrassment or demythologizing explanations of the omissions of exorcisms. John is not averse to mentioning angels, the devil and also charges of demonic possession. Cf. R. Piper, 'Satan, Demons', 261–263.

12. Plumer, 'Absence of Exorcisms', 360–361.

13. For an alternative explanation of John 7:20, 8:48, 52 and 10:20, see below.

14. R. Piper, 'Satan, Demons', 265, 267–270.

world view, posing the important question raised by the reference to the apparent defeat of the ruler of this world at the cross in John 12:31.[15] What exactly happens to the devil in the world view of the Fourth Gospel? His suggestion is that the devil is confined to this world, not cast out from this world, and therefore has no influence on believers who are 'not of the world' (John 17:14, 16). The question becomes one of identity and how believers define themselves with respect to both the devil and the world. Piper correctly draws attention to the need to explain both the presence of the language of demon possession and the devil, as well as explaining the absence of exorcisms. One wonders if his own explanation relies too heavily on the reconstruction of a conflict between the Johannine community and its opponents, and upon the categories of group identity and boundary maintenance. Further, in focusing on the interpretation of the Fourth Gospel in this context, it seems that the focus is taken off the stated purpose of the Gospel; that is, presenting Jesus as the Christ (John 20:30–31). Piper's construction, however, does raise the important questions of the devil's influence, relationship to 'this world' and the nature of his defeat.

### Graham Twelftree

Arguably the majority of reflections on this matter suggest that there must be theological reasons for the omission of the exorcism material. This is tied to some aspect or other of the presentation of John's Christology and the point he is trying to make. A key writer in this respect is Twelftree, who suggests three interconnected reasons for the omission. First, he says that the exorcisms are not spectacular enough; that is, that they are a fairly mundane example of a work being performed with a regular degree of frequency in Jesus' time.[16] Undoubtedly the recipients of Jesus' ministry in this regard did not consider the work mundane, but perhaps that is beside the point. More importantly Twelftree's point concerning frequency is also disputed.[17] As to whether they are not spectacular

---

15. Ibid., 271–276.

16. Twelftree, *In the Name*, 192–193.

17. See e.g. Ferdinando, *Triumph of Christ*, 312–313.

enough, it is certainly true that John makes a small selection of very impressive miracles to include among the collection of signs he records to demonstrate Jesus' identity. However, it is a matter of opinion as to how spectacular the Synoptic account of the exorcism of 'Legion' is in Mark 5, and perhaps this would rank as a candidate for Johannine inclusion?

The second suggestion Twelftree makes is that in John the theme of the kingdom of God is considerably downplayed. He notes that in the Synoptics the theme of exorcism is closely tied to the coming of the kingdom. While the theme of 'kingdom' is not entirely absent from John (cf. John 3:3–5; 18:33–37), it is true that this is another noticeable difference from the Synoptic presentation. John's focus is far more on the role of Jesus as King than the coming of the kingdom per se, though it is also often noted that the language of eternal life does some sort of duty for the Synoptic concept of the kingdom of God and what it means. This 'solution' only replaces the mystery of one absence with another.[18] However, it also opens the possibility that if John's focus is on kingship and the identity of Jesus as Christ or King, then the reason for the absence of exorcisms is not so much because of the absence of the kingdom theme, but rather that John is focusing on the battle between rival kings or princes that takes place between Jesus and Satan in the Gospel.

Twelftree's third suggestion is that in the Fourth Gospel the defeat of Satan is connected with the events that transpire on the cross and not with the defeat/exorcism of evil spirits. He further suggests that this theme is hinted at in Matthew's Gospel, but largely absent from Mark and Luke. This is arguably the most fruitful of the three suggestions and will be pursued in what follows. Piper's observation that it is one thing to try to explain an absence of demonic activity, but that in the Fourth Gospel this must be done while also accounting for the presence of language concerning demons and Satan, rings true. It is suggested that matters of theology, especially Christology and the Johannine perspective on

---

18. Cf. also Piper's comments on this suggestion, R. Piper, 'Satan,
    Demons', 266.

these matters, will give the best account.[19] Attention will therefore be given to the presentation of the person and work of Christ and the contribution to that presentation of the various mentions of the devil/Satan.

## Thinking through the Gospel of John

### *Observing the texts*

As Piper noted, while demons do not feature as characters in the Gospel, the figure of the devil or Satan does and there are several accusations of demonic possession made in debate (6:70; 7:20; 8:48–52; 10:20; 12:31; 13:27; 14:30; 16:11; 17:15). Observations from these texts can be collated under a number of headings.

### *The reality of the devil*

The first observation is that while John does not speak often about the devil or Satan, he does so at significant moments in the Gospel. A variety of terms are used: *diabolos* (the devil, 6:70; 8:44; 13:2), *satanas* (Satan, 13:27) and *ho archōn tou kosmou toutou* ('the ruler of this world', 12:31; 14:30; 16:11), *ponērōs* ('the evil one', 17:15).[20] All of these terms refer to the same character/reality throughout the Gospel. Three of the terms overlap with Synoptic and broader NT usage, with *ho archōn tou kosmou toutou* being the novel expression.[21]

The devil is mentioned in chapter 6, at the moment of a great Christological confession by the disciples; in 8:44 in connection with the Jews' rejection of one of Jesus' great Christological claims; at 12:31 where the turning point of the Gospel is reached with the announcement of the advent of the much-anticipated hour; in John 13:2, 27 with regard to the treason of Judas, which leads to

---

19. Piper appears to underestimate the value of theological explanations in favour of 'boundary-related' reasons (ibid., 265).

20. Note that all English translations are from the Holman Christian Standard Bible.

21. Coetzee, 'Christ and the Prince', 104.

the cross; in chapter 16 as the future ministry of the Holy Spirit is mentioned the judgment of Satan is mentioned; and then finally in the context of Jesus' final prayer for his disciples (17:15).

The point here is simply to underscore the reality of the devil as depicted in the Fourth Gospel. He is an effective power, active on the stage of world history and not a mere figure of speech or a faded mythological conception.[22]

### The 'character' of the devil

From a narrative point of view three observations can be made about the character of the devil as he is presented in the Fourth Gospel.

First, his title *ho archōn tou kosmou toutou* (ruler of this world) can be considered. Only John uses the precise title, though there are glimpses of similar concepts in the temptation narratives in Matthew and Luke and the mentions of the 'god of this age' at 2 Corinthians 4:4 and 'the ruler of the atmospheric domain' in Ephesians 2:2.

In the Fourth Gospel the phrase 'this world' usually designates the world in the more negative Johannine sense of humanity enslaved in sin and living in enmity with God. The title occurs three times in the Fourth Gospel and this usage suggests that John sees the devil as a person of great power.[23]

Secondly, while the title might suggest power, there are also real limitations on this power. The limitation of the devil's power is particularly shown in the 'defeat' passages (12:31; 14:30; 16:11). Further, in one of the main descriptions of his character the devil is described as a murderer from the beginning (*ap' archēs*) and not a murderer in the beginning (*en archē*), as is said of the *logos* in John 1:1. The prepositions hint at the fact that the devil is not an eternal, autonomous cosmological power. There is, however, an ambiguity about his ongoing power and potential threat to the disciples of Jesus expressed in the fact that Jesus prays in John 17:15 that they will be protected from 'the evil one'.

---

22. Kovacs, 'Now Shall the Ruler'.
23. Coetzee, 'Christ and the Prince', 106.

Thirdly, the major description given to the devil occurs in John 8, where he is described as a murderer and the father of lies. These are significant descriptions that presuppose the devil's animosity towards both the Father and the Son. As this statement suggests, he stands opposed to the two major things that Jesus and the Father stand for in the Gospel: life and truth. He destroys the life that God creates and denies the truth that God reveals.[24]

While there is some discussion as to precisely which murder might be in mind, the background here is clearly Genesis 1 – 3. The combination of 'murderer' with the description 'father of lies' suggests that the ancient story of the serpent's encounter with Adam and Eve is in view, and the implication is that they were murdered through the devil's lies about God. The father of lies utters the mother of lies and is the original murderer.[25] He murders through the propagation of lies.

The echo of this ancient narrative is important in a Gospel where so much emphasis is placed on the truth and where the truthfulness of Jesus' word and testimony is a significant point at issue throughout the numerous trial scenes that populate this Gospel, especially between chapters 5 and 12. In the immediate context of this description of the devil, Jesus has been accused of offering a testimony that is not true (8:13); he has gone on to assert that his judgment is in fact true (8:16); he has asserted that if his audience do not believe that Jesus is who he has said he is, they will die in their sins (8:24); and that this is true because he is speaking the words of one who is true (8:26). Jesus then goes on to say that if they continue in his words, they will know the truth that sets them free. This truth involves the knowledge that the Son can set them free from slavery to sin to become sons who remain in God's household for ever (8:33–36). The Jews claim to be children who have God as their father, but this claim is invalidated by their behaviour in denying the truth of Jesus' words and in attempting to kill him. Questions of truth and lies abound in this encounter. The prospect of life is therefore connected to the truth of his testimony.

---

24. Barrett, *John*, 348.

25. Tonstad, 'Father of Lies'. See also Moberly, 'Did the Serpent?'

This therefore makes questions concerning the nature and content of truth in the Gospel important ones. To ask Pilate's question, perhaps a little more sincerely, what is truth?[26] In brief it is observed that as Jesus speaks during the Fourth Gospel, he is the subject of his own speech, his own words.[27] He speaks words about himself, his identity and his origins: that he has come from the Father as the Son. The truth of the Gospel is that Jesus is the Son of the Father and that, therefore, the Father is the Father of the Son. Everything else that might be included in the truth that Jesus brings springs from this basis.

In John 8:18 Jesus says that he testifies about himself and the Father testifies about him as well. The implied testimony of the Jews, as they contest the claims of Jesus, is that Jesus has not come from the Father. Jesus retorts that in saying this they speak the language of their own father: lies.

Some key questions are therefore raised for the readers as well as the various participants as Jesus and the Jews interact. Can the testimony of the Father and Son be trusted? Can the word of the Father and Son be abided in with the prospect of life held out for those who do so? These questions take us back to the original lie, to the 'mother of all lies'. The original lie prompted doubt concerning the truth of God's word and the integrity of his character. In short, could God be trusted? The figure of the devil in the Gospel is characterized as the father of lies.

*The relationship between the 'world' and the devil*
Rather than demons or unclean spirits appearing in the story, it is the devil himself who is presented at work and there are strong suggestions in the narrative that he works through individuals and groups, chiefly Judas and the rulers of the Jews.

Judas first appears in the narrative at 6:70, where Jesus has been deserted by a number of followers after he has spoken to them of the necessity of eating his flesh and drinking his blood if they

---

26. It is in the immediate context of Pilate's question that Jesus states that he was born to be a king and has come into the world in order to testify to the truth (John 18:37).

27. Gundry, *Jesus the Word*, 49–50, summarizing his argument in 1–50.

want to have eternal life. Jesus turns to the Twelve and asks if they too wish to leave. Peter replies on their behalf that they will remain because they know that Jesus is the Christ and that there is nowhere else to go to gain access to the words of eternal life. The relief and triumph of this moment are immediately undercut by Jesus' words that one of them is the devil.[28] This could be simply a description anticipating Judas' later role in the betrayal of Jesus, but as the narrative moves on it is more sinister and it is seen that the direct influence of the devil will be exercised upon Judas.

The relationship between Judas and the devil is continued in 13:2, where the devil puts it into Judas' heart that he ought to betray Jesus and then is described as entering him (13:27), after Judas takes the morsel of food offered to him by Jesus.[29] The verb used here for entering is used of demons in the Synoptics (*eiserchomai*; e.g. Mark 5:13), but the suggestion that it is Satan (the only time this name is used in John) that enters here is, apparently, without parallel in later Judaism (cf. Luke 22:3 however for a parallel perspective in the Gospels).[30] The devil is depicted as entering and controlling Judas' actions, but there is also a sense in which Judas' accountability in the action is preserved through the description of Jesus' offering the morsel of food, which is to be seen as a gesture of honour and friendship.[31] It then perhaps

---

28. Should this be translated as 'a devil' or 'the devil'? Wallace, *Greek Grammar*, 29, considers this an example of a monadic noun and this, plus the fact that it precedes the equative verb (Colwell's rule: a definite predicate nominative that precedes the verb is usually anarthrous), suggests that it should be treated definitely. Carson, *John*, 304, comments that *diabolos* invariably refers to Satan in the NT, and the parallel with a similar statement to Peter in the Synoptics confirms the identification. Köstenberger, *John*, 222, demurs and suggests, on the grounds of context, that 'a devil' is adequate.

29. However the potential ambiguity in 13:2 is decided, that is, whether the devil puts the suggestion into his own heart or that of Judas, it is clear that the devil and Judas are now in a conspiracy. See Raymond Brown's discussion in *Gospel according to John*, 2: 550. The next reference is more explicit in any case.

30. Köstenberger, *John*, 417. Note that Acts 5:3 has Satan filling Ananias' heart.

31. Beasley-Murray, *John*, 238–239.

constitutes a final appeal to Judas. Satan and Judas are therefore connected; but Judas is not unwitting, as the offering of the morsel forces a moment of decision. A sequence is described whereby Satan suggests, Judas decides and Satan enters. At the same time, however, even at this point of betrayal John is concerned to show us the control, or sovereignty, exercised by Jesus in the situation as he commands Judas to be on his way. A complex set of relations is therefore established, which sees human responsibility, the possession of a human being by an evil personality and divine sovereignty all in play.

Finally, in 14:30 Judas may again be in view, but if so his personality has been totally subsumed by the ruler of this world.

The devil is portrayed as working through an individual in specific circumstances to achieve specific goals, in this case the death of Jesus. The devil is also portrayed as working in a broader context, through groups as well as individuals. Two lines of thought are suggestive here. The first is the unique title *ho archōn tou kosmou toutou*. It is an unusual title. The only other characters designated as rulers in the Gospel are the Jews (John 3:1; 7:26, 48; 12:42) and in view of the verbal linkage at least one writer has posited a tentative connection between 'the ruler' and the 'rulers'.[32]

Whatever the likelihood of this particular connection, there are other suggestive connections to be explored. It has already been observed that while there are no demons as such in the Fourth Gospel, the language of demonic possession is present. This language occurs repeatedly as an accusation in polemical contexts (7:20; 8:48–49, 52; 10:20–21).[33] Observing this language in its context opens up some further fruitful lines of enquiry.

In the context of John 7:20 Jesus is in dispute with the Jewish authorities, who are looking for a way to arrest him.[34] The crowds appear to know nothing at all of these machinations and question Jesus when he states that some want him dead or are trying

---

32. Moloney, *John*, 354–355.

33. The main lines of the following discussion are indebted to Twelftree, *In the Name*, 198–204.

34. Von Wahlde, 'Johannine "Jews"', 33–60, suggests the designation 'the Jews' (*hoi Ioudaioi*) generally refers to the Jewish authorities.

to kill him. The charge of demon possession that ensues is often assumed to be madness, but the context shows it may also be an expression that suggests Jesus is not believable, that he is not telling the truth.[35]

The reader is aware of the error in the charge because the answer to the crowd's question is known. At least twice earlier in the narrative the reader has been told that the Jews are trying to kill Jesus. On the basis of this earlier knowledge the reader is invited to conclude that Jesus is telling the truth and that he does not have a demon.

The main cluster of accusations concerning Jesus being demon possessed occurs in John 8:48–52, where the dual charge is that Jesus is a Samaritan and has a demon. It is in this context of course that Jesus also makes his own accusations as he charges the Jews as not loving him (8:42), not accepting his word (8:43) and having the devil as their father (8:44). At least two of Jesus' accusations are clearly correct from the narrative and so the reader is invited to reject the implication in the question the opponents pose in 8:48.

Jesus' own reply is a 'catch-all' response, indicating that the two charges are related if not synonymous. He does not have a demon and also implicitly rejects whatever is inferred in the charge that he is a Samaritan.

The charge of being a Samaritan is unique and to some extent opaque. The charge most likely implies a cluster of ideas surrounding the antipathy of the Jews and the Samaritans. Jews avoided Samaritans because they were despisers of true religion; they had false prophets and were known to be prone to idolatry and sorcery. They misrepresented God. In the context of John 8 the slight again looks to be directed at Jesus' teaching and his claim to be telling the truth. He is in fact 'acting the Samaritan', teaching falsely about God and therefore the Jewish people, whom he has just insulted by denying their claim to legitimate worship of the one true God.[36] The accusation of deception is echoed in the charge of having a demon. The two-part accusation amounts to Jesus' being a liar.[37]

---

35. Twelftree, *In the Name*, 199.

36. See Schnackenburg, *John*, 2: 218; Ridderbos, *John*, 319.

37. Twelftree, *In the Name*, 201.

There is irony in this charge, especially in the light of the fact that Jesus has just accused the Jews of having the 'father of lies' as their father. Earlier in the Gospel we have seen a group of Samaritans accepting Jesus' testimony and acclaiming him correctly as the Saviour of the world (John 4:39–42). Jesus' non-rebuttal of the charge of being a Samaritan is positive towards the Samaritans, but also picks up on the high view of the Samaritans expressed in the Gospel. In fact the implication is that the Jews are demon possessed and not the Samaritans. In this Gospel it is they, and not the Samaritans or Jesus, who falsely testify to God.

The final charge occurs in John 10:20–21, where Jesus is accused of having a demon and being out of his mind. The impression created by the charge in chapter 8 is carried through here as well. The verb used to describe Jesus as mad is used only a handful of times in the New Testament and its use in Acts especially is in the context of utterances given that are unbelievable for the listener. Again the implication is that Jesus is not telling the truth. The charge of having a demon here is a charge akin to being a deceiver, a liar and a false prophet.

In John 8:44 the Jews are accused of 'lying' in the image of their father. If the implication is that in some sense they are the ones 'possessed by a demon', then we see that John is meaning to say that there is a sense in which to be demon possessed is to be in error. To be in error is the problem of many and not just a few who are possessed 'individually' by a single demon, or even a company of demons. This immediately signals that, in the Johannine perspective, there is a more universal problem to be dealt with in respect of the influence of the devil. It is at this broader level that the Gospel seems to operate.

This is a more expansive realm of influence ascribed to the devil as well as an insight into the way that he operates; that is, through lies and untruth. If this association of demon possession and lies and the father of lies being the father of the Jews is correct, then we begin to see the Johannine way, at least, of how the devil is to be opposed. To be demon possessed is to be in error and is to be combated with the truth, the truth that, as Jesus says, will set one free (John 8:32).

If I may extrapolate slightly further, one of the interesting features of the Fourth Gospel that has often been noticed and commented upon is the relationship between the Jews and the *kosmos* (world), such that the Jews instantiate the world and show what it means to belong to the world.[38] The Jews are of their father, the devil, while the world is eventually described in Johannine terms as lying in the influence of the evil one (1 John 5:19). The Gospel prepares the ground for this final observation with its implicit relationship between the Jews and the world. This world lies in the power of the devil. The inhabitants of this world can be described as subjects under a foreign power as well as children reflecting the image of their own 'father'. The bifocal perspective is important, suggesting a need for liberation as well as forgiveness for complicity in the 'family image'.

However, we need to note again the cautious terms in which this is expressed. There are careful qualifications made, so that the correspondence is not exact. God's children are begotten by him (John 1:12–13); this is not so with the devil's children. The devil takes life; he does not propagate or generate it. The children of the devil are shown to be his children by their own sin. The Jews act in conformity with their father's character but are nonetheless responsible for all they do. The devil is always subject to Christ's/ God's sovereignty, throughout the Gospel.

Perhaps here is a hint as to why John does not record Jesus' casting out unclean spirits. If John recorded these incidents, then he would be undercutting his insight that the devil has a hold on many and not a few; and that truth is fundamental to the battle: salvation and knowing and remaining in Jesus and the truth that he brings is the antidote to error and the demonic, not a healing encounter reserved for a few.[39]

### John 12:31: the climactic moment

In a Gospel that does not waste words and is full of climactic moments this is a huge moment. The request of some Greeks to see Jesus signals the arrival of the much-heralded hour that has been foreshadowed a number of times in the previous narrative (John 2:4; 7:30; 8:20). The moment is used by Jesus to unfold the

---

38. Salier, 'What's in a World?'
39. Twelftree, *In the Name*, 204.

meaning of the hour to which the Gospel has been proceeding. It will involve a fruit-bearing death, as Jesus tells the 'parable' of the seed falling to the ground and dying in order to produce fruit. In terms of Christ's victory it is what Jesus says in verse 31 that is most significant, where he declares that he sees the ruler of this world cast out. At this moment a veil is lifted to show a cosmic conflict ensuing, which will be decided at the cross.[40] Numerous writers have observed that what appears to be in view here, with the use of the verb *ekballō*, is a 'great exorcism'.[41] At least two questions are posed by this passage: (1) From whence is the prince of this world cast out? And (2) how is he cast out?

In terms of the place from which the ruler is cast out, it is initially tempting to conclude that this is heaven, with the account in Revelation 12 providing a comparison. However, the context suggests that it is 'this world' that is in mind. Jesus goes on to speak of his being lifted up from the earth and drawing all people to himself. Judgment for the world is salvation for all types of people who are drawn to him. The ruler's expulsion is therefore a metaphorical allusion to the fact that he cannot keep his victims enslaved. He still exercises power in the world, but his domination is broken and he cannot stop people being drawn to Christ.[42]

In a single act the devil is dealt with directly by Jesus. In this way the Fourth Evangelist is able to affirm that the devil's control of this world is far more pervasive than the possession of individual people, and that the defeat of the devil requires more than isolated activity against individual demons by Jesus.[43]

Whatever interpretation we might make of the details, the overall point is clear. One aspect of the cross-work of Jesus is to secure the liberation of humanity from the devil's control. A major element

---

40. Kovacs, 'Now Shall the Ruler', 231–233; Tonstad, 'Father of Lies', 195–196.
41. Michaels, *John*, 227.
42. Ferdinando, *Triumph of Christ*, 324–326. See also Barrett, *John*, 427. A close reading of Rev. 12 suggests a two-part victory that coordinates with this reading.
43. Twelftree, *In the Name*, 204.

of both John's and Jesus' understanding of the cross, then, is the destruction of the works of the devil (cf. 1 John 3:8). The casting out of demons and unclean spirits as recorded in the Synoptics may have been eschewed in order to convey the grand cosmic scale and other-worldly setting of the battle the Fourth Evangelist wished to convey was taking place and was won in the cross event.[44]

How is the ruler cast out? And what is the relationship of Jesus' lifting up to this understanding? In terms of classical understandings of the atonement, is this then a 'Christus Victor' theory? And if it is, then what is the nature of this victory? The two other 'ruler of this world' passages and a broader consideration of what the cross achieves in the Fourth Gospel will help to answer these questions.

### John 14:30

In John 14:30 Jesus states that he will not speak much longer with his disciples because the ruler of this world is coming. He then states that this ruler 'has no power over Me' (*kai en emoi ouk echei ouden*). The idiom used is an obscure one. One persuasive line of thought sees the idiom as translation of a Hebrew phrase often used in legal contexts.[45] That is to say that the prince of this world has no legal claim on Jesus. This understanding works on a number of levels as the Gospel unfolds. Certainly in the trial before the only other group designated as rulers, the Jews, it is clear they have no case (John 8:46). In the trial before Pilate at the end of the Gospel, he several times declares the charges of the Jews against Jesus to be baseless (John 18:38; 19:4, 6). Pilate, also, has no hold on Jesus and no authority of his own, as Jesus points out in John 19:11.

The devil ultimately has no claim on Jesus. In the context Jesus is speaking of his departure by way of death. Elsewhere in the Gospel the reader has been told that this cannot be a death because of Jesus' own sin, because it has already been intimated that he is without sin (John 8:46). Rather it occurs because he is the good shepherd who lays down his life for the sheep, who has

---

44. Ibid., 198.
45. Köstenberger, *John*, 445.

authority to lay it down and take it up again, who attributes his death to his love for the Father, and the obedience to the Father's will that this love involves (John 10:14–18). The pervasive legal motif of the Gospel suggests that the devil has no hold (14:30) on Jesus in a legal sense.[46] Jesus is without sin, so no accusation can be laid against him and no claim made on him by an accuser.

### John 16:11

In John 16:11 the reference to the judgment of the ruler of this world occurs in the midst of another concentrated cluster of legal language as the future ministry of the Holy Spirit with respect to the word is outlined. The Spirit will convict the world with respect to sin, righteousness and judgment. The point made in John 12:31 is reiterated and cast into an explicit legal framework. The cross is once again seen as a judgment on Satan, and this passage establishes the ruler of this world's own guilt and judgment as well as anticipating his final destiny.

### What does the cross achieve in John's Gospel?

The question has been posed earlier as to how the victory over the devil at the cross is to be understood in John's Gospel. This poses the broader question concerning the understanding of what Jesus' death achieves in the Fourth Gospel. This remains a controversial question in Johannine scholarship. The parameters of the debate were set by Bultmann and Käsemann, who both claimed, though for different reasons, that the death of Jesus was more or less the inevitable end of trajectories through the Gospel, but contributed very little to John's understanding of salvation. For Bultmann especially, and many who have followed him, the cross was the moment of supreme revelation of the identity of the Father and therefore the culmination of the Son's mission, which was to reveal the Father. Salvation comes through this revelation, not through any particular work of atonement or even victory over the devil that might have been won on the cross.

---

46. For the most thorough exposition of the legal motif in the Fourth Gospel, see Lincoln, *Truth on Trial.*

However, there is ample evidence from John's Gospel to suggest that the death of Jesus is to be seen as a sacrificial, fruit-bearing death, where one dies as a substitute for many in order to procure forgiveness of sins. Some of this evidence includes the timing of the crucifixion at the Passover and the 'Passover plot' that runs through the Gospel, the good shepherd references to laying down one's life for the sheep and numerous other references using the preposition *hyper*, Caiaphas' prophecy in John 11, Jesus' statement concerning the seed dying in John 12.[47]

References to sin occur at the beginning, middle and end of the Gospel. John the Baptist's announcement is that Jesus is the Lamb of God who will bear away the sins of the world. This programmatic revelation/testimony may be, initially, a little unclear, but as the Gospel goes on it becomes clearly tied into the Passover references that pervade the Gospel's chronology, so that it is clear that the death of Jesus at Passover is the death of the Lamb bearing the sins of the world. In John 8 there is an intense discussion on sin whereby Jesus states that his listeners will die in their sins unless they believe him (8:21–24). Finally, at the end of the Gospel, following the resurrection, Jesus breathes on his disciples and sends them out with the message of forgiveness of sins (John 20:21–23).

The message of forgiveness of sins as procured by a substitutionary death is a major understanding, if not the major understanding, of the cross in the Fourth Gospel.

### Towards a synthesis: trials, truth and forgiveness

In attempting to draw some threads together, it is suggested that the description given of the character of the devil in John 8 is essential to an understanding of both the absence of exorcisms from the Fourth Gospel as well as John's contribution to thinking about the relationship of Jesus to the 'powers'.

The presentation of the defeat of the devil is necessarily cosmic and cross-related because of the backdrop assumed in his description. The defeat of the devil is linked to his original murdering through the lie, via the important character description in John

---

47. For a more detailed account, see Salier, 'Obedient Son'.

8:44. Jesus comes as the truth to reveal the truth and prove the lie wrong. In doing so Jesus breaks the devil's power in two ways. First, he reveals the truth that he is the Son of the Father. Jesus' death on the cross reveals the truth that he is the Son of the Father because it is the expression of the love and obedience of the Son for the Father. Secondly, he enables the forgiveness of sins through his death on the cross as the Lamb of God.

The plight of the Jews, as outlined by Jesus in John 8, demonstrates that the world is enslaved due to sin. The Jews, and by implication humanity more generally, lie and believe lies about God and his Son. It is assumed that it is sins that give the devil power over human beings and it is because they are sinners that he can destroy them. All people are drawn to Jesus as the source of forgiveness of sins and the devil loses his power to accuse. He is 'cast out' in this sense. Salvation is from sin and the defeat of the devil is a secondary effect (but nonetheless real and important). The pervasive legal motif of the Gospel helps to frame this understanding.

The Synoptic exorcisms are not 'big enough' and cannot prefigure the 'big exorcism' in the way that Lazarus' death and resurrection might prefigure Jesus' own death and resurrection because of the nature of the Satan/devil portrayed.[48]

## Applying the Gospel of John

As Clement famously stated, John composed 'a spiritual gospel' (Eusebius, *Ecclesiastical History* 5.4–8). The Fourth Gospel seeks to give a complementary perspective on the Synoptic tradition, born of long years of preaching and reflection, and no doubt apologetic engagement with hearers over the central and controversial claim that Jesus is the incarnate, divine Son of God, glorified in the resurrection.

So John takes the opportunity, through his own eyewitness account, to emphasize the King, his origins and destiny, his surpassing greatness; to show through his narrative, especially the

---

48. Twelftree, *In the Name*, 205.

conflict with the devil, that the stronger man is Jesus by his victory on the cross. In doing so he makes explicit what is implicit in the Synoptic accounts; or at least describes the same concept in his own way or key.[49]

In thinking about the application of the teaching of the Fourth Gospel to contemporary practice it is helpful to consider briefly the purpose of the Gospels in presenting their portrait of Jesus. The Gospels first and foremost present a portrait of Jesus 'for us'; that is, Jesus achieves on behalf of the reader that which they cannot do for themselves. Occasionally Jesus is presented as a model for action (John 13:14–15; but note that this is only after a careful application of what the foot-washing achieves for the believer; see John 13:7–11), but there are also elements of his work that only he can do. The defeat of the devil as outlined in the Fourth Gospel is one such example. Jesus has achieved this defeat on behalf of his followers. The first response then is to rejoice and appropriate what Jesus has achieved. There is no special imperative to be obeyed in regard to any action with respect to the devil, and certainly not with respect to demons, on the believer's behalf in the Gospel.[50]

This suggests that the instinct to call on the name of Jesus and power in his name when confronted by anything that appears to be a manifestation of the powers of darkness is the correct one. In relation to modern preoccupations with confronting the powers of darkness it may be well to remember the perspective of Jesus' absolute control and mastery as shown by John in his narrative. And perhaps ponder the thought that it is inadvisable to send children out to do the stronger man's work.[51]

---

49. Cf. Painter, 'Memory Holds the Key', 229–245, esp. 236, where he talks about the relationship between John and the Synoptics.

50. Arguably this aspect of Johannine teaching is more clearly seen in 1 John. An analogy to the point being made here is seen in the careful work of Köstenberger, *Missions of Jesus*, where he differentiates the similarities and differences between the mission of Jesus and the mission of those who are sent and therefore participate in mission in Jesus' name.

51. Twelftree, *In the Name*, 294, wisely observes that the Fourth Gospel invites that our attention be placed on the healer and not the disease.

The second point for reflection concerns the importance in the Gospel of forgiveness of sins and the apparent place of such forgiveness in the defeat of the devil as implied by the Gospel's narrative. The proclamation of forgiveness of sin in Jesus' name and the pastoral application and exploration of the implications are clear implications of the Johannine presentation. It may be tempting, at times, to downplay the importance and impact of forgiveness, but this is a function of a failure to grasp the enormity, pervasiveness and destructiveness of sin in a personal and corporate sense, let alone its eternal consequences, the implications of guilt and shame for sins committed, and the debilitating effects of the remembrance and effects of sins past. The glorious words of Romans 8:33–34 eloquently encapsulate the implications of the Johannine exposition of the 'casting out' of the devil in legal terms, reminding the believer that any attempt by him to use their sin before the throne of God to accuse or shame will be dismissed because of their advocate with the Father (1 John 2:1–2).

John's emphasis on the truth gives pause for thought as to how to compare the 'Lying Ruler' with the 'Truth-Telling King'. The importance of truth-telling, especially unfolding the truth that Jesus is the divine Son and all its implications for knowledge of God and self, seems paramount. It is the sonship of Jesus and his revelation of God as Father that lays the basis for the believers' knowledge of their own status as children of God, being able to call God their own Father (John 1:12; 20:17). Reminding oneself and others that Jesus is the eternal Son, that on this basis he truly reveals the Father and enables life, reinforces this truth against the lies of the 'father of lies'. The truth of the believers' own status as children with respect to God is integrally tied to the truth concerning Jesus' own Sonship. Perhaps the chief attack and temptation of the devil for the Christian today is echoed in the words of the tempter to Jesus: 'if you are the Son of God' (Matt. 4:3, 6). This is a temptation to be met with the truth: 'Look at how great a love the Father has given us, that we should be called God's children. And we are!' (1 John 3:1).

## 4. 'YOU HAVE OVERCOME THE EVIL ONE': VICTORY OVER EVIL IN 1 JOHN

Matthew Jensen

### Introduction: the evil one and the believer

The New Testament (NT) contains a number of scattered statements about the present power of the evil one (Satan or the devil) and the believer's response to him. For instance, the evil one can tempt (1 Cor. 7:5), scheme (2 Cor. 2:11; Eph. 6:11) and masquerade (2 Cor. 11:14), and trap some people to do his will (2 Tim. 2:26). As a result, believers are warned:

> Put on the full armour of God so that you can take your stand against the devil's schemes. (Eph. 6:11)[1]

> Submit yourselves, then, to God. Resist the devil. (Jas 4:7)

> Be self-controlled and alert. Your enemy the devil prowls around like a roaring lion looking for someone to devour. (1 Pet. 5:8)

---

1. All biblical quotations are taken from the NIV unless otherwise noted.

Yet the NT also teaches that the evil one's power has been destroyed, resulting in freedom and victory for the believer:

> Since the children have flesh and blood, he [Jesus] too shared in their humanity so that by his death he might destroy him who holds the power of death – that is, the devil – and free those who all their lives were held in slavery by their fear of death. (Heb. 2:14–15)

> In addition to all this, take up the shield of faith, with which you can extinguish all the flaming arrows of the evil one. (Eph. 6:16)

> But the Lord is faithful, and he will strengthen and protect you from the evil one. (2 Thess. 3:3)

And if we include the whole of James 4:7, rather than leaving the last part out, we have 'Submit yourselves, then, to God. Resist the devil, *and he will flee from you*' (emphasis added).

In the light of this situation where the evil one has been conquered yet remains a threat, this chapter seeks to answer two connected questions. First, how was the victory over the evil one achieved? Secondly, how is this victory experienced in the present? It is this second question in particular that seems relevant to this volume, as it seems to be a main point of difference between 'deliverance ministries' and evangelicals in general.

In order to answer these questions, the chapter will narrow its focus and take 1 John as a case study. There are three reasons for the decision to examine 1 John. First, the scattered teaching of the rest of the NT about the present power of the evil one and the believer's response to him is found collected in 1 John. Just as the evil one is a threat and has some power, 1 John states that the evil one has control of the present world (5:19). Yet, like the rest of the NT, 1 John also teaches that believers have overcome the evil one (2:13–14) with the result that the evil one cannot harm them (5:18).

Secondly, John states twice that he is writing because his readers have overcome the evil one (2:13, 14). So an examination of 1 John may reveal how this victory was won and how it is experienced.

Thirdly, the vocabulary of victory (*nikaō, nikē*) is significant in this letter, being used to affirm the believer's victory over the evil one

(2:13–14). It occurs with a greater rate of frequency in 1 John than any other book in the NT (apart from Revelation), marking it as a theme in the work.[2] Further, the vocabulary is used in conjunction with not just the evil one (2:13–14), but with other themes associated with him – antichrists (4:4) and the world (5:4–5). So examining this theme along with the book's teaching about the devil or evil one (3:7–12; 5:18–19) should provide a more holistic answer to the questions of how the victory was won and how it is experienced.

## The structure of 1 John

One of the features that causes difficulties in understanding 1 John is its apparent lack of an obvious structure. So, in order to clear the ground, it is necessary to outline 1 John's structure briefly.

The most obvious self-contained unit in 1 John is the short poem of 2:12–14:

> I am writing to you, little children, because your sins are forgiven for his name's sake. I am writing to you, fathers, because you know him who is from the beginning. I am writing to you, young men, because you have overcome the evil one. I write to you, children, because you know the Father. I write to you, fathers, because you know him who is from the beginning. I write to you, young men, because you are strong, and the word of God abides in you, and you have overcome the evil one. (ESV)

This poem stands out as a unit due to its form but also for two other reasons – its *multiple vocatives* that directly address its readers, and its *purpose statements* that outline why John is writing. The poem contains six lines made up of two sets of three. This is evident from the tense of the verb *graphō* (the first three in the present, the second three in

---

2. *Nikē* occurs only in 1 John 5:4 in the NT, and *nikos*, which occurs four times elsewhere (Matt. 12:20; 1 Cor. 15:54–55, 57), is not used by 1 John. The verb occurs more often in 1 John (2:13–14; 4:4; 5:4–5) than any other book (Luke 11:22; John 16:33; Rom. 3:4; 12:21) except Revelation (2:7, 11, 17, 26; 3:5, 12, 21; 5:5; 6:2; 11:7; 12:11; 13:7; 15:2; 17:14; 21:7).

the aorist); the parallel groups addressed in the vocatives (children, fathers, young men);[3] and the repetition of reasons in lines 2 and 4 (you know the Father), and in lines 3 and 5 (the particular reason of interest for this chapter: you have overcome the evil one).

However, the change in the tense of *graphō* is more significant than just marking two parts of this poem. It also seems to indicate two parts of 1 John as a whole. Until 2:14 all the occurrences of *graphō* are in the present (1:4; 2:1, 7–8, 12–13). From 2:14 until the end of the book, *graphō* occurs only in the aorist (2:14, 21, 26; 5:13). That is, this poem seems to mark a transition in the book and indicates that it has two main parts: an *introduction*, 1:1 – 2:11, and a *body*, 2:15 – 5:21.

Once this is observed, key themes in each part are evident that support this division of the book. The language of light and dark (*phōs, skotos/skotia*) occurs in a prominent place at the start of the introduction (1:5). This language appears again at the end of the introduction, forming an inclusio (2:8–11). Further, the language is not used in the rest of the book. The first paragraph of the body of the book acts as a topic paragraph by introducing its key theme: 'the world'. *Kosmos* occurs twenty-three times in 1 John, all but one of which occurring in the body of the book.[4] This provides the broad context within which the themes of the body of 1 John are to be read and understood. Though these themes are contained to their relative parts, they are nevertheless connected. In the only two occurrences of *paragō* in 1 John, both themes are described as passing away (2:8, 17).

The vocabulary of victory, the evil one and the devil occur in the poem and the second part of 1 John; that is, from 2:13 onwards. Even though the introduction does not contain the victory vocabulary, or any references to the evil one, it still requires discussion.

---

3. Even though the two nouns used in addressing the children are different (*teknion, paidion*), both are from the same semantic domain.

4. *Kosmos* occurs more frequently per thousand words (9.22×) in 1 John than in any other NT book. The book with the second highest frequency is the Gospel of John, where it occurs 4.29× per thousand words, which is less than half of 1 John's rate.

## The introduction of 1 John (1:1 – 2:11)

There are two reasons not to pass over the introduction. First, introductions establish the context for the interpretation of a work by the reader. They often introduce key themes, characters, setting, purpose and any conflict to be resolved. To start reading a work part way through opens readers up to misinterpretation as they lack this context. In the opening section of 1 John the author introduces himself, makes two purpose statements (1:4; 2:1), provides significant Christological statements and discusses two main themes (sin and love).

Secondly, the similarities in form and content between the introduction and the poem suggest some of the introduction is about victory over the evil one even though the specific vocabulary is not used. In terms of the formal similarities, the verb *legō*, which forms the backbone of the first part, occurs in two groups of three, differentiated by a change in tense, just like *graphō* in the poem.[5] The phrase *ean eipōmen hoti* occurs in 1:6, 8 and 10, while the phrase *ho legōn* starts 2:4, 6 and 9. Thus there are two clearly demarcated units in the first part: 1:6 – 2:2 and 2:4–11. In terms of content, each of these units exhibits a theme. Sin and forgiveness is the theme of the first unit (1:6 – 2:2), and love in obedience to God's commands, as the evidence of knowing God, is the theme of the second unit (2:4–11). The vocabulary of sin (*hamartia, hamartanō*) and love (*agapē, agapaō*) occur exclusively in their units, reinforcing the formal division. This is parallel with the poem because the first two lines of the poem have the same two themes – sin and forgiveness in 2:12, and knowledge of God in 2:13. Since the first three lines of the poem in 2:12–14 share the present tense of the verb *graphō* with the introduction, it appears that the first part of the poem summarizes the themes of the introduction, suggesting that some link exists between the victory over the evil one in the third line and the only other part of the introduction not yet discussed, namely verses 1:1–4.

---

5. The tense change is from aorist to present, which is the opposite to that in the poem, where it is from present to aorist.

## The glorified incarnate Christ (1:1–4)

> That which was from the beginning, which we have heard, which
> we have seen with our eyes, which we have looked at and our hands
> have touched – this we proclaim concerning the Word of life. The life
> appeared; we have seen it and testify to it, and we proclaim to you the
> eternal life, which was with the Father and has appeared to us. We
> proclaim to you what we have seen and heard, so that you also may have
> fellowship with us. And our fellowship is with the Father and with his
> Son, Jesus Christ. We write this to make our joy complete.

Scholarship has usually interpreted these opening verses of 1 John
as an affirmation of the incarnation, for two reasons.

First, the historical situation is reconstructed so as to identify
those who have gone out from the community (2:19) as docetic or
proto-gnostic. This reconstruction usually starts with 4:2–3 as the
clearest statement of the 'opponents' and then reads other selected
passages in the light of this definition. However, recently these
identifications have begun to be questioned. This is because there
is little or no literary evidence of these groups existing in the first
century; the method for reconstructing the situation is circular so
without other external evidences it is hard to verify; and because
the method does not read 1 John in the order in which it is written,
these opening verses are understood in the light of the latter 4:2–3
rather than the other way around.

Secondly, the similarities of these verses with the prologue of
John's Gospel (1:1–18) then strengthens scholarship's identification of these verses with the incarnation. The starting phrase
'from the beginning' is reminiscent of John 1:1. The stress of the
eyewitness testimony to the hearing, seeing, looking at and touching reinforce the opinion that the physicalness of the incarnation
is in view. The use of the phrase *peri tou logou tēs zōēs* at the end of
verse 1 even sounds like the language of John 1:1–3 and 14. The
second verse continues to echo the Gospel prologue, as the life
appears from 'with the Father'. This last phrase has an unusual
use of *pros*, being understood not as 'to' but rather 'with', an
unusual use that has a parallel in John 1:2. However, given the
uncertainty about the historical situation behind 1 John, to limit

these similarities to the incarnation is suspect. I would like to suggest that the message preached in 1:1–4 is more than just the incarnation, but, instead, the message preached is about the glorification of the incarnate Christ.

Let me explain what I mean by 'the glorification of the incarnate Christ' and then give the evidence for this line of thinking. I understand 'glorification' in the usual Johannine sense as referring to Jesus' death, resurrection and ascension.[6] The reason for using this Johannine category lies in the similarities in vocabulary and writing style between 1 John and John's Gospel, which suggest at least a common school or circle of thought, if not a common authorship. The glorified Christ in John is the incarnate Christ. This is the purpose of the resurrection narratives, especially the Thomas incident. Jesus' resurrection and ascension were not spiritual but physical, so his glorification was physical. So by the phrase 'glorification of the incarnate Christ' I mean the death, resurrection and ascension of the incarnate Christ.

The evidence for this understanding requires one change in approaching the text: to read it in the light of not just John 1:1–18 but also John 20 – 21. Without denying the parallels with John's prologue, it seems problematic to stop at those parallels and not also to acknowledge the parallels with John 20 – 21. Like any good narrative, John 1:1–18 was written to introduce the reader to the themes that find their culmination in John 20 – 21. For instance, the prologue of John's Gospel introduces the theme of Jesus' divinity (1:1–3) that is affirmed explicitly at the climax by Thomas (20:28). The parallels in 1 John 1:1–4 with John 1:1–18

---

6. In commenting on John 12:16, Carson, *John*, 434, states, 'This verse closely resembles John's remark about what the disciples did not understand when Jesus talked about destroying the temple and raising it in three days [. . .] (2:22). There, the crucial turning point in their understanding took place "after he was raised from the dead"; here, it is after Jesus was glorified. But this amounts to virtually the same thing. Jesus' death marked the turning point. It was part of the movement that led on to his resurrection and exaltation, i.e. his glorification, and the bestowal of the Spirit that was conditioned by it (7:39; 16:7).'

do affirm the incarnation. However, the incarnation is assumed in the climax of John's Gospel, in chapters 20 – 21. To read 1 John 1:1–4 in the light of John 1:1–18 only is to half read the text and so to misread it.

Once this change is made a number of features support this reading. Due to considerations of space, I will outline only five. First, the verbs of perception with their corresponding sense organs are reminiscent of the resurrection narratives. The vocabulary occurs in combination in Jesus' post-resurrection appearance to Thomas in John 20:24–27 (where *horaō* and *cheires* are used repeatedly) and to the disciples in Luke 24:39–40 (where *psēlaphaō*, *cheires* and *theōreō*, the cognate of *theaomai*, all occur). This is especially the case with *psēlaphaō*, for, when used of Jesus, this word is used with reference to his resurrection only (Luke 24:39).[7]

Secondly, the parenthetical comment that explicates the phrase *peri tou logou tēs zōēs* does not explain what is meant by *tou logou* but *tēs zōēs*. This suggests that *tou logou* should be translated with something like 'message' rather than 'Word'. The content of the message is the focus of the phrase. Since the relative clauses prepare the reader for this phrase and since they were reminiscent of the resurrection, it follows that 'life' is the emphasis of the phrase.

Thirdly, the first parenthetic description of the life is that it appeared (*ephanerōthē*). This verb *phaneroō* is used to describe Jesus' resurrection appearances to his disciples in John 21:1 and 14.[8] This understanding is further supported when the second occurrence of the verb in 1 John 1:2 is examined. Here the life is described as being with the Father and appearing to the authors from beside the Father (*pros ton patera*). This sounds like a reference to John 1:3, where the Word was with God and thus to the incarnation. However, the same phrase (*pros ton patera*) is used in 1 John 2:1 to describe the present place of Jesus – in heaven with the Father, where he acts as our *paraklētos*. So it seems that the

---

7. See also Ignatius, *Smyrnaeans* 3.1–3.

8. *Phaneroō* also occurs twice in relation to the resurrection in the longer ending of Mark (Mark 16:12, 14).

appearances referred to here are Jesus' resurrection appearances
that he made after going to the Father.[9]

Fourthly, the author describes his actions in terms of speech –
testifying (*martyreō*) and announcing (*apangellō*) to the audience 'the
life'. These verbs again are reminiscent of the actions of the apostles as a result of their experience of the resurrection. According to
Acts, the risen Jesus commissions the apostles to be his witnesses
(1:8), witnesses of everything Jesus said and did; in particular, witnesses to his resurrection (1:21–22).[10]

Fifthly, the Christological references that immediately follow
this prologue fit well with the suggestion that the glorification of
the incarnate Christ is in view. For instance, the death of Jesus is
referred to in 1:7, 9 and 2:2 and his present heavenly session is
referred to in 2:1.

Since this unit stands at the very start of 1 John, it sets the glorification of the incarnate Christ as the main context for interpreting
the rest of the book. When this is combined with the third line of
the poem that concludes the section, it is suggestive that the glorification of the incarnate Christ is how the victory over the evil one
for us was achieved and preaching the message of Jesus' glorification is how it is experienced by us. An examination of the body of
1 John may further support or deny this suggestion.


## The body of 1 John (2:15 – 5:21)

We will now examine each of the four passages that speak of the
evil one and victory found in the body of 1 John. The first of these
passages primarily speaks about how victory over the evil one was
achieved (3:7–12). The second (4:4) and third (5:4–5) indicate how

---

9. It should be noted that the phrase (*pros ton patera*) occurs ten times in John
   and on all but one occasion (5:45) refers to Jesus' ascension to the Father
   after his death and resurrection, i.e. the final part of his glorification (13:1;
   14:6, 12, 28; 16:10, 17, 28; 20:17 twice).

10. The cognate *martys* occurs in relation to the apostles' task to testify to
    Jesus in Luke 24:48; Acts 1:8, 22; 2:32; 3:15; 4:33; 5:32; 10:39, 41; 13:31.

this victory is experienced. The last passage acts as a summary of this theme (5:18–19).

### Victory over the evil one: achievement (3:7–12)

The first passage that speaks explicitly of the devil is 3:7–12:

> Dear children, do not let anyone lead you astray. He who does what is right is righteous, just as he is righteous. He who does what is sinful is of the devil, because the devil has been sinning from the beginning. The reason the Son of God appeared was to destroy the devil's work. No one who is born of God will continue to sin, because God's seed remains in him; he cannot go on sinning, because he has been born of God. This is how we know who the children of God are and who the children of the devil are: Anyone who does not do what is right is not a child of God; nor is anyone who does not love his brother. This is the message you heard from the beginning: We should love one another. Do not be like Cain, who belonged to the evil one and murdered his brother. And why did he murder him? Because his own actions were evil and his brother's were righteous.

These verses are part of a unit that starts at 2:28 and extends down until 3:12. Two features give the unit coherence. First, at the formal level, the words *pas ho* are followed by a participle seven times in these verses (2:29; 3:3–4, 6 [2×], 9–10).[11] Secondly, the unit has an underlying logic – a link between Christ and those born of God. So in 2:29, knowing that Jesus is righteous results in knowing that those who do righteousness are born of God. In 3:1 the world does not know those born of God because it did not know Jesus. In 3:2 the children of God will be made like Jesus when he returns because they will see him as he is. In 3:3 the child of God holding on to the hope of being made like Jesus makes himself holy just as Jesus is holy. In the passage of particular interest, 3:7, the one who does what is right is righteous just as Jesus is righteous.

The unit of 2:28 – 3:12 is also linked to 1:5 – 2:2 in two ways. First, 2:28 – 3:12 starts with Jesus' being in heaven, from whence

---

11. R. E. Brown, *Epistles of John*, 118.

he will appear (2:28; 3:2). This picks up the thought of the end of
1:5 – 2:2, where Jesus was described as the advocate (*paraklētos*)
in heaven in 2:1. This link between units is further evident in the
description of Jesus as righteous. In 2:29 Jesus is described as
righteous, the same description used of Jesus in 2:1, a description
that has not occurred between 2:1 and 2:29.[12] This description of
Jesus as righteous is restated at the start of the verses of interest
in 3:7. So this unit's Christology has the righteous Jesus in heaven
as the advocate who will return. The second link between 2:28 –
3:12 and 1:5 – 2:2 is the theme of sin. Sin has not been discussed
since 2:2 and is reintroduced in 3:4. This discussion dominates
3:4–9.[13] These two links are significant because they provide the
background for understanding the unit as a whole, and 3:4–9
in particular.

The first few verses (3:7–9) that refer to the devil (*diabolos*)
form the second part of a series of parallel statements. There are
parallels between 3:4–6 and 3:7–9. Both start with discussions
of sin (3:4, 7–8a), move to reasons for Jesus' appearing (3:6, 8b),
and then return to discuss sin, apparently affirming the ability to
stop sinning (3:6, 9). These parallels suggest that they should be
read together and interpreted in the light of each other. Thus the
destruction of the devil's work should be understood in terms of
taking away sins. This understanding also fits with the first half of
3:8, where the devil is described as sinning from the beginning.[14]

The two verses that then speak of the victory over the devil (3:5
and 8) both describe it as occurring by the 'appearing' (*phaneroō*)
of Jesus. In 3:5 Jesus appeared in order to take away sins and
in 3:8 the Son of God appeared in order to destroy the works of
the devil.

---

12. The *dik-* word group does not occur between 2:1 and 2:29.

13. There is one reference to sin in 2:12. As suggested above, because this
   reference is in the poem it seems to act as a summary of the theme in the
   introduction, i.e. a summary of 1:6 – 2:2.

14. This is a reference to Gen. 3, where it was the devil who instigated the
   first sin, resulting in humanity being under the curse of God, outside the
   garden, born in sin, and under the judgment of death; cf. Rom. 5:12–14.

Under the influence of reading 1:1–4 as being about the incarnation, due to historical reconstructions assuming docetic or proto-gnostic opponents, the 'appearing' (*phaneroō*) of Jesus in these verses is usually taken to refer to his coming into the world.[15] Jesus appeared on earth to take away sins and destroy the works of the devil. This view sits uncomfortably with evangelicals, as it seems to downplay the significance of the death and resurrection of Jesus, who therefore tend to read the death of Jesus into these verses on the basis of the links with 1:5 – 2:2 being grounded in the doctrine of forgiveness of sins.

However, if 1:1–4 is about the glorification of the incarnate Christ, as argued above, there is another option that could be in view in these verses. The appearing of Jesus, the one who bears the sin of the world and destroys the devil's works, is his appearing in heaven to present his perfect sacrifice for us. There are three lines of evidence that support this suggestion.

First, to interpret appearing (cf. *phaneroō*) as always referring to Jesus' incarnation is suspect. The verb does not specify where the appearing takes place. This is evident in this unit where it is used with reference to Jesus' return to earth to judge in 2:29 and 3:2. Since the default location of Jesus in this section is in heaven, it seems that 'appear' in 3:5 and 8 refers to Jesus' appearing in heaven.

Secondly, the links in Christology between this unit and 2:1 indicate a high-priestly activity for Jesus in heaven. The discussion of the theme of sin in 1:6 – 2:2 takes place in Old Testament cult terms, so when Jesus' present role in heaven is described as the advocate (*paraklētos*), it is describing Jesus' priestly action. Just as the priest entered the temple and God's presence to present the sacrifice of atonement for his people, so Jesus entered God's presence with his sacrificial blood to bring forgiveness for sins. This understanding matches the order of the verses in 2:1–2 where the session occurs before the crucifixion in the description of Jesus. Since 2:28 – 3:12 starts with Jesus in heaven and contains the cultic

---

15. Marshall, *Epistles of St John*, 185, commenting on 3:8, is a good example: 'Here John assumes the reality of the incarnation, which was accepted by his adherents but doubted by his opponents.'

language of holiness (3:3) that then gives way to the discussion of sin (3:4–9), it seems that 3:5 and 8 should be understood in the same vein. The affirmation of Jesus' righteousness in 3:7 links this section in particular with the Christology of 2:1–2. Hence Jesus' 'appearing' in 3:5 and 8 is his appearing in heaven as the high priest to bring the sacrifice that deals with sin. This understanding is corroborated by two elements in 3:5. The description of Jesus as bearing (using *airō*) sins is reminiscent of the high priest's carrying the sacrifice of atonement for sins into the holy of holies. Further, the description of Jesus as sinless could be taken to refer to Jesus' sinless sacrifice of himself. However, it could also be referring to the qualification he required in order to appear as the high priest in heaven to bear the sin offering (Heb. 4:15; 7:26–28).

Thirdly, this understanding has parallels with the teaching of Hebrews 2:5–18 and 9:24–28. In Hebrews 2:14, where the defeat of the devil is explicitly addressed, it is the death of the incarnate Christ that destroys him who holds the power of death; that is, the devil. This statement about the defeat of the devil is in the midst of other teaching similar to the understanding of 1 John 3 proposed here. For instance, Hebrews 2:17–18, Jesus' present situation is as the high priest for his people. In Hebrews 9:11–28 Jesus enters heaven (9:11–12, 24) to 'appear' for his people in God's presence.[16] There he presents the sacrifice of himself for sin once for all.

So the victory over the devil was achieved through the glorification of the incarnate Christ. Jesus died a sacrificial death for the sins of his people, he was raised up into heaven where he appeared as the high priest before the Father, bearing the blood of his sacrifice that atones for sins and destroys the works of the devil – his ability to accuse God's people of sin and hold the power of death over them.

This understanding of 1 John 3:5 and 8 helps to explain the difficulties experienced in reading 3:6 and 9, where Christian sinlessness is affirmed. This section desires that the readers remain in

---

16. 'Appear' in 9:24 is not *phaneroō* but *emphanizō*. However, Ellingworth, *Hebrews*, 480, comments, 'There is no sharp distinction or contrast in Hebrews between *emphanizō* and *phaneroō*.'

Christ (2:28). Since Christ is righteous, holy and sinless, believers are also seen to be these things by God because Christ is in heaven representing them as their high priest. So 3:6 can say that no one who remains in Christ sins, because the perspective of this section is of Christ in heaven bearing his blood for his people. Similarly, in 3:9 everyone born of God from the heavenly perspective does not sin, because they have received the Spirit – that is, the seed of God remains in them, so they are unable to sin in God's sight. They have a *paraklētos* with the Father who holds the sacrificial blood that pays the penalty for sin.

Yet, as believers live in this world waiting to be made completely like Jesus at his return (3:2), there is still the issue of how the children of God and the children of the devil can be recognized. 1 John 3:10–12 concludes the unit with a test and an example. Everyone who does not do what is right or love his brother is not from God (3:10). The reason for this (*hoti*) is found in the message they have heard from the beginning, the message that they should love one another (3:11), not follow the example of Cain, who, under the influence of the evil one, killed his brother (3:12), but be under the influence of the glorified, incarnate Christ, who died for his people (3:16). The message of the glorified, incarnate Christ, which they have heard from the beginning, has an imperative element – love for one another.

So, from the first passage where the devil is explicitly mentioned in 1 John, it is evident that the victory over the devil was achieved by the glorification of the incarnate Christ – his death for sin, his physical resurrection and ascension into heaven, where he presents his blood to bear sin and destroy the works of the devil. This victory is experienced through hearing the message of Jesus' glorification and is expressed in lives of righteousness and brotherly love.

## Victory over the evil one: experienced

### *Victory over antichrists: confession by the spirit (4:1–6)*
Not only are believers victorious over the devil because of the glorification of the incarnate Christ, but they are also victorious over the antichrists in the world. The second passage to

investigate is 1 John 4:1–6, because of its use of the victory word group (*nikaō, nikē*).

In 1 John 4:4 the readers are assured of their victory over the antichrists: 'You, dear children, are from God and have overcome them, because the one who is in you is greater than the one who is in the world.'

This verse has two parts – the affirmation of the readers' identity and victory over the antichrists, and the reason for this affirmation and victory.

The identity of the readers is that they are 'from God'. This little phrase (*ek tou theou*) is significant in this unit, being used six times. The unit opens with two imperatives – do not believe every spirit, but test the spirits in order to ascertain if they are 'from God'. The reason for this command is the existence of false prophets in the world. These false prophets are called antichrists at the end of verse 3. A test is provided in verses 2 and 3a to discern whether a spirit is 'from God' or not 'from God'. The test is two lines in parallel, with the second line 'gapping' some contents of the first line for brevity (see the table below).

| 4:2 | 4:3 |
| --- | --- |
| Every spirit that confesses Jesus Christ has come in the flesh / | Every spirit that does not confess Jesus / |
| is from God | is not from God |

If scholarship is followed and this test is taken in isolation from the rest of 1 John, then it seems to indicate that anyone who denies the incarnation of Jesus is an antichrist. The phrase 'come in the flesh' is understood as 'come into the world'. However, when the verse is read in the light of the Christological statements already made in 1 John (the message of the glorification of the incarnate Christ [1:1–4], who is presently in heaven acting as a high priest [2:1–2], a message some deny because they deny that Jesus is the Christ [2:22–23],[17] yet it is the means by which

---

17. There are two reasons for understanding the denial that Jesus is the Christ

sins are borne [3:5] and the works of the devil are destroyed
[3:8]), the antichrists in 4:3 are denying that Jesus Christ came in
the flesh to heaven, that the crucified body of Jesus was raised up
into heaven to act as the high priest. This understanding builds
on the observation that *erchomai* does not indicate the direction of the movement (to earth or, in this case, to heaven) but
just movement. The Christological context of 1 John suggests
heaven as the end point of the movement. This use of *erchomai*
to refer to the glorification of the incarnate Christ is not without
precedent, since it occurs on Jesus' lips as he speaks of his glorification in his prayer to the Father in John 17:11 and 13.[18] It
is somewhat akin to understanding the Son of Man in Daniel 7
(and NT quotes and allusions) as coming to the Ancient of Days
in heaven.

Thus the test reveals who is 'from God' and who is not, through
the confession about Jesus that they are able or not able to make.
So when verse 4 starts with the description of the readers as being
'from God' it is saying that they are people who have the Spirit
who is able to make the confession of Jesus' incarnate glorification.[19] Since they can make this confession, they have overcome
those who deny Jesus is the Christ.

The reason they can make this confession is given in the second
statement in verse 4 – because the one in the reader(s) is greater
than the one in the world. The Spirit from God who is in the
readers, who enables the confession, is greater than the spirit of

_____

as a denial of the message of 1:1–4. First, the vocabulary of Father and
Son first occurred in 1:3 and has not occurred explicitly again until 2:22.
Secondly, the argument that Jesus is the Christ because he was glorified by
God is evident elsewhere in the NT; see e.g. Acts 2:22–36, Rom. 1:4 and
Phil. 2:5–11.

18. *Poreuomai* is used to speak of Jesus' glorification throughout the Upper
Room Discourse, but Jesus in his prayer changes to use *erchomai*.

19. Paul outlines a similar test of spirits in 1 Cor. 12:3, where only someone
speaking by the Holy Spirit is able to make the confession that Jesus
is Lord. Taking into account the way these different authors express
themselves, Paul's 'Lord' seems equivalent to John's 'come in the flesh'.

the antichrists that is in the world.[20] The next two verses (4:5–6) further explain what this means.

Verse 5 speaks about the antichrists and their origin – they are from the world. This phrase 'from the world' (*ek tou kosmou*) occurs only in this verse and in the topic paragraph of the body of 1 John; that is, in 2:16. There John states that 'the cravings of sinful man, the lust of his eyes and the boasting of what he has and does' comes from the world. Here we can add the antichrists to this list – they are from the world. Since they are from the world, they speak in terms drawn from the world and the world listens to them. In contrast to this the author and his readers are from God, so that everyone who knows God listens to them and those who do not know God do not listen. The reactions to the message of the glorification of the incarnate Christ (its confession or denial, the ability to hear it or not) reveal the true Spirit and the false spirit.

In these verses the believer's victory over the antichrists is through the message of the glorified incarnate Christ. Victory is experienced through the Spirit of God, who is greater than the spirit of the antichrist and who enables them to confess and hear the message of the glorification of the incarnate Christ.

### Victory over the world: faith (5:4–5)

Believers are also victorious over the world. The victory word group (*nikaō, nikē*) also occurs in 5:4–5:

> for everyone born of God overcomes the world. This is the victory that has overcome the world, even our faith. Who is it that overcomes the world? Only he who believes that Jesus is the Son of God.

The first sentence in these verses is a reason (*hoti*) for why God's commands are not burdensome (5:3) – because 'everyone born of God overcomes the world' (v. 4). Back in 5:1 the readers were

---

20. That the masculine article is used instead of the neuter in referring to the Spirit in 4:4 draws attention to whose Spirit it is – God's. The Spirit is from God (4:2), since he gave him to the readers (3:24).

told that 'everyone who believes that Jesus is the Christ is born of God'. This is in contrast to the antichrists, who were saying that Jesus is not the Christ (2:22). That is, everyone who believes the message of the glorification of the incarnate Christ has been born of God. In 5:4 this person is the one who has overcome the world. Belief in the message of the glorification of Jesus is how someone conquers the world.

If the readers are in doubt of this, John repeats the logic in the rest of verses 4 and 5. The rest of verse 4 links the victory to our faith: 'This is the victory that has overcome the world, even our faith.' Verse 5 then asks the question about the identity of the person who has overcome the world and answers in terms of belief that Jesus is the Son of God. That the title 'Christ' is not used here, but rather 'Son of God', is not problematic since both can refer to the position of God's chosen king.[21] Belief in the message of the glorification of Jesus, that he is now the Son of God enthroned in heaven, is how someone conquers the world.

So victory over the world is experienced by faith in the message of the glorification of the incarnate Christ.

### Summary: the evil one, sin and safety (5:18–19)
The last references to the evil one are in the concluding section of I John, in 5:18–19. These verses repeat the main teaching already discussed and introduce little that is new to the discussion:

> We know that anyone born of God does not continue to sin; the one who was born of God keeps him safe, and the evil one cannot harm him. We know that we are children of God, and that the whole world is under the control of the evil one.

The references in 5:18 to being born from God remind the reader of 5:4, where it is affirmed that they are born by faith in the message of the glorified incarnate Christ. The statement that they

---

21. See e.g. the apposition of the title 'Son of God' with 'King of Israel' in the confession of Nathaniel in John 1:49. Kruse, *Letters of John*, 174, notes, 'In 1 John "the Son of God" is virtually equivalent to "Christ" (cf. 2:22, 23; 5:1, 5).'

do not sin links back to the heavenly perspective of Christ's work discussed in 3:4–9. The concept that the readers are from God, in contrast to the world, which is under the control of the evil one, is linked back to the discussion of 4:1–6, where the Spirit-empowered confession of the glorification of the incarnate Christ is the basis for knowing that someone is from God. Further, the conceptualization of the world as either from God or from the evil one – either listening to the message or ignoring it – is the basis of the second part of verse 19, where it is said that the whole world is under the control of the evil one.

These verses contribute the idea that the one born from God keeps believers safe so that the evil one cannot harm them. Given the context of praying for fellow believers, this verse seems to affirm that the prayers of believers for other believers keeps them safe from the evil one.

## Conclusion

Having examined the references to the evil one and victory in 1 John, we are now in a position to answer the two questions posed in the introduction to this chapter.

First, the victory that the believer has over the evil one was achieved by Jesus' glorification – his death for sin, his physical resurrection and ascension into heaven, where he has presented his sacrificial blood to make atonement for their sins, thus conquering the devil and destroying his works.

Secondly, this victory is experienced by faith in the message of the glorified Christ, a faith that leads to the confession under the power of the Spirit. This victory is not only over the evil one, but also over antichrists, the world and even sin from the perspective of heaven.

# 5. NO CHARGE ADMITTED: JUSTIFICATION AND THE DEFEAT OF THE POWERS

**Mark D. Thompson**

The gospel brings assurance of our justification, but is this message strong enough in the face of spiritual evil?

In what is perhaps the critical New Testament (NT) text dealing with the defeat of the principalities and powers, Colossians 2:13–15, Christ's triumph is associated with three things: the giving of life to those dead in trespasses and the uncircumcision of their flesh, the forgiveness of all our trespasses, and the cancellation of the record of debt that once stood against us 'with its legal demands (*tois dogmasin*)'. It is a highly significant conjunction of ideas and a somewhat puzzling one. How exactly are they, 'the rulers and authorities (*tas archas kai tas exousias*)', disarmed and put to shame by these things which are directed at us and our situation? *We* are made alive together with him, forgiven, freed from the record of indebtedness that once determined our destiny, and as this is done *they* are decisively defeated.

If we step back a little, we find that these crucial verses are nestled between three bold imperatives. In Colossians 2:8 Paul's readers are called upon to 'see to it that no one takes you captive (*mē tis hymas estai ho sylagōgōn*) by philosophy and empty deceit, according to human tradition, according to the elemental spirits of the world, and not according to Christ'. There is a very real danger of being deceived, of falling into slavery and of departing from the truth about Christ, which Paul has been outlining in this letter. Paul's answer, it would seem, is to point them once again to the magnificent person of Jesus Christ and what has been accomplished for them 'in him'. On the other side of the verses that concern us is a second imperative: 'let no one pass judgment on you (*mē tis hymas krinetō*) in questions of food and drink, or with regard to a festival or a new moon or a Sabbath' (v. 16). The danger Paul warns of here is of being deceived into thinking that these shadows really have a part to play in determining our life before God and our future. But, in addition, the folly and perversity of this suggestion is shown by considering again the nature of what was accomplished for us in the cross of Christ. Going back to the structures of everyday life under the old covenant is thoroughly inappropriate in the light of what he has done. This second imperative is followed rather quickly by a third, in verse 18: 'let no one disqualify you (*mēdeis hymas katabrabeuetō*), delighting in humility and the worship of angels, going into things he has seen, without reason puffed up by the mind of his flesh and not holding fast to the head'.[1] The danger here is more subtle still: the danger of believing yourself to have missed out, to have failed to attain real, genuine spirituality. It is allowing others to suggest, either by word or simply by conspicuous practice, that there is an advanced level of Christian living, to which you have so far failed to attain. And once again the answer lies in considering just who it is who has acted for us, and what it is that he has done.

Reflection upon these three imperatives suggests that each involves a misjudgment, an accusation, which those redeemed in and by Christ are not to entertain for a moment. Each involves the suggestion that something is lacking from the life of faith

---

1. This more literal translation was suggested by Dr John Woodhouse in a sermon given in the Moore College chapel in Sept. 2008. I would like to record my debt to him for that stimulating series of sermons.

as Paul taught it and as the Colossians understood it. Whether
it be a wisdom that promises some kind of connection with the
elemental powers of the universe, the impressive and distinctive
regimen of Jewish piety, or spiritual experiences of various kinds,
the accusation Paul calls on his readers to resist is of a critical deficiency in their lives, which, if remedied, will enable them to live
as God intends. And in the midst of countering these diversions
from walking in Christ Jesus the Lord 'as you received' him (2:6),
Paul explains:

> you, who were dead in your trespasses and the uncircumcision of your
> flesh, God made alive together with him, having forgiven us all our
> trespasses, by cancelling the record of debt that stood against us with
> its legal demands. This he took from our midst, nailing it to the cross.
> He stripped the rulers and authorities and put them to open shame, by
> triumphing over them in it. (2:13–15, my tr.)

How exactly does Paul expect this to be an effective counter to the
misjudgments that threaten his readers? How is the cross both the
means of stripping and shaming the powers and the answer to any
suggestion that the life of faith needs support or embellishment in
any of these other ways?

The answer to these questions is profitably considered
with reference to the biblical doctrine of justification by faith
– indeed, by faith alone. So before returning to look more
carefully at Colossians 2:13–15, we turn to consider the doctrine of justification and its function within the wider body of
Christian doctrine.[2]

---

2. A lot of ink has been spilled attacking and defending a view of the powers
   mentioned in Colossians and elsewhere as 'personal, supernatural agen-
   cies'. The arguments have been carefully canvassed by Peter O'Brien, who
   concludes that they are 'personal, supernatural intelligences, emissaries
   of the god of this world, which seek to influence the world and mankind
   for ill at every level, using every resource at their disposal' (O'Brien,
   'Principalities and Powers', 146).

## Justification: its basic shape

### Soteriological

In contrast to some contemporary suggestions, justification is understood in Scripture as primarily a soteriological doctrine rather than
an ecclesiological one. That is to say, for all its *implications* for who
forms the Christian community and how we live together within it
(implications which at points might even be presented as necessary
consequences, as in Gal. 2), the biblical doctrine of justification is
first and foremost about the believer's standing before God. This
much is clear in Jesus' parable of the Pharisee and the tax collector.
The climax of that parable is Jesus' pronouncement 'I tell you, this
man went down to his house justified, rather than the other' (Luke
18:14). This is the blessing received by the man who can only cry,
'God, propitiate me, the sinner!' (v. 13 my tr.). His concern was
not – at least not primarily – the way he was ostracized by those
who saw themselves as holy and righteous before God. Even less
was he concerned about overcoming the salvation-historical divide
between Jew and Gentile. This man knew he deserved nothing but
wrath from God and knew there was nowhere to turn in those circumstances but to God himself: 'God, propitiate me, the sinner!'

It is this fundamental soteriological orientation that characterizes Paul's explanations of the doctrine as well. The classic
instance of Paul's letter to the Romans in fact begins with a reference to the gospel, which remains 'the power of God for salvation
to everyone who believes' (Rom. 1:16). To be sure, Paul is insistent that this 'everyone' includes both Jews and Greeks, and even
that the priority of the Jew remains in some sense ('to the Jew first
and also to the Greek') but that is not the focus of Paul's attention in this and the next seven chapters. Paul's prior concern is to
expound the gospel of salvation, and the fact that this will necessarily establish the ground upon which a proper discussion of the
Jew–Gentile question might proceed (as it will, in one form, in chs
9 – 11) is an important but secondary consideration.

In Romans in particular Paul's exposition of the gospel begins
with an explanation of the universal human predicament. Every
man and woman who has walked the face of the earth stands
accountable to God, complicit in Adam's choice to disobey him

and reiterating that choice in their own lives. The first premise upon which Paul will build his argument for a full, rich and impregnable salvation is this simple yet indisputable conclusion based on the evidence adduced in chapters 1–3: 'all' (those with the law and those without it) 'have sinned and fall short of the glory of God' (Rom. 3:23). To that premise is added another, that God has acted in Christ to remedy this situation. The righteousness that all have failed to demonstrate has now been provided by God himself 'through the redemption that is in Christ Jesus, whom God put forward as a propitiation by his blood, to be received by faith'. In this way God is able both to be just (in line with his own eternal character) *and* 'the justifier of the one who has faith in Jesus' (Rom. 3:24–26). The dire predicament of the entire race has been matched by the extraordinary mercy and love of God. The just Judge of all the earth has borne the cost so that he might be the one who 'justifies the ungodly' (Rom. 4:5). 'Therefore,' Paul says, 'since we have been justified by faith, we have peace with God through our Lord Jesus Christ' (Rom. 5:1). 'Since, therefore, we have now been justified by his blood, much more shall we be saved by him from the wrath of God' (Rom. 5:9). 'There is therefore now no condemnation for those who are in Christ Jesus' (Rom. 8:1).[3]

It has become rather standard in some circles, at least since Krister Stendahl's seminal article was published in English in 1963, to dismiss the Reformation concern with personal salvation as an imposition on the text of the NT.[4] Paul simply had other, larger concerns than the personal search for a gracious God. Luther's question was not Paul's question. The persuasiveness of this suggestion rests in part upon our proper concern to respect the historical location of the NT texts and to avoid jumping too quickly to our own situation and its particular interests. However, the way

---

3. The same soteriological context for the discussion of justification can be found in Paul's letter to the Galatians. Even though the argument is substantially different, with a different 'universe of discourse' (so Thiselton, *Hermeneutics*, 352), justification and salvation are also connected in the epistle of James (2:14–26).

4. Stendahl, 'Apostle Paul', 214. This article first appeared in Swedish in 1960.

Paul casts his exposition of the gospel, with special prominence given to the universal human predicament in terms of guilt, corruption and enslavement, raises the question of how anyone might be saved. The saving power of God in the gospel, which so delights Paul in Romans 1, is seen as urgent and necessary against the backdrop of the just condemnation we all deserve. As Henri Blocher comments, 'When one catches the power of Paul's vision of the human plight (as Luther was able to do), one can hardly imagine that it was eclipsed by the Jew–Gentile issue', notwithstanding the passion with which Paul introduces the latter in Romans 9.[5] In addition, contemporary theologians are rightly concerned to avoid a distortion of Christian soteriology by the anthropocentric and individualist preoccupations of our cultural environments, but still concede the fundamental appropriateness of Luther's question. As Bruce McCormack paraphrases Barth, '"How do I lay hold of a gracious God?" is not the only question to be asked in Christian soteriology [. . .] but it is an inescapable one.[6] Whatever else might be said about the doctrine of justification, then, it is important to acknowledge its basic soteriological context.

### Forensic
Justification is also an essentially forensic notion: it has to do with judgment in the heavenly court (*in foro Dei*). This is not simply a matter of observing that the basic vocabulary is taken from legal discourse, in both the Old Testament and the New. Studies of that vocabulary by Mark Seifrid have indeed concluded that the hiphil of *ṣdq* is often used of an act of judgment, where '"justice pronounced" is regularly joined to "justice done"' and also that Paul's use of the verb *dikaioō* is consistently forensic and positive in meaning (i.e. it speaks of a favourable verdict, an acquittal).[7] In the NT the antonym of 'justification' is 'condemnation' (e.g. Rom. 8:33–34). However, the context in which these terms are used points in precisely the

---

5. Blocher, 'Justification', 486–487.

6. McCormack, '*Justitia aliena*', 176.

7. Seifrid, 'Paul's Use of Righteousness Language', 41, 52. Both Calvin and Barth agree at this point; see McCormack, '*Justitia aliena*', 184.

same direction. The human condition to which justification answers contains an irradicable legal element. God has 'fixed a day', Paul told the Athenian intellectuals, 'on which he will judge the world in righteousness by a man whom he has appointed; and of this he has given assurance to all by raising him from the dead' (Acts 17:31). The Corinthians heard the same message from him: 'we must all appear before the judgment seat of Christ, so that each one may receive what is due for what he has done in the body, whether good or evil' (2 Cor. 5:10). Yet it was the writer to the Hebrews who most explicitly connected this truth with the salvation provided in Christ: 'just as it is appointed for man to die once, and after that comes judgment, so Christ, having been offered once to bear the sins of many, will appear a second time, not to deal with sin but to save those who are eagerly waiting for him' (Heb. 9:27–28).

Apart from Christ, we stand guilty before God. God's perfect law condemns us. Our own consciences accuse us. Sin brings not only the corruption of ourselves and all around us (Mark 7:20–23; Eph. 4:22), not only enslavement to our own desires and the purpose of those powers who have risen in rebellion against God and his rightful rule (Eph. 2:1–3); it brings guilt, real, objective, unfudgeable guilt. And in that condition we face the fearful prospect of an exacting, righteous and unavoidable judgment. So whatever else salvation entails, it must deal with this facet of our predicament. It must deal with the simple fact that we deserve nothing but condemnation. Justification by faith – or rather, justification by grace through faith – is God's answer to this fundamental aspect of our condition.

To say that justification is essentially a forensic notion is not to say that the analogy between a human courtroom and the heavenly court is exact or straightforward. There are very significant differences between the two, which need to be considered if we are not to distort the uniqueness of God's relationship with men and women.[8]

---

8. Agreeing with D. A. Carson, Bruce McCormack writes, 'every attempt to assess the "legality" of the trial described in Romans 3:19–26 on the basis of an appeal to the situation that pertains in even the best human courtrooms is bound to mislead. Such analogy as exists between them is simply too inexact' (McCormack, '*Justitia aliena*', 185).

In the human courtroom there is an important distinction between the judge and the law, which he administers. The human judge is bound by laws, which are in a very significant way external to him. In a modern state the legislature and the judiciary are distinct from each other and properly kept at some distance from one another. Judges are servants of the law rather than masters of it. Furthermore, an appeal process exists to remedy any deficiency in a particular judge's application of the law of the land. In contrast, God is not bound by anything external to him. As Karl Barth puts it:

> The God who is present and active in the justification of man and therefore as the gracious God, has right and is in the right. Not subject to any alien law, but Himself the origin and basis and revealer of all true law, He is just in Himself. This is the backbone of the event of justification.[9]

God always judges justly, not because he is constrained to do so by a law that stands above him, but as a proper expression of his being and character. 'What God does is right because what God is seen to be doing here manifests perfectly what God is as the one who is always just in himself.'[10] In other words, the standard of judgment is internal to God rather than external to him. However, this does not mean that it is an arbitrary standard. Rather, it is the standard which alone makes sense of reality, as it is constituted by the perfect union of God's being and his will. It is the righteousness embodied in Jesus of Nazareth, the incarnate Son.[11]

Affirming the basically forensic character of justification is

---

9. K. Barth, *CD* IV.1, 530–531.

10. McCormack, '*Justitia aliena*', 186.

11. Barth made much of this too: 'This is the right of God which is maintained in the justification of sinful man, which marks it off even as a free act of grace from the caprice and arbitrariness of a destiny that apportions blindfold its favour and disfavour, which clothes it with majesty and dignity, which gives to the knowledge of faith an infallible certainty – that in the first instance God affirms Himself in this action, that in it He lives His own divine life in His unity as Father, Son and Holy Spirit. But in it He also maintains Himself as the God of man, as the One who has bound

not the same as claiming that it is an *exclusively* forensic notion.[12]
For instance, the language of judgment and acquittal is tempered
in Luther's treatment of the subject by the language of personal
relationship. In a famous sermon from 1519, 'On the Twofold
Righteousness', Luther began to develop the notion of 'the happy
exchange (*der frölich wechßel*)' between Christ and the believer in
justification that can be understood on analogy with marriage.
Seeking to elaborate the connection between the righteousness
conferred by God in Christ and the response of faithful and
obedient living, Luther proclaimed, 'Therefore through the first
righteousness arises the voice of the bridegroom who says to the
soul, "I am yours," but through the second comes the voice of
the bride who answers, "I am yours".'[13] Luther understood that
our justification is more than a legal transaction. Beneath those
undeniable and indispensable legal elements are more personal
and relational ones. Melanchthon was undoubtedly more single-
minded in his advocacy of legal categories for understanding
justification than Luther; however, the criticism he received even
in his own time suggests others were more cautious.[14] Law and

---

Himself to man from all eternity, as the One who has elected Himself for
man and man for Himself. In the action of His grace He executes that
which He willed and determined when to man as this creature He gave
actuality and his human nature' (K. Barth, *CD* IV.1, 532).

12. This is conceded even by those most committed to the forensic understanding of justification. So François Turretin: 'Now although we do not
deny that this word has more than one signification and is taken in different ways in the Scriptures [. . .], still we maintain that it is never taken for
an infusion of righteousness, but as often as the Scriptures speak profess-
edly about our justification, it always must be explained as a forensic term'
(Turretin, *Institutes* 2.634).

13. Luther, 'Twofold Righteousness', 300.

14. One should note in passing that the sharp distinction made between
Luther and Melanchthon on this subject, in the early twentieth century
by Karl Holl and later in the same century by Lowell Green, is somewhat
overplayed. Luther consistently used the legal image from the time of his
1515–16 Romans lectures. Melanchthon, for all his emphasis on the

justice are not ultimate in the universe. At the heart of the universe we find the *person* of God, who is indeed a just Judge but also a loving Creator and a merciful Father.

### Christological

The doctrine of justification is properly located within the Bible's teaching on salvation. It deals with the question of how we are saved from the condemnation we deserve. However, we are not saved by a doctrine or even by a theological principle. We are saved by the powerful and merciful action of God in Jesus Christ. This much should have been evident already. The tax collector in Jesus' parable prays to be propitiated (Luke 18:13). In Romans we are 'justified by [God's] grace as a gift, through the redemption that is in Christ Jesus' (Rom. 3:24). The doctrine of justification is inseparably bound to the cross of Christ. In fact, as we shall see in a moment, the function of the doctrine of justification by faith is to keep our attention focused on Christ rather than ourselves.

The doctrine of justification by faith is open to caricature whenever it is dealt with apart from this focus on Christ and his work. Our redemption is redemption 'in Christ' (Rom. 3:24). He 'was delivered up for our trespasses and raised for our justification' (Rom. 4:25). We have been justified 'by [*en*; literally, 'in'] his blood' (Rom. 5:9). It is this anchor in our union with Christ in his death and resurrection that prevents our justification from being merely a legal fiction. It is this anchor in our union with Christ that prevents the doctrine from being distorted into a licence to keep sinning, as Paul makes clear in Romans 6. It is our union with Christ that ensures we take seriously the implications of this doctrine, not least the implications for our life together as the one people of God. It is our union with Christ that undergirds the assurance this doctrine generates, and connects it to the other aspects of what

---

Footnote 14 (*cont.*)

forensic character of justification, did not entirely exclude more personal images, such as that of the exchange that occurs upon marriage. Holl, 'Luthers Bedeutung', 544–582; Green, *How Melanchthon Helped*; Blocher, 'Justification', 492; McGrath, *Iustitia Dei*, 235–258.

God has done for us in him. Calvin realized the critical importance of understanding justification – and indeed all of what God has done for us – under the rubric of union with Christ.[15] This insight became particularly important among Calvin's heirs in Scotland. As T. F. Torrance insisted, 'union with Christ lies at the heart of our righteousness in him, for it is through that union that we actually participate in his holy life'.[16] Since this supremely important idea is explored in detail elsewhere in this volume we will not spend more time on it here.[17] Suffice to say, with Anthony Thiselton, 'Being in Christ is the horizon of understanding within which the various "problems" associated with justification by grace through faith alone become simply questions that receive intelligible answers.'[18]

As one might expect, Karl Barth was especially attuned to the need to understand this doctrine (and everything else!) in the closest possible relation to the person of Jesus Christ. He was particularly concerned about a dualistic tendency he discerned in some Protestant theology, which stressed far too strongly a distinction between 'an objective achievement of salvation there and then and a subjective appropriation of it here and now'.[19] When justification is treated as part of an *ordo salutis*, as one step in a series, either in the Spirit's application of the benefits of Christ's work or the believer's appropriation of it, the danger arises that we begin to speak of two discrete actions rather than of 'the one totality of the reconciling action of God, of the one whole and undivided Jesus Christ, and of His one grace'.[20] The cross then

---

15. 'First, we must understand that as long as Christ remains outside of us, and we are separated from him, all that he has suffered and done for the salvation of the human race remains useless and of no value to us' (Calvin, *Institutes* 3.1.1).

16. Torrance, 'Justification', 151.

17. See Campbell's chapter (6) in the present volume.

18. Thiselton, *Hermeneutics*, 349.

19. K. Barth, *CD* IV.2, 502–503.

20. Ibid., 502. Barth was certainly aware that a number of the most significant expositions of the *ordo salutis* in Lutheran and Reformed circles did stress the temporal simultaneity of the various elements (he quotes J. A.

becomes the ground for a potential justification, a possibility that needs to be made actual, real or effective by a further act of God in the Spirit. Alternatively, a religious and moral psychology takes over, with the spiritual experience of the Christian in a sense supplementing the work of Christ. Either way, Christ ceases to be at the centre of our exposition of the doctrine. Barth's answer was to insist that both the objective and subjective dimensions of our justification are accomplished in Christ. Jesus has become our righteousness (1 Cor. 1:30) in a much more profound sense than is usually imagined. Torrance follows Barth when he writes:

> Not only was the great divine act of righteousness fulfilled in the flesh of Jesus, in his life and death, but throughout his life and death Jesus stood in our place as our Substitute and Representative who appropriated the divine Act of saving Righteousness for us [. . .] in justification, Jesus Christ was not only the embodiment of God's justifying act but the embodiment of our human appropriation of it. In that unity of divine and human, justification was fulfilled in Christ from both sides, from the side of justifying God and from the side of justified man – 'He was justified in the Spirit', as St Paul put it [1 Tim. 3:16]. Justification as objective act of the redeeming God and justification as subjective actualization of it in our estranged human existence have once and for all taken place – in Jesus.[21]

There are certainly questions that need to be raised about Barth's Christological exposition of the doctrine of justification. It presupposes a particular understanding of election and of a covenant of grace with humanity, which renders all discussion of imputation unnecessary.[22] It acknowledges the importance of

---

Footnote 20 (*cont.*)

   Quenstedt in this connection), but is convinced that on the whole this was not taken seriously.

21. Torrance, 'Justification', 156–158.

22. McCormack, '*Justitia aliena*', 192–193. The brevity of Barth's discussion of this concept of imputation (and of Gen. 15:6) in §61 of *Church Dogmatics* is remarkable, especially in the light of the prominence of both in NT discussions of justification.

union with Christ but locates this union in the incarnation (the eternal Son's real ontological union with the race) rather than as a work of the Spirit through his gift of faith.[23] Consequently, and because he rejects the usual distinction between the accomplishment of salvation and its application, Barth insists:

> There is not one for whose sin and death He did not die, whose sin and death He did not remove and obliterate on the cross, for whom He did not positively do the right, whose right He has not established. There is not one to whom this was not addressed as his justification in His resurrection from the dead. There is not one whose man He is not, who is not justified in Him [. . .] Again, there is no one who is not adequately and perfectly and finally justified in Him [. . .] There is not one whose right has not been established and confirmed validly and once and for all in Him.[24]

There are other issues too, chiefly surrounding the nature of faith and an attenuated doctrine of the Spirit and his work. Nevertheless, perhaps in some measure because Barth's account does not quite reflect the proportions of the biblical material, we are bound to take more seriously the need to keep the person and work of Jesus Christ at the centre of our own accounts of the doctrine.

## Justification: its central truth

The doctrine of justification is the biblical teaching about salvation from the condemnation we deserve by means of the life, death and resurrection of Jesus Christ. The contours of the doctrine are determined by its soteriological, forensic and Christological concerns. Yet given that basic shape, how might we describe the truth at the heart of it? At this point, concentrating our attention on what is generally regarded as the most enduring systematic

---

23. This is even more pointed in some of Barth's former students, e.g. Torrance, 'Justification', 156.

24. K. Barth, *CD* IV.1, 630.

treatment of the doctrine of justification by faith, that of John Calvin in Book 3 of the *Institutes*, should prove helpful.

Calvin's explanation continues to commend itself as a fruitful account of the biblical teaching on the subject, not least because it remains sensitive to the concerns just mentioned. In particular, as already noted, Calvin is aware of the critical importance of union with Christ and sets his discussion of how we receive the salvation that has been won for us in that proper context.[25] Further, Calvin explains the nature of this union by reference to both the work or 'secret energy (*arcana efficacia*)' of the Spirit and, especially, the Spirit's gift of faith. For this reason, before Calvin turns to what he describes as the twofold grace which proceeds from our union with Christ (that of justification and sanctification) he discusses in some depth the nature of faith.[26] Recalling his well-known definition of faith will prove valuable for the analysis of what follows:

> Now we shall possess a right definition of faith if we call it a firm and certain knowledge of God's benevolence toward us, founded upon the truth of the freely given promise in Christ, both revealed to our minds and sealed upon our hearts through the Holy Spirit.[27]

---

25. To the critical passage from *Institutes* 3.1.1, which I have already quoted (n. 15 above), could be added 3.11.10: 'Therefore, that joining together of Head and members, that indwelling of Christ in our hearts – in short, that mystical union – are accorded by us the highest degree of importance, so that Christ, having been made ours, makes us sharers with him in the gifts with which he has been endowed. We do not, therefore, contemplate him outside ourselves from afar in order that his righteousness may be imputed to us but because we put on Christ and are engrafted into his body – in short, because he deigns to make us one with him. For this reason, we glory that we have fellowship of righteousness with him.' See also Gaffin, 'Justification'.

26. In these chapters of the *Institutes* Calvin uses the term 'regeneration (*regeneratio*)' for the concept later theologians would describe as 'sanctification (*sanctificatio*)'. For helpful discussion of the 'twofold grace' and its relation to 'union with Christ', see Garcia, *Life in Christ*.

27. Calvin, *Institutes* 3.2.7.

The significance of this definition lies in the way it brings together ideas of confidence, knowledge, the promise of Christ and the work of the Holy Spirit, centring them around 'God's benevolence toward us (*erga nos benevolentiae*)'. Faith is not simply an assent to doctrine, though it is properly understood as a species of 'knowledge (*cognitio*)'. It is not trust either, if that is understood in abstract terms. Faith, in Calvin's estimation, has this particular focus: the goodness of God towards us. God is not only good in himself; he is determined for our good. He is not against us as our adversary. He is *for us*.

When Calvin turns to the subject of justification, he spends eight chapters of the *Institutes* expounding the doctrine and countering what he sees as the distortions of it. Such distortions come from various quarters, of course, but those who receive Calvin's special attention are the theologians of the Roman church and one particularly eccentric Lutheran (eccentric on this issue at any rate), Andreas Osiander.[28] Quite early on in the discussion Calvin provides his definition, one that repays careful scrutiny.[29] He starts by enunciating the basic principle 'He is said to be justified in God's sight who is both reckoned righteous in God's judgment and has been accepted on account of his righteousness (*acceptus est ob suam iustitiam*).'

Simply put, it is only the righteous who are justified. Sinners can expect only wrath and vengeance, but those whom God judges to be righteous are accepted. In the context 'to be accepted' is synonymous with 'to find favour (*invenire gratiam*)', an expression he uses in the very next sentence. God's favourable judgment is reserved for the righteous person. Calvin sums up, 'justified before God is the man who, freed from the company of sinners, has God to witness and affirm (*testem et assertorem*) his righteousness'.

Calvin does not immediately proceed to demonstrate that no one is in this position (he does that elsewhere).[30] At this stage he

---

28. Osiander had published his *De Iustificatione* in 1550 while he was Professor of Theology at the new University of Königsberg, but died in 1552.

29. Calvin, *Institutes* 3.11.2.

30. E.g. ibid. 3.11.15: 'Now we confess with Paul that the doers of the law are justified before God; but, because we are all far from observing the law,

is simply working with the definition of the word 'justification', which he insists is properly used to describe God's endorsement of the righteous person's behaviour. God cannot fail to recognize and endorse this behaviour where (one might even say 'wherever') it is found. This becomes significant as Calvin takes the next step to explain what it means to be justified *by faith*:

> justified by faith is he who, excluded from the righteousness of works, grasps the righteousness of Christ through faith (*Christi iustitiam per fidem apprehendit*), and clothed in it, appears in God's sight not as a sinner but as a righteous man.[31]

Three things are worth noting briefly. The first is that the person Calvin has in mind is 'excluded from the righteousness of works'. Justification by faith is always the justification of the ungodly (Rom. 4:5), the justification of those who have nothing to plead before God's judgment seat, not even their own faith. They can make no claim to God's favour. What is in view here is the justification of those who know that all roads to favour with God have been blocked and can only cry with the tax collector, 'God, propitiate me, the sinner!' It is the justification of those who have been excluded from justification any other way.

The second thing to notice is that a genuine and substantial righteousness lies at the heart of justification by faith. The righteousness reckoned to the believer is no mere invention, an 'as if' righteousness. It is no legal fiction nor is it simply a 'book entry'. The righteousness of Christ is genuine and substantial. He is and always was 'the Holy and Righteous One' (Acts 3:14). And it is his righteousness, 'the righteousness of Christ', that is grasped through faith and that clothes the believer. God does not have to pretend that the sinner before him is really righteous. The profound union of the believer with Christ that comes about through faith, a union

---

Footnote 30 (*cont.*)

> we infer from this that those works which ought especially to avail for righteousness give us no help because we are destitute of them.'

31. Ibid. 3.11.2.

every bit as real and ontologically significant as the union of Christ and the race in the incarnation, means that the believer really does now stand before God as a righteous person.

And yet it is and remains 'the righteousness of Christ'. It comes from him and not from within me. It is genuinely mine, but only because it is first and always his. The happy exchange that Luther loved to talk about has taken place: I am clothed in his righteousness and this profoundly impacts my life at every level. However, I am always in the position of a receiver rather than an achiever. This realization that our justification is anchored in a righteousness extrinsic to us, an alien righteousness, is one of the great legacies of the Reformation.[32] It was exegetically grounded in 1 Corinthians 1:30, where we are told that God made Christ Jesus 'wisdom', 'righteousness', 'sanctification' and 'redemption', and in Philippians 3:9, where Paul longs to be found in Christ 'not having a righteousness of my own that comes from the law, but that which comes through faith in Christ, the righteousness from God that depends on faith'. Here is one of the cornerstones of the inescapably forensic character of justification by faith.

Thirdly, we should notice the means (what others would later speak of as the instrumental cause) of our justification. The righteousness of Christ is grasped *by faith*. Calvin had prepared for this reference to faith in an earlier chapter of the *Institutes*, from which we have already quoted. Faith, as Calvin explains it, is oriented towards God's goodness and mercy. It is, as one moving paraphrase put it, 'the conviction that, no matter what happens around you, the face of your heavenly Father is turned towards you in love'.[33] However, Calvin does not consider faith to be a simple matter of abstract knowledge or mere acknowledgment.

---

32. Barth insists that our justification is always 'a matter of the rule of the righteousness of God in Him, which, although it rules over us and applies to us, is always a strange righteousness: *iustitia aliena*, because first and essentially it is *iustitia Christi*, and only as such *nostra, mea iustitia*' (K. Barth, *CD* IV.1, 549).

33. The paraphrase is one offered by Dr Peter Jensen when lecturing a third-year doctrine class in 1985.

God's mercy is not simply a reality in the universe viewed at some distance from us and our circumstances. It is not 'merely to know something of God's will'.[34] In the long chapter on faith he would also explain what he called 'the chief hinge on which faith turns': 'we do not regard the promises of mercy that God offers as true only outside ourselves, but not at all in us; rather that we make them ours by inwardly embracing (*intus complectendo*) them'.[35]

Yet this inward embrace is not a natural human phenomenon. As Calvin's definitional statement makes clear, this knowledge of 'God's benevolence toward us' is 'both revealed (*revelatur*) to our minds and sealed (*obsignatur*) upon our hearts through the Holy Spirit'.[36] Faith in the believer is always a work of God, a gift rather than an achievement. But that is not to say that faith is powerful in itself. Calvin will later labour this point, agreeing momentarily with Osiander:

> faith of itself does not possess the power of justifying, but only in so far as it receives Christ. For if faith justified of itself or through some intrinsic power, so to speak, as it is always weak and imperfect it would effect this only in part; thus the righteousness that conferred a fragment of salvation upon us would be defective. Now we imagine no such thing, but we say that, properly speaking, God alone justifies; then we transfer this same function to Christ because he was given to us for righteousness. We compare faith to a kind of vessel; for unless we come empty and with the mouth of our soul open to seek Christ's grace, we are not capable of receiving Christ. From this it is to be inferred that, in teaching that before his righteousness is received Christ is received in faith, we do not take the power of justifying away from Christ.[37]

Calvin certainly recognizes that in this age faith exists side by side with doubt, assurance with anxiety.[38] But even if it did not, we

---

34. Calvin, *Institutes* 3.2.7.
35. Ibid. 3.2.16.
36. Ibid. 3.2.7.
37. Ibid. 3.11.7.
38. 'Surely, while we teach that faith ought to be certain and assured, we cannot imagine any certainty that is not tinged with doubt, or any

must be careful in the way we think about it. We are not powerfully saved by our faith, but by Christ. Faith is critical because of
its object and because by its very nature it orients us towards that
object. But it must not become its own object. It must not shift
from being the *instrument* to being the *ground* of our justification.[39]
This would be to return to justification by works under another
guise and, as Calvin would later say, 'faith righteousness so differs
from works righteousness that when one is established the other
has to be overthrown'.[40]

Having said all this, we come at last to Calvin's summary of the
Christian doctrine of justification:

> Therefore, we explain justification simply as the acceptance (*acceptionem*)
> with which God receives us into his favour (*in gratiam receptos*) as
> righteous men. And we say that it consists in the remission of sins and
> the imputation of Christ's righteousness.[41]

He does not repeat here what he has just said about faith as the
means through which the righteousness of Christ is apprehended
and the remission of sins embraced. That is not necessary given the
context we have been examining. But, when everything else is pared
back, this lies at the heart of justification: God's favourable verdict,
properly being considered righteous in his sight, because sin and its

---

assurance that is not assailed by some anxiety. On the other hand, we
say that believers are in perpetual conflict with their own unbelief' (ibid.
3.2.17). Again, 'in the course of the present life it never goes so well with
us that we are wholly cured of the disease of unbelief and entirely filled
and possessed by faith' (ibid. 3.2.18).

39. 'Therefore I say that faith, which is only the instrument for receiving
righteousness, is ignorantly confused with Christ, who is the material
cause and at the same time the Author and Minister of this great benefit'
(ibid. 3.11.2). Paul Helm draws attention to the fact that in this subsection
Calvin is prepared to defend his account of justification by using elements
of the Aristotelian fourfold causal schema (Helm, *Calvin's Ideas*, 400).

40. Calvin, *Institutes* 3.11.13.

41. Ibid. 3.11.2.

guilt have been dealt with and the righteousness of Christ has been imputed to us. Justification is the judicial aspect of 'God's benevolence toward us', which can never be separated from Christ.[42]

Here, and in the rest of this chapter, Calvin is insistent that Christ's righteousness is imputed to us. This is particularly important in the light of Osiander's suggestion that because of union with Christ, his righteous, divine essence is infused and we are right to talk about our 'essential righteousness'. The notion of imputation undercuts any notion of merit or of faith as a new kind of religious 'work'. It guards the alien or extrinsic character of the righteousness that is ours. Of course the warrant for its use comes from the classic texts on the subject in the NT. Paul makes use of *logizomai*, 'to reckon' or 'impute', and its cognates thirty-four times in his letters, fifteen times with God as the explicit or implied subject (Rom. 2:26; 4:3, 5–6, 8–11, 22–24; 9:8; 2 Cor. 5:19; Gal. 3:6; 2 Tim. 4:16). It is also the word used in the Septuagint to translate *ḥšb* in Genesis 15:6.

It has been of particular interest over the centuries that Calvin speaks of two elements in justification: the remission of sins and the imputation of Christ's righteousness. Robert Gundry has challenged the conventional correlation of these elements with the passive and active obedience of Christ.[43] Generations of Lutheran and Reformed scholars, in particular, have spoken of Christ's obedient suffering in the place of sinners (*obedientia Christi passiva*) as that which secures the forgiveness of our sins and of his life of obedience, his fulfilment of all righteousness (*obedientia Christi activa*), as that which is imputed to us.[44] Gundry finds this correlation of Jesus' obedience throughout his life and the righteousness imputed to us to be without any

---

42. While justification is the focal point of this chapter and has this critical role to play in our salvation, it is important to remember that justification is not the only aspect of our salvation. A fuller treatment would need to coordinate this with other aspects such as adoption, sanctification and the indwelling Spirit of God.

43. Gundry, 'Nonimputation'. See in response Carson, 'Vindication', and J. Piper, *Counted Righteous*.

44. So the Lutheran Johann Gerhard in response to the work of Johannes Piscator (McGrath, *Iustitia Dei*, 272).

explicit exegetical warrant. Those who have responded to him have insisted that the concept is woven deeply into the NT. However this debate is decided, Calvin's insistence remains that our justification is grounded in a righteousness not intrinsic to us.

There is more that can and perhaps should be said about the nature of justification. However, enough has been said to draw our attention to the heart of the matter: God's benevolent acceptance of those who deserve nothing but condemnation, based solely on the person and work of Christ and grasped by the Christian with the hand of faith. Before we return to the issue of how the principalities and powers have been defeated, and, more specifically, how the doctrine of justification contributes to our understanding of that defeat, it remains simply to explore for a moment the *dogmatic function* of this doctrine.


## Justification: its dogmatic function

How does the doctrine of justification by faith alone function within the body of Christian doctrine? It is well known that Martin Luther described the doctrine of justification as 'the article of the standing or falling church (*articulus stantis et cadentis ecclesiae*)'.[45] In 1530 Luther explained what he meant by this statement:

> If this one teaching stands in its purity, then Christendom will also remain pure and good, undivided and unseparated; for this alone, and nothing else, makes and maintains Christendom. Everything else may be brilliantly counterfeited by false Christians and hypocrites; but where this falls, it is impossible to ward off any error or sectarian spirit.[46]

---

45. This standard formula is a slight modification of what Luther actually said: 'when it stands by this article the church *stands*, when [this article] falls the Church falls (*quia isto articulo stante stat Ecclesia, ruente ruit Ecclesia*)' (emphasis added). From a comment on Ps. 130:4 in Martin Luther, 'In XV Psalmos Graduum' (1532), *D. Martin Luthers Werke*, xl–iii, 352.1–3.

46. M. Luther, *Commentary on Psalm 117* (1530), *D. Martin Luthers Werke*, xxxi-i, 223–257 = *Luther's Works* 14, 1–39.

According to Luther, the health of the churches is to a very large measure determined by the clarity with which they proclaim *this* biblical truth. What is more, evangelical doctrine more generally takes its shape from its coherence around God's gracious act of justification by faith. To the degree to which a particular doctrine stands in conflict with the basic shape and content of justification by faith, it should not be considered genuinely evangelical. Melanchthon went a step further, arguing in effect that the doctrine of justification operates as a hermeneutical key, which 'alone opens the door to the whole Bible'.[47]

Karl Barth famously disagreed, though he hinted that his disagreement was with the standard formula rather than with what Luther said and thought on the issue:

> The *articulus stantis et cadentis ecclesiae* is not the doctrine of justification
> as such, but its basis and culmination: the confession of Jesus Christ, in
> whom are hid all the treasures of wisdom and knowledge (Col. 2:3); the
> knowledge of His being and activity for us and to us and with us.[48]

Barth was willing to concede that 'there never was and there never can be any true Christian Church without the doctrine of justification'. However, he believed that when this doctrine itself is taken seriously we cannot make it the centrepiece of all.[49] It is not a theological formula but a person who stands at the centre of the Christian faith, and from the early church onwards all Christian doctrine has been structured around our confession of him as Lord and Christ (Acts 2:36).

---

47. Melanchthon, *Apology of the Augsburg Confession* IV, translated in Jüngel, *Justification*, 17–18.

48. K. Barth, *CD* IV.1, 527.

49. 'It is the justification of man itself, and our very confidence in the objective truth of the doctrine of justification, which forbids us to postulate that in the true Church its theological outworking must *semper, ubique et ab omnibus* be regarded and treated as the *unum necessarium,* the centre or culminating point of the Christian message or Christian doctrine' (ibid., 523–524).

There is, it would seem, truth in both observations. Jesus Christ, the incarnate Son and Israel's Messiah, is at the centre of God's purposes. All things were created through him and for him (Col. 1:17). He is the one before whom one day every knee will bow (Phil. 2:10–11). God's plan for the fullness of time is to sum up all things in him (Eph. 1:10). Barth's concern to keep Christ at the very centre of our attention resonates with the teaching of the NT and with the preoccupation of the Christian heart. And yet the doctrine of justification by faith gives a particular shape to our understanding of the gospel and the Christian life, which, in fact, safeguards the central place of Jesus Christ, who he is, what he has done and the promises he has given us.

Perhaps rather than asking what lies at the centre of Christian theology we would be better served by the question 'What is the relation between this doctrine and others that go to make up the body of Christian doctrine?' The point can be made with reference to one of the better-known legacies of Reformation theology. The great Reformation slogans *solus Christus, sola fide, sola gratia* and *sola scriptura* (Christ alone, by faith alone, by grace alone, and by Scripture alone) are too often treated in isolation from one another or as a series of affirmations that arose in the same tumultuous period but are otherwise unrelated. Yet they are profoundly related. Eberhard Jüngel, who prefers *solo verbo* (by the Word alone) to the better known *sola scriptura*,[50] makes this point emphatically:

> The meaning of 'Christ alone' (*solus Christus*) admittedly only becomes sufficiently clear when we use the three other exclusive formulae. These, in turn, have no other function than to guarantee a correct understanding of the 'Christ alone' formula.[51]

If we follow this line of argument, and I think we should, the doctrine of justification functions to keep our attention focused on Christ, the object of our faith and the one who rescues us from

---

50. Jüngel, 'Justification', 198–204.
51. Ibid., 168.

condemnation by clothing us in his righteousness. It supports the primacy of grace, since faith is not a work and is indeed the antithesis of religious achievement. It directs us to the promise of God, made in Christ and conveyed to us in the Scriptures, for comfort and confidence and freedom from our frantic attempts at self-justification. The doctrine of justification by faith keeps us from placing ourselves, our works, our piety, and even our faith, at the centre of God's purposes or the Christian life. In the end we do not need to make the choice between the doctrine of justification and the confession of Christ because rightly understood the doctrine of justification is a confession of Christ.

## The triumph of the cross over every accusation

So how does this rich piece of biblical teaching help us to understand those powerful yet perplexing words in Colossians 2:13–15? Earlier we noticed three imperatives surrounding these verses and I suggested that each of these was a response to a judgment or accusation which the Colossians, and all who read these words after them, are encouraged to dismiss immediately. However, there is in fact another accusation standing amid these three. It is the accusation of verse 13: 'you, who were dead in your trespasses and the uncircumcision of your flesh'. This is not the only letter of Paul where he repeats this accusation (Eph. 2:1). So profound was their entanglement (our entanglement) with all that characterizes rebellion against the living God that our condition could rightly be described as death. Beyond hope of a change, beyond resuscitation, out of reach of any human assistance – a case closed, a hospital bed emptied.

While Paul called on his readers not to entertain any of the other three accusations, even for a moment, this one is different. The other three, Paul hopes he has shown them, are unambiguously false. Faith in Christ does not need to be supplemented by the secret wisdom of the ages, which would put you in touch with the elemental powers of the universe. Faith in Christ does not need to be given substance by the observance of Jewish rules, regulations, ceremonies and festivals. Faith in Christ is not developed by 'spirituality' or spiritual experiences. But the accusation Paul repeats in verse 13 is profoundly true. We were ensnared by sin. We lived as those without any relation at all to the God who made and sustains us. We deserved nothing but condemnation. And a day of reckoning was unavoidable. A record had been kept. All that we owe to God, as his creatures, as those utterly dependent upon him, as those who have received so many good things from his hand and yet have returned all this with enmity or apathy or some other form of idolatry – all that could be legally demanded of us has been fully recorded. *This* accusation has documentary evidence to support it. This accusation can be proven.

And yet even this accusation did not prevail. Though there was substance to this one while the other three had none, this one too cannot stand in the light of the person of Jesus Christ and what he has done. We who were dead have been made alive with him. Our transgressions have been forgiven, swallowed up by grace. The legal record has been completely erased, wiped clean. Calvin, when expounding this part of Paul's letter, remarked 'this is full liberty, that Christ has by his blood blotted out not only our sins, but every handwriting which might declare us to be exposed to the judgement of God'.[52] Elsewhere he observed that in this one word 'blotted out' (*exaleiphō*) resides 'nearly the whole of our redemption'.[53] Certainly at this point, as Paul explicitly says, the legal dimensions of our human predicament have been dealt with. The cross of Christ, the atoning death of the obedient and righteous Son, secures our acquittal. The accusation can no longer be sustained. We have been made alive. Our transgressions have been forgiven. The legal record of our debt has been wiped clean. And if this has indeed been done, then how can any other accusation stand?

Here is the point of the connection between justification and the defeat of the powers. In the Old Testament and the New, Satan in particular is presented as a liar and a false accuser. In the garden he accused God of self-interest as he tempted the woman and her husband: 'You will not surely die. For God knows that when you

---

52. Calvin, *Epistles of Paul, Commentary on Colossians 2.14*.
53. Calvin, *Institutes* 2.7.17.

eat of it your eyes will be opened, and you will be like God, knowing good and evil' (Gen. 3:4–5). In the opening chapters of Job, Satan accuses Job before the heavenly court: Is Job's faith not merely self-interest (Job 1:9–11; 2:4–5)? Jesus labelled him the 'father of lies' and 'a murderer from the beginning' (John 8:44; did his lies in the garden not lead to the death of the man and the woman?), and one whose very character is revealed when he lies. In the book of Revelation, victory is celebrated over 'the accuser of our brothers' who 'accuses them day and night before our God' (Rev. 12:10).

The chief instrument of Satan's power is the lie that God is against us, that there is no such thing as divine benevolence, that we cannot expect anything good from the just and fearsome Judge of all the earth. A tantalizing and spectacularly successful combination of seduction and accusation has been his stock in trade from the beginning. This lie is, of course, infinitely malleable. It can involve a false appeal to the law of God, an exploitation of the subjective awareness of guilt that is meant to cause us to flee to Christ.[54] It can involve a manipulation of the word of God, a tactic that succeeded in the garden (Gen. 3) but not in the wilderness of Judea (Matt. 4). It can take the form of a suggestion that there is something missing, some power not yet acquired, some experience not yet explored, some vital key to success not yet taken up, and until it is, the final verdict of God on our life and ministry is in doubt. Or it might just be the insinuation that there is something still left undone, a victory still to be won.

Yet such a thing has happened in the cross of Christ that God's final, unalterable judgment has been given. So thoroughly has our sin been dealt with, so real and appropriate is our union with Christ, so undoubted and pure is his righteousness that has been imputed to us, that no accusation against us can succeed.[55] 'Who shall bring any charge against God's elect?' Paul asked the Roman Christians. 'It is God who justifies. Who is to condemn?' (Rom.

---

54. Satan's recourse to the law of God is explored in a helpful but slightly different way by Blocher, 'Agnus Victor', 83–84.

55. This is what Bolt, *Living with the Underworld*, 116–117, provocatively calls the indirect 'neutralization' of the demonic powers.

8:33–34). The weapon has been stripped from the Accuser and those in league with him; the rulers and authorities have been disarmed. As Jesus faced what he was about to do in Jerusalem, he told his disciples, 'Now is the judgment of this world; now will the ruler of this world be cast out' (John 12:31). And when it was done, having taken upon himself our sin and all that it entailed, he said 'It is finished' (John 19:30). As one of Calvin's more distinguished successors put it, Christ did this '"in himself" for us [. . .] by his incarnation and death, by which he so most fully satisfied divine justice and expiated our sins as to take away from Satan all right of accusing men afterwards: "Through death he destroyed him that had the power of death" (Heb. 2:14, 15)'.[56]

The doctrine of justification by faith keeps the focus of our understanding of salvation on the cross of Christ, on the redemption secured by his shed blood, rather than anything we could or can do. It points us to a judgment delivered outside us, which changes finally and for ever who we are and where we stand with God. Colossians 2 shares this same preoccupation. So magnificent is Christ Jesus our Lord, so effective is his death and resurrection, that those who share the circumcision of Christ (v. 11), who have been buried with him in the baptism of Christ (v. 12), who have been made alive with him (v. 13), need listen to no lies and fear no false accusations. The rantings of the principalities and powers are empty and powerless.

Lies will still be told, of course, and they will sound wise. The accusations will still be made. But they cannot stand. They and the liar who stands behind them have been unmasked. And 'there is therefore now no condemnation for those who are in Christ Jesus' (Rom. 8:1). Is the message of justification by faith strong enough in the face of spiritual evil? It most certainly is – because at its heart is a confession of the victorious Christ.

> For I am sure that neither death nor life, nor angels nor rulers, nor things present nor things to come, nor powers, nor height nor depth, nor anything else in all creation, will be able to separate us from the love of God in Christ Jesus our Lord. (Rom. 8:38–39)

---

56. Turretin, *Institutes* 2.221.

# 6. WITH CHRIST OVER THE POWERS

**Constantine R. Campbell**

## Introduction

### *Preamble*

This chapter investigates the nexus between two themes that are sometimes neglected by New Testament (NT) exegetes. Both themes, 'the powers' and 'union with Christ', are assumed by Paul in various contexts, and yet are nowhere defined or explicitly expounded. While some interesting work has been produced on both themes,[1] an issue that has not frequently been explored within scholarship is the intersection between the powers and union with Christ.

In order to explore the connection between the powers and union with Christ, I will begin with a brief sketch of the theme

---

1. See e.g. Adams, *Constructing the World*; Berkhof, *Christ and the Powers*; Horton, *Covenant and Salvation*; MacGregor, 'Principalities and Powers'; D. G. Powers, *Salvation through Participation*; Tannehill, *Dying and Rising*; Van Kooten, *Cosmic Christology*.

of union with Christ as found in Colossians and Ephesians. I will then explore the nature of the nexus between union with Christ and Christ's victory over the powers.

### Union with Christ?

The concept of union, or participation, with Christ defies simplistic definition. As Markus Barth reflects:

> This key term of Paul's theology is a puzzle that has been treated in any number of monographs and excurses. Mythical (Schlier in his commentary), mystical (Schweitzer), existential, sacramental (Bouttier), local (Deissmann), historical and eschatological (Lohmeyer, Neugebauer, Bouttier), juridical (Parisius), and ecclesiastical (Grossouw) interpretations compete for recognition or are grouped together in various selections [. . .][2]

Indeed, there have been many and varied attempts to classify this theme, but Barth's conclusion on the matter is sober: 'The impossibility of elaborating a final definition of the meaning of "in Christ" may well have a simple cause: namely that Paul used the formula *in more than one sense*.'[3] Having said as much, however, this does not mean that it is impossible to delineate a broad outline of the concept as it is employed in Paul's thought.

Some of the language that relates to union with Christ includes phrases such as 'in Christ', 'in him', 'in the Lord', 'in whom' (when Christ is the antecedent of the relative pronoun), 'with Christ', 'with him', 'with whom', 'through Christ', 'through him', 'through whom' and so on. It is important to recognize the scope of such phrases, since some studies tend to focus simply on the phrase 'in Christ', as though the theme can be reduced to a single expression.

When we explore the uses of these, and related, phrases, through the Pauline canon, there are a few key subthemes that rise to prominence. The language is often connected to the expression of things achieved for, or given to, believers in Christ. That is, 'in Christ'

---

2. M. Barth, *Ephesians*, 69.
3. Ibid. (emphasis original).

and related phrases are employed with reference to our salvation, reconciliation, the bestowal of blessings, and other such matters. Language connected to union with Christ is also employed in relation to the actions and characteristics of believers. Paul exhorts his readers to do certain things 'in Christ', and to conduct themselves in a manner befitting those who are in the Lord. Obviously, such language is also used to depict faith 'in Christ', which simply denotes the object of our trust. Union-with-Christ language also depicts the solidarity with Christ that believers share. We are *baptized* with Christ, *raised* with Christ, *seated* with Christ in the heavenlies and *suffer* with Christ. Finally, union-with-Christ language is used simply as a periphrasis – or what Schweitzer describes as a brachylogy – to refer to someone who is a *Christian*.[4] Rather than use the term 'Christian', Paul refers to people as being 'in Christ'. While the language related to union with Christ demonstrates other uses also, these five subcategories are the most common and important for Paul. We turn now to survey briefly some of the key references in Colossians and Ephesians that refer to the concept of union with Christ.

### Union with Christ in Colossians

Union with Christ is seen primarily in chapters 2 and 3 of Colossians. Believers are to walk in him (2:6); they have been circumcised in him (2:11), buried and raised with him (2:12), made alive with him (2:13), and they died with him (2:20). Their lives are hidden with Christ (3:3), and will be revealed with him in glory (3:4). And of special significance for this chapter, the fullness of God dwells in him, and believers have been filled by him who is the head over every ruler and authority (2:9–10).[5]

Of the various uses of the language associated with union with Christ, it is evident from this summary that *solidarity* with Christ is prominent in Colossians. Believers are circumcised in him, buried, raised and made alive with him. Their lives are hidden with him,

---

4. A. Schweitzer, *Mysticism of Paul*, 122–123.

5. All direct Scriptural quotations are taken from the Holman Christian Standard Bible, and paraphrases retain the language of the HCSB in most instances.

and will be revealed with him in glory. We also see the conduct of believers addressed ('walk in him'), and things achieved for believers ('you have been filled').

### Union with Christ in Ephesians

Union with Christ is seen primarily in chapters 1 and 2 of Ephesians, occurring no fewer than eleven times in 1:3–14. Believers have been blessed in Christ (1:3), chosen in him (1:4) and adopted through Jesus Christ (1:5). God favoured us in the beloved (1:6), and provided redemption in Christ and the forgiveness of trespasses (1:7); he made known to us the mystery of his will, according to his good pleasure that he planned in him (1:9). Everything is to be brought together in Christ (1:10). Believers have been made God's inheritance in Christ (1:11), have their hope in Christ (1:12) and are sealed with the Holy Spirit (1:13). In chapter 2 we see that believers have been made alive with Christ (2:5), raised up with him and seated with him in the heavens (2:6), were created in Christ Jesus for good works (2:10), and have been brought near in Christ Jesus (2:13). The whole building of God's people is fitted together in him, and is growing into a holy sanctuary in the Lord (2:21), being built together in him (2:22). From this summary we may observe that things achieved for believers are prominent (believers are 'blessed', 'chosen', 'adopted', 'favoured' etc.). Solidarity with Christ is also featured ('made alive', 'raised up', 'seated').

Having briefly surveyed some of the key occurrences of the language that relates to union with Christ in Colossians and Ephesians, we turn now to consider the nexus between the themes of union with Christ and Christ's victory over the powers.

## Colossians

### The 'Colossian heresy'

It is commonplace in NT scholarship to regard Paul's writing of Colossians as a response to a so-called 'Colossian heresy'.[6]

---

6. See e.g. E. Schweizer, *Colossians*, 125–134.

Even though there is no formal exposition of the heresy in Colossians, it has been reconstructed by scholars based on Paul's apparent reaction against it. It is argued that this heresy is set forth as a 'philosophy' based on 'tradition' (2:8), which seems to have been Jewish in origin, but mixed with forms of asceticism and mysticism. It was reserved for the spiritual elite, who were urged to press on in wisdom and knowledge so as to attain true 'fullness'. Ascetic practices (2:18, 23) were encouraged for the receiving of visions of heavenly mysteries, and for participation in mystical experiences. Entrance to heaven was for the 'mature', who would join in the 'angelic worship of God' as part of their present experience.

Some scholars, however, remain sceptical about the existence of a Colossian heresy. Morna Hooker, for instance, argues that Paul is far too positive in tone towards the Colossian believers for there to have been a serious heresy within their midst.[7] Compared to Galatians, Colossians is much lighter in tone, and lacks specific accusations of error. Furthermore, scholars have had some difficulty identifying the heresy, once all its elements are collated, since the eclectic mix of things that Paul warns against does not really match any particular religious system known to us. Consequently, it seems more likely that Paul is simply warning the Colossians about the dangers of being seduced by various tendencies of the culture that surrounded them. Some people worshipped angels; some were engaged in ascetic practices; some were proto-gnostics.

### Paul's response to the 'heresy'

Whatever false forms of worship concerned Paul, it is clear he regarded all such things as having their root in the powers and principalities, who are opposed to God. His basic imperative is that the Colossians should not submit to the powers associated with such practices. In order to address the problem of these powers, Paul writes of the cosmic Christ (1:15–20), who is Lord over all creation, including those principalities and powers that

---

7. Hooker, 'False Teachers?', 315–331.

were so prominent in the 'Colossian heresy'. All things were created in, through and for him – he is the ultimate goal of creation (1:16). Paul warns the Colossians so that no one will deceive them with 'persuasive arguments' (2:4), nor take them captive by philosophy and empty deceit, which are based on the 'elemental forces' of the world, but not based on Christ (2:8). Of particular interest is 2:15, where Paul declares the dominance of Christ over the powers. He disarmed the rulers and authorities, put them to shame and triumphed over them.

The last phrase in 2:15, *thriambeusas autous en autō*, presents a minor translational issue regarding the antecedent of *en autō*. The ESV translates the phrase as 'triumphing over them *in him*'. The NIV has 'triumphing over them *by the cross*', while the HCSB has 'triumphed over them *by Him*'. Any of these options is possible, and there are decent arguments to be mounted for each. On the one hand, 'in him' is similar to the language used throughout the passage, and fits with the interest in union with Christ. However, in the immediate context, 'by the cross' is probably better since the cross is the last-named substantive that is a possible candidate (2:14), and is therefore a more natural antecedent to the pronoun. In any case, the context makes clear that by the cross God's enemies are defeated. The forces of evil are defeated by the cross, because through it the penalty for sin has been vanquished. The accuser and those forces under his influence are unable to accuse God's people of sin once it has been definitively dealt with upon the cross. With sin dealt with, the grip of evil is loosed, as G. B. Caird observes: 'It is the cancelling of the legal bond, the acquittal of men whom the law declares to be sinful and deserving of death, that renders the principalities impotent.'[8]

Furthermore, translations cause us to miss something in 2:15. The phrase 'triumphing over' (*thriambeusas*) refers to a 'triumphal procession',[9] which denotes a victory march after a great conflict.[10] The Romans would stage a procession to celebrate their military

8. Caird, *Principalities and Powers*, 43.

9. Bauer, *Greek-English Lexicon*, 459.

10. O'Brien, *Colossians*, 128–129.

victory, sometimes with their defeated enemy on display – humiliated, mocked, despised.[11] Moreover, the word often translated 'disarmed' (*apekdysamenos*) in 2:15 can be translated literally as 'stripped'. This coordinates with 'triumphing over', such that the image conveyed is one of enemies stripped naked, put to public shame and led in a triumphal procession. Paul's point in 2:15 is, of course, that this is the kind of victory that Jesus' cross achieved over the dark powers of evil.

At this point there is a profound irony embedded in 2:15, since Jesus' defeat of the powers is depicted in a manner that evokes his own experience. Jesus was stripped naked, put to open shame and paraded in a victory procession to the place of his execution. He was mocked, humiliated, shamed and defeated. Yet the irony is that through these events the reverse was taking place. By his cross Jesus' enemies were defeated. They were exposed, humiliated and conquered. This, indeed, is the paradox of the cross: while Jesus was defeated and shamed, through his death he conquered evil and put the powers to shame.

This apparent paradox between Jesus' appearance of defeat and the actuality of victory reveals Paul's apocalyptic framework. A useful summary of this framework is provided by Harink:

> The understanding of Paul as an 'apocalyptic' theologian goes back as far as the work on Paul by Albert Schweitzer. It has been given a vigorous revival by Ernst Käsemann, J. Christian Beker, and J. Louis Martyn. [. . .] the emphasis in the apocalyptic interpretation of Paul is on *God's action*. In the death and resurrection of Jesus Christ, the giving of the Holy Spirit, and the creation of the new community of God's people among the nations, God acted decisively to deliver humanity and the cosmos from the powers of 'this present evil age' and inaugurated 'the age to come' in which God's triumph over the powers is revealed or 'apocalypsed' to Paul and among the nations.[12]

---

11. An apt example of this may be seen in the Roman soldiers' treatment of Vitellius, as portrayed in Dio Cassius, *Histories*, 8.20–21.

12. Harink, *Paul Among the Postliberals*, 16–17.

From the point of view of Paul's apocalyptic framework, Jesus' death had the *appearance* of weakness and shame, but the *reality* was one of power and victory.

### Supreme and sufficient

It is recognized that Colossians 'underscores the supremacy and pre-eminence of Christ'[13] – he is supreme in authority over all things. As such, Paul was concerned to protect the Colossian believers from thinking that Jesus was somehow insufficient; he sought to protect them from looking elsewhere to fulfil certain spiritual needs. This makes good sense of 2:9–10: 'For in Him the entire fullness of God's nature dwells bodily, and you have been filled by Him, who is the head over every ruler and authority.' Those incorporated into Christ have fullness of life; thus there is no need to seek perfection elsewhere. All the treasures of wisdom and knowledge are hidden in him (2:3), and believers are united to him through his death, burial and resurrection (2:11–12).

And so we see that Paul draws a connection between the *supremacy* of Christ and the *sufficiency* of Christ. No other spiritual power is necessary to achieve full salvation. Because Christ is supreme, he is also sufficient. There is no one, or nothing, more powerful than Christ; so if Christ cannot provide what a believer needs, *no one* can. And Paul's point is that Christ does provide, so the Colossians should not go looking elsewhere.

From Paul's perspective, it would be foolish for the Colossian believers to be misled into thinking it necessary to obey the angelic powers, or the principalities and powers that had held them in their grip. God has stripped these evil authorities, cancelling their bond over the Colossians, nailing it to the cross. Christ put these powers on parade so that all the world might see the magnitude of his victory (2:13–15). Those who have faith in Christ have shared in his death and resurrection; they are not to serve the elemental forces Christ conquered. Why should those whom Christ had freed submit again to such a yoke of bondage?

---

13. Thompson, *Colossians and Philemon*, 11.

Because believers are united to Christ by faith, they are filled by him, and the fullness of God dwells within him. Thus, by our union with Christ, believers have the fullness of God. Christ is supreme over all; he is the fullness of God; we are united to him.

## Ephesians

### *Dominion and reconciliation*

The theme statement of Ephesians is found at 1:9–10: 'He made known to us the mystery of His will, according to His good pleasure that He planned in Him for the administration of the days of fulfillment – to bring everything together in the Messiah, both things in heaven and things on earth in Him.'[14] Here we see that the concept of cosmic reconciliation is key to the message of Ephesians. All things in heaven and earth are brought together in Christ.

This concept of cosmic reconciliation should be read together with 1:20–23:

> He demonstrated [this power] in the Messiah by raising Him from
> the dead and seating Him at His right hand in the heavens – far
> above every ruler and authority, power and dominion, and every title
> given, not only in this age but also in the one to come. And He put
> everything under His feet and appointed Him as head over everything
> for the church, which is His body, the fullness of the One who fills all
> things in every way.

This passage brings forward another key theme in the message of Ephesians: cosmic domination. All things in heaven and earth are placed under Christ's rule. Within this cosmic dominion Christ is the head of the church, his body. Thus the church is under Christ in a special way. While the rest of the cosmos is submitted to Christ, the church is Christ's body and has grown from (and into) him.

---

14. O'Brien, *Ephesians*, 58.

Reading these two statements into each other – cosmic *reconcili-ation* (1:9–10) and cosmic *domination* (1:20–23) – it is apparent that reconciliation of all things is achieved through the submission of all things under Christ. Cosmic reconciliation means that everything is put in its proper place. The church is in its proper place: it is Christ's body. The church is united and reconciled to him in a special way, as his body. This means that, in some sense, if Christ is over all creation, believers are there with him, since we are joined to him as his body. It is to this issue we now turn.

### Sharing dominion

Two essential elements in the concept of sharing Christ's dominion are that believers have been raised with Christ, and that the church forms his body.

### Raised with Christ

Ephesians 2:5–6 says that believers have been made alive with Christ, raised up with him, and have been seated with him in the heavens. Due to their union with Christ, where Christ is, there they are also. He is seated in the heavens at God's right hand, and so believers are also seated in the heavens. Consequently, it follows that believers, like Christ, are also far above every ruler and authority, power and dominion (1:20–21).

### His body

Part of Christ's lordship over all things is his headship of the church, his body (1:22–23). This relationship between the body and her head is developed later in the epistle, with ethical and theological implications. The body is to grow into him who is the head, Christ (4:15); from him the whole body promotes the growth of the body (4:16); Christ is the head of the church and the Saviour of the body (5:23); the church submits to Christ, who is her head (5:24); we are members of his body (5:30); a man will leave his father and mother and be joined to his wife – and Paul is talking about Christ and the church (5:31–32).

A profound ingredient of our union with Christ is that we are his body. The body is under his headship. The body grows out from Christ. The body grows into Christ. The body is joined to

Christ as a wife to her husband. Since the church is 'married' to Christ, she shares in her husband's elevated position. She is *under* him, but also *with* him over everything else.

And so we see that being raised with Christ and being Christ's body are important contributions for our understanding that believers share his dominion over the powers. Furthermore, this all has implications for how we read the final section of Ephesians.

### *Dominion and battle*

It is sometimes claimed that Ephesians lacks a now–not-yet eschatology, but rather elucidates a realized eschatology.[15] The main reason for such claims is that believers are regarded as already seated in heaven – it is not a future reality, but this has already taken place. However, Ephesians 6:10–18 counters claims to a fully realized eschatology, because it pictures an ongoing spiritual battle still being waged. Even though Christ is Lord over the spiritual forces opposed to God, there nevertheless exists a battle between believers and the forces of evil.

There are three ways in which union with Christ relates to this battle. First, believers are seated with Christ in the heavenlies, yet remain active in this world in which the evil powers are still at battle. Second, while all the battle armour listed in Ephesians 6:10–18 is well known from Roman warfare, each item conveys a double entendre. Each piece of armour is worn by the Lord or his Messiah in the Old Testament (OT), mostly with Isaiah as background.

Paul instructs his readers to stand with truth like a belt around their waists (6:14).[16] The Roman soldier wore a leather apron that hung under his armour and protected his thighs. But we also discover in Isaiah 11:4–5 (Septuagint) that the Messiah will be girded with righteousness around his waist, with truth bound around his sides. Thus the belt of truth reflects a double entendre: the image of the Roman soldier is immediately grasped, while the Isaianic

---

15. See e.g. Lincoln, *Ephesians*, lxxxix–xc. Lincoln does, however, acknowledge that the eschatology of Ephesians nevertheless contains some future elements.

16. Much of this section is dependent upon O'Brien, *Ephesians*, 472–482.

background provides a theological meaning as well. This pattern is repeated throughout the passage for each item of armour. Believers are to wear the breastplate of righteousness (6:14). The Roman soldier wore armour that covered the chest, but we also learn that Yahweh himself puts on 'the breastplate of righteousness', as he comes to deliver his people and punish his enemies (Isa. 59:17). Paul says they should stand with their feet sandalled with readiness for the gospel of peace (6:15). The Roman soldier would wear footwear appropriate to his task. The *caliga*, for instance, was a half-boot that soldiers would wear for long marches since it was especially suited to that task. But in Isaiah 52:7 we read, 'How beautiful upon the mountains are the feet of him who brings good tidings, who publishes peace.'

In every situation, Paul says, take the shield of faith (6:16). The Roman soldier bore a shield that was large enough to cover his whole body, being shaped like a door. It was usually made of wood, and covered with canvas and calfskin. But we note that in the OT a shield is used by God to protect his people (e.g. Gen. 15:1). Moreover, Paul says that this shield of faith is able to extinguish the flaming arrows of the evil one (6:16). Roman shields were designed to quench flaming arrows, and were often soaked in water for this very purpose. Nevertheless, flaming arrows represented an extremely dangerous threat to soldiers; while they were able to defend themselves, there was no room for cavalier attitudes in the face of such danger. Thus Paul uses this image of extreme danger to represent the attacks launched by the devil. He views these attacks as very serious indeed, even though there is adequate protection available to believers.

In 6:17 Paul says to take up the helmet of salvation. The Roman soldier wore a solid helmet made of bronze, but in Isaiah 59:17 we also see that Yahweh is the victorious warrior who wears the 'helmet of salvation'. Finally, in 6:17 Paul instructs his readers to take the sword of the Spirit, which is God's Word. Here we encounter the only offensive weapon among this catalogue of weaponry. In Isaiah 11:2–4 the Spirit of the Lord rests upon his Messiah, who will smite the earth with the word of his mouth and destroy the wicked with the breath of his lips. His word is a menacing weapon. Furthermore, Paul uses the lexeme for a short sword (*machaira*), which was important for close-combat battle. In other words, declaring the Word of God is not done from a distance; rather, it is front-line fighting.

Bringing these images together now, we may conclude that believers battle against the forces of evil while wearing the armour of the Lord, which he himself wears into battle. Our union with Christ means that we share in his instruments of battle; they are ours in him, and we are to 'put them on'. Consequently, we see that in this battle believers are to be 'active' ('put on the full armour of God'; 'take up the full armour of God'; 'so that you may be able to resist in the evil day'; 'and having prepared everything, to take your stand'; 'Stand, therefore' etc.), but there is also a dimension that reflects their 'passive' solidarity with Christ.

The third way in which union with Christ affects the way we understand this passage is that it counters our individualism. Usually Ephesians 6 is interpreted individualistically, which is reasonable given that each Roman soldier would put on his own armour. But we should keep in mind that a Roman army would fight together as one man in battle. Given the extensive discussion concerning the church as the body of Christ, are we not supposed to regard each item of Roman armory as protecting our body; that is, *the* body – the church? This is not to deny the exhortation to each believer to take up arms – just as each part of the body does its work – but that a corporate protection of *the body* against the forces of darkness is in part what Ephesians 6 is about.

As the body of Christ, then, united though faith in him who is our head, we are in heaven with him; we share in his battle armour as we remain active in this world, and we battle as one body. Reinhard states this well:

> Therefore, putting on God's armor is an aspect of putting on Christ, that is, being united with Christ through the work of the Holy Spirit, recognizing the riches that he has lavished upon us and responding appropriately by standing firm as a united Church against those dark forces that strive against God's will.[17]

---

17. Reinhard, 'Ephesians 6:10–18', 531.

## Conclusion

From this exploration of the themes of union with Christ and Christ's victory over the powers in Colossians and Ephesians, it has been argued that they might profitably be read together. Christ's victory over the powers means that he is also sufficient, and offers the fullness of God to those who trust in him and do not succumb to the empty deceit of the defeated powers of darkness. Furthermore, the church shares in the dominion of Christ and is seated in heaven with him; whatever is under his feet is also under hers. She is his body, and shares in his battle armour as she faces off against the spiritual forces of darkness in the battle that has already been won, but is not yet ended. By way of conclusion, it will be useful to reflect on some of the pastoral implications that arise from these facts.

### Supremacy

Ephesians 6 makes it clear that believers are engaged in a spiritual battle against the dark forces of evil, which represent a serious threat and are not to be taken lightly. And yet Ephesians 1 and Colossians 2 teach us that this battle has been decisively won. The forces of evil have been conquered, though not yet destroyed. Some believers may underestimate the enemy, and as a result play loose with a real threat. They may not take seriously the damage that might be inflicted by the forces of evil, nor the warnings of Scripture. Others may overestimate the enemy, and consequently live in fear of Satan and his influence. They might not enjoy the assurance that Christ provides in the face of spiritual danger. Both extremes, it seems, are wrong. Yes, we face a dangerous enemy, but it is an enemy who has been defeated once and for all. Because we are in Christ, all that is under his feet is under ours.

### Fullness

Many people in our culture and age are looking for something more – something that gives more meaning to their lives and that makes sense of the apparent randomness of life. Some seek this unintentionally and perhaps subconsciously, filling the void

with money, entertainment or sex. Others deliberately investigate various spiritualities and philosophies, looking for truth or a
higher plane of existence. Whatever version of 'filler' is explored,
however, in so far as they seek to substitute idols for God, they
all find their ultimate source in the spiritual forces of evil, sup-
planting the truth with lies and misleading people into corrupted
versions of wholeness. Yet in Christ the whole fullness of God
dwells bodily, and believers in Christ are filled by him. Since we
are created for relationship with God, only he can complete our
needs. In Christ he is ours, and ours in full.

### Identity

Union with Christ denotes inclusion with the Messiah and unity
with each other. We share in a corporate union with Christ, which
has all kinds of practical implications. Since we are in Christ, we
are part of his body, and Paul spells out in Ephesians 4 and 5
what this should look like in community and family. But for now
let us reflect upon just one of these implications – *identity*. How
are we to define ourselves? How do we identify who we are?
Many people will define themselves according to their profes-
sion, popularity, the nature of their relationships, their abilities,
power or through their community. People so often identify
themselves through such categories, which affect self-esteem,
their sense of worth and value, and their apparent standing with
others. Often their experience of happiness is directly associated
with their success or otherwise in these matters. This is all the
more serious in relation to instances of family dysfunctionality,
as well as various forms of abuse. It is virtually impossible to
emerge from such situations without some degree of brokenness
and disfigured identity.

But who are we *really*? Clearly, those of us who trust in Christ
are *in*. We have been created in God's image, and are in Christ.
Now, in him, our insecurities and brokenness are addressed as we
are renewed into the image of God. This must define us and shape
our understanding of ourselves. This is how we may assess our
'worth' and standing: in Christ we have been chosen, predestined,
redeemed, forgiven, blessed, sealed with the Spirit. In Christ we
belong to him and therefore belong to each other.

## Ministry

In terms of serving others in Christian ministry these truths provide us with some of the most important ingredients that people yearn for in life. First, we have *confidence* in Christ in the face of fear. Second, we have the *real* thing in Christ, as opposed to empty deceit. Third, we have *identity* in Christ, in the face of shifting, superficial cultural values. These three things present a powerful combination, and believers need to be reminded of them. We are to trust in Christ in our battle against the evil spiritual forces – the victory is ours in Christ. We are to look to Christ for fulfilment, turning away from the false promises of the world, the flesh and the devil. We are to rest assured in Christ, knowing that our identity is eternally bound to him; we no longer need to be defined by passing, godless measures of self-worth.

Believers are reminded of these things through the Word of God. While, on the one hand, our proclamation may appear as weakness (few may respond and our efforts are sometimes feeble), nevertheless, it is the sword of the Spirit. The Word of God is the key offensive weapon in our arsenal against the forces of evil. We wield this sword as we share Christ's weaponry. It is the Spirit's sword, and the voice of God.

Moreover, we must remember the apocalyptic nature of Christ's triumph. He defeated the powers and authorities through his apparent 'weakness' – through suffering, triumph is achieved. It may have the appearance of weakness, but the reality is no less than cosmic domination. Paul follows the mode of triumph that Jesus established – victory is achieved through suffering. Paul will suffer as he proclaims the word of the gospel, but in so doing captives are set free, and slaves of the devil become slaves of Christ. We too must suffer in our proclamation of the Word. It will have the appearance of weakness – it may seem a small thing – but it is the power of God for salvation.

# 7. CHRIST'S VICTORY OVER THE POWERS: CROSS-CULTURAL PERCEPTIONS AND OPPORTUNITIES

**Greg Anderson and Jonathan Lilley**

## Background to 'the powers' in missiology

In missionary encounters in many parts of the world the issue of Christ's victory over the powers seems particularly relevant. In many cultures there is a perception of the spiritual realm that has almost ceased to exist among the descendants of the Enlightenment. As missiologists seek to develop ways of relating the good news of Jesus that engage with the world views and concepts of the world's unreached people groups, the issue of spiritual powers has come to the fore in recent decades, although it has not been completely absent in any era of the history of Christian mission. Some of the major proponents of what has come to be called the 'spiritual warfare' movement worked in cross-cultural mission settings for many years: including Peter Wagner in Bolivia for sixteen years, and Charles Kraft in Nigeria.

In the history of mission the usual flow has been 'from the West to the rest'. This has meant that differences in world view between Western missionaries and the people they go to have been a significant factor in the missionary encounter, including both the way that cross-cultural missionaries have evaluated the people they have gone to, and also in the way that the phenomena missionaries have encountered have sometimes confused or challenged their own presuppositions.

We can trace the discussion of these differing world views and their implications for cross-cultural mission through some key events since the early 1980s.

### The 1980s: Hiebert's 'flaw of the excluded middle'

Paul G. Hiebert was a missionary and missiologist who served in India for six years, and subsequently taught at Fuller Theological Seminary and then Trinity Evangelical Divinity School until his retirement. In 1982 he wrote about an 'excluded middle' in the world view of Western missionaries – missionaries believed in God, miracles and a spiritual world, but there seemed a big gap between that and the naturalistic explanations that they would habitually give for a range of phenomena that others might ascribe to spiritual powers. He wrote:

> Because the Western world no longer provides explanations for questions on the middle level, it is not surprising that many Western missionaries have no answers within their Christian world view. What is a Christian theology of ancestors, of animals and plants [used as omens or to convey supernatural power], of local spirits and spirit possession, and of 'principalities, powers and rulers of the darkness of this world' (Eph 6:12).[1]

Hiebert's paper challenged Western missionaries to develop a theology of this 'middle area', including 'divine [. . .] healing; [and . . . ] ancestors, spirits and invisible powers of this world'.[2] The motivation for developing such a theology was primarily so that they would be able to respond appropriately and missionally into the situations that Hiebert fully expected them to find themselves in – situations, implies Hiebert, that they would probably have no experience of at home.

---

1. Hiebert, 'Flaw', 198.
2. Ibid.

At about the same time, this middle area was being anything
but neglected by another group of evangelists and missionaries in the North American context, including John Wimber and
Peter Wagner, who began teaching the 'Signs and Wonders and
Church Growth' course at Fuller in the same year that Hiebert's
paper was published, 1982. While it was not exclusively related to
cross-cultural mission, there were clearly implications for that area.
As the Signs and Wonders movement expanded and developed,
particularly under Wagner's leadership, the emphasis on spiritual
warfare and encounters with spirit beings increased, so that it was
believed that certain techniques, such as claiming a geographical
territory in prayer and binding the territorial spirits would have an
enormous effect on the progress of evangelistic outreach. Wagner's
influence was apparent in the AD 2000 and Beyond Movement,
which sought to facilitate the evangelism of the unreached peoples
of the world between the Lausanne II Conference in Manila in
1989 and the end of the twentieth century.[3]

### The 1990s: Evangelical Missiological Society's debate
A few years later, in 1994, the American-based Evangelical
Missiological Society (EMS) annual conference heard a paper
that raised concern over the lack of biblical basis for many claims
that were being made by Christian missionaries and missiologists
about the spiritual world. Such claims included detailed accounts
of spirit-possession or spirit-oppression, territorial spirits, exorcisms or deliverance and evangelistic breakthroughs as a result.
In that paper, Priest, Campbell and Mullan place themselves not
as 'enlightenment rationalists who refuse to accept the valid-
ity of any account of the supernatural',[4] but as 'Biblicists who
refuse uncritically to trust reported experiences of the supernatural which advance "new doctrine"'. In response to a published
version of this paper, Charles Kraft, Professor of Anthropology
at Fuller School of World Mission in California, rejected Priest,
Campbell and Mullan's position as 'barely [. . .] supernaturalistic'

---

3. See e.g. <http://www.ad2000.org>, accessed 18 Sept. 2008.
4. Priest, Campbell and Mullan, 'Missiological Syncretism', 25.

and spoke about his own paradigm shift, or as he calls it 'practice shift' into much greater credulity about what he calls 'biblical supernaturalism'.[5] From Kraft's point of view, Priest, Campbell and Mullan were still excluding the middle, while from their perspective Kraft was overstuffing the middle with material that had little or no biblical basis.

In 2000 a wider representation than the EMS was drawn together when the Lausanne movement convened a consultation in Nairobi, to discuss the implications of the range of views on spiritual powers on world evangelism. Although all sixty participants defined themselves as evangelical, a wide range of views was represented among them, and among the papers presented. Consequently, the Statement produced at the end of the consultation was inconclusive at points, including in areas such as prayer concerning 'territorial spirits', the place of experience relative to biblical revelation in developing an understanding of spiritual powers, and whether Christians could be the subject of demonic affliction. There was no lack of clarity, however, in laying the blame on the Enlightenment for lack of engagement with spiritual forces on the part of some missionaries, when the Statement asserted:

> The unwillingness/inability of the contemporary western church to believe in the reality of the spiritual beliefs and engage in spiritual conflict arose out of a defective Enlightenment-influenced world view, is not representative of the total history of the church in relation to spiritual conflict nor has it been characteristic of Christianity in the Two Thirds World in contemporary history.[6]

If the target of this criticism was the same kind of missionaries that Hiebert had criticized, a balancing criticism was also levelled at another group of missionaries who also failed to engage with local world views, but in the opposite way. The Statement accused this second group of 'hit-and-run ministries of spiritual conflict',

---

5. Kraft, 'Christian Animism', 109.

6. Lausanne Movement, 'Deliver us from Evil', Common Ground/Spiritual Conflict in Practice, par. 1.

presuming that they had 'superior knowledge of the local reality'.[7]
The impression is given of outsiders, possibly Westerners, coming
into a local setting for short periods of time, ministering in a dramatic way in apparent spiritual warfare, but riding roughshod over
the understanding and practice of the local believers.

### The division between West and 'South'

In a significant number of accounts of 'Christ's victory over the
powers' and 'spiritual warfare' in cross-cultural mission contexts,
including some of the examples just given, the different views
taken of spiritual power issues are seen as a product of the difference between Western Enlightenment and non-Western world
views. Clearly, however, this description is too simplistic. People
like John Wimber, Charles Kraft and Peter Wagner are evidence
that for some Western Christians there is no 'excluded middle'.

### A blurred line

It may be that the accusations against the West are accurate and
that Westerners who advocate spiritual techniques against powers
and spirits have simply abandoned their Enlightenment heritage and turned to an irrational, non-scientific and superstitious
world view. This is not how the situation presents itself, however.
People like Charles Kraft, who are such strong advocates of direct
encounters with spiritual entities and powers, still seek to present
their case from within a world view that derives from European
rationalism – they appeal to evidence which they describe as verifi-
able and replicable; they argue their case in classical Western form
and using the terms of Enlightenment discourse; they accuse their
opponents of ignoring evidence and being bound by presuppositions in their analysis of the data.[8]

Indeed, some in non-Western areas are accused of being influenced by Western Pentecostals, rather than their own traditional
religious background, when they become advocates of spiritual
warfare practices. Hwa Yung, former principal of the Malaysian

---

7. Ibid., par. 11.
8. See e.g. Kraft, 'Christian Animism'.

Theological Seminary, and subsequently Methodist Bishop in
Malaysia, says that for him

> what is rather distressing is that often the theological interpretations used
> by Asian Christians to understand the work of the Holy Spirit in their
> churches today have been borrowed almost wholesale from Western
> Pentecostals and charismatics.[9]

Of course, it is impossible to know precisely where the lines of relative influence are to be drawn among people who have travelled,
lived, worked and been educated in places with very divergent
world views.

### The place of the West in global theology

Nevertheless, the West continues to have a great influence on
Christian opinion and mission practice in the world. While the
number of missionaries from 'everywhere to everywhere', including what has been called 'South–South mission', has increased,
there are still huge numbers of Western Christians interacting
with non-Western people, including immigrants to the West. For
reasons that include the economics of publishing, the economics
of travel and the dominance of English as a world language the
influence of the West is likely to continue for some time. Whether
this is desirable or not will not be canvassed here.[10]

It is worth noting also that, while evangelicals may tend to think
of missionaries as coming from evangelical backgrounds because
of their commitment to the uniqueness of Christ and their concern
for the lost, Western influence has been considerable in promot-
ing liberal theology in the Majority World as well. Some would go
as far as to say, with Vanhoozer, that because so much of both
evangelical and liberal theologies have their roots in Western
history and culture, 'the really significant dividing line is no longer

---

9. Hwa, *Mangoes and Bananas*, 238–239.
10. A starting point for this discussion is Ott and Netland, *Globalizing Theology*,
    where the dichotomy 'the West v. the rest' seems more prominent than
    any other.

that between conservative and liberal Western Christians but that between Western and non-western Christians'.[11]

## The need to listen

The disagreement over spiritual powers in the cross-cultural mission context has not gone away in the few years since the Nairobi consultation. A further dimension is that in recent years, with the shift of Christian numbers from the West to the global south, there has been a call for greater participation of Majority World theological and missiological views in the discussion. Tite Tiénou, for example, challenges Western theologians to be better listeners to the rest of the world.[12] Because the Majority World remains a place where many have first-hand experience of spiritual forces, especially when compared with the West, Tiénou's call is particularly relevant as we think about Christ's victory over the powers. Indeed, historian Philip Jenkins asserted, 'If there is a single key area of faith and practice that divides Northern and Southern Christians, it is this matter of spiritual forces and their effects on the everyday human world.'[13] The Nairobi Consultation Statement made the same point: 'We particularly call the churches in the West to listen more carefully to the churches in the Two Thirds World and join them in a serious rediscovery of the reality of evil.'[14]

## Listening in Australia

Whatever may be the case in a globalizing world, it is certainly the case in Australia that 'Western' theology is dominant and will remain so. Although the percentage of people from non-Western backgrounds in Australia is increasing, and although there is obvious interaction between people from Western and non-Western heritages within evangelical circles, the balance of demography, not to

---

11. Vanhoozer, 'One Rule to Rule Them All?', 88.

12. Tiénou, 'Christian Theology', 48.

13. Jenkins, *Next Christendom*, 123.

14. Lausanne Movement, 'Deliver us from Evil', Frontiers That Need Ongoing Exploration, par. 8.

mention education patterns, suggests that Western models will remain well entrenched. As a consequence, Western people on this continent would have to take special steps to be aware of the global issues and to do the kind of listening that Tiénou and the Nairobi Consultation advocate. It might be better to say that together we should listen to what the Bible has to say, being open to hearing God's word through the ears of others as well as our own.

In this chapter we are seeking to respond to that challenge of listening by bringing an Aboriginal Christian voice into the discussion of Christ and spiritual powers. From our own lives and work among and with Aboriginal Christians for many years, the two of us are aware that they have a range of beliefs and consequent practices concerning spiritual beings and spiritual power, with points of similarity and dissimilarity with their pre-Christian beliefs. Many have stories about their own experiences of phenomena that correspond to their beliefs.

As we listen we are asking questions about the perceptions that Aboriginal Christians have about the meaning of Christ's victory over spiritual powers in their context, and how that might shape the way the gospel is communicated, as we remain open to the word of God as we hear it, and as others hear it.

## Background to the powers in Aboriginal Australia

### Aboriginal diversity
#### Diversity of background
The Aboriginal community in Australia is extremely diverse. It includes tertiary-educated professionals who value both their own indigenous traditions and traditions that have come from other places, including Westernized or mainstream Australia. It includes people who live in rural areas of the southern half of the Australian continent, perhaps living for some periods in the bigger cities, and who place less value on non-Aboriginal ways of knowing and being. It includes people who live in remote parts of Queensland, the Northern Territory, South Australia and Western Australia, whose language and world view have remained little changed from the times before white people came to dominate their horizons.

It is to be expected that such a range of people, even when they are Christians, will have a range of views about spiritual matters.

It might be expected that Aboriginal people who have lived in closest contact with mainstream Australia would be more influenced by the mainstream way of thinking about spiritual issues. To some extent this is true, but, on the other hand, the closer proximity to the mainstream often increases the value of indigenous knowledge and belief systems for those people. As indigenous identity is threatened by assimilation to the mainstream, through education, employment and life circumstances, it becomes more important to be differentiated from the mainstream in some ways, and spiritual beliefs can be part of that differentiation.

In remote parts of Australia there may be less consciousness of the 'Aboriginality' of beliefs and practices (although there are no parts of Australia where the effect of Western intrusion is absent), beliefs and practices that are in a sense taken for granted as 'the way the world is, and the way we are'. Ironically, perhaps because Aboriginal identity is at less risk of assimilation, some people will discard traditional views with surprising ease.

*Diversity of views*
While the diversity of backgrounds is a significant factor in describing Aboriginal Australia, it is also important to recognize that among people from a similar background there is a diversity of views. Sometimes it is the Christian faith of a person that will change what he or she believes about certain things, including issues of spiritual entities and spiritual power. There are people in various Anglican churches in Arnhem Land for whom this is clearly true. Christians have made decisions not to attend traditional ceremonial practices, not to incorporate traditional religious paraphernalia into Christian practices, or have stipulated that when they die they do not want traditional ceremonies carried out with respect to them. In each case these decisions are made because of what they believe Christian allegiance requires, and at some cost to relationships and community equilibrium.

On the other hand, Philip Clarke, an Adelaide-based anthropologist who has related closely to Nungga people of South Australia, makes the point that

> The degree to which Aboriginal people consider themselves to be Christians does not seem to overly impact upon the strength of their beliefs in ghosts or other spirits. Aboriginal people believe that most European-Australians are not in tune with the Spirit World; that is, they are oblivious to the presence of spirits.[15]

That is, Christian Aboriginal people do not see the maintenance of traditional beliefs in spirits as out of accord with their Christian faith, nor do they see any difference between their views and the views of 'whitefellas' as due to Christianity, but rather to other aspects of 'Western-ness'. Other factors are influential as well, including personal standing and power in the community, relationships with outsiders, education and life experience. Even within quite small groups there are likely to be differences of opinion, with some people having strong views, and others feeling more uncertain or confused.

In our experience, however, despite all this diversity, Aboriginal Christians across a broad range of locations, experience, education, language and world view have a strong belief in supernatural beings and powers that seems deeply intertwined with Aboriginal identity.

### *The present listening*
*Method*
Apart from reflecting on our own experience, we have attempted to conduct interviews with several Aboriginal Christians, nominated by their church leaders and willing to speak for the purposes of this chapter.[16] Our methodology was to use three open-ended questions, as a stimulus for eliciting stories and opinions about spiritual beings or powers, and the difference Christ was perceived to have made in that context. The first was simply asking for stories about experiences with spiritual beings or forces. We acknowledge that simply asking this question may skew the results towards the extraordinary rather than the more usual. The second

---

15. Clarke, 'Indigenous Spirit', 153.
16. This research was conducted after approval from the Moore College Human Research Ethics Committee.

was what their knowledge of God was at the time of those experiences, and what difference becoming a Christian had made to their understanding of the experiences. The third was what they thought were helpful ways to talk about Christ's victory over the powers when talking about Christian faith. These three questions provided a framework for the interviews, but were also supplemented with other questions to stimulate the flow of conversation. Interviews were recorded electronically, and there was the provision of a follow-up interview if this was required, although we did not make use of this provision.

*Stories*
The people who were interviewed all had stories to tell about first-hand experiences that they understood as engagement with spiritual beings or powers. The stories were told matter-of-factly rather than embellished with a lot of detail, and did not bring about a reliving of the emotions that may have been associated with the experience at the time. As a typical story, one interviewee recollected a time when he had been away from home at a Christian convention, which had also been attended by many Aboriginal people from 'tribal' backgrounds, who still maintained their cultural traditions. He had an experience of a dark shape entering his room as he was going to sleep and pressing down on his chest and throat. He wrestled with it unsuccessfully, but when he called on the name of Christ, the being left. His interpretation of the event was that this was a spirit being, which was somehow attached to the tribal Aboriginal people who were perceived as even more closely in touch with spiritual powers than the interviewee, and this spirit being was trying to frighten him because of the Christian environment of the convention.

A similar story was of an interviewee camping in rural New South Wales at a Christian site, seeing three figures enter the camp, coming to him, and physically lifting him up. The interviewee had no doubt that these were spirits; he recognized what was happening to him, but was not overwhelmed with fear by it.

There were a number of other stories of unexplained phenomena – doors or gates opening for no reason, stones being thrown out in the country when nobody was around, lights at night following people. There were also stories of being brought up in an environment where older relatives taught children about the reality of the spiritual world and its dangers, for example warning them not to wander around at night.

Apart from the stories that interviewees reported, the interviews and our other experiences of Aboriginal communities reflect a fair degree of thought and even analysis of spiritual forces. We will try to bring some of these threads together, before considering the implications of Christ's victory for this issue.

## What we have heard

### *The importance of spiritual powers*

All the interviewees, as well as many other Aboriginal Christians we know, speak of spiritual powers and spirit beings as an intrinsic part of Aboriginal culture. It is seen as one of the things that marks Aboriginal culture as distinct from Anglo-Australian culture. The view is widely held that spiritual powers and spirit beings – Hiebert's 'excluded middle' – are real, and that belief in them is taken for granted and thoroughly unremarkable. 'They are just a part of our culture' is what one Aboriginal Christian said.

### *Kinds of spirit beings and powers*

A number of interviewees in their stories spoke of spirits in a way that implied the existence of different kinds, almost a taxonomy. This categorization differentiated spirits of the dead, spirits that belong to a particular location, spirits associated with natural phenomena such as shooting stars or min-min lights, totemic spirits associated with groups of people, and other kinds of named spirits, such as *duranggin* in northern New South Wales or *namor-rortto* or *wirrijih* in central Arnhem Land, which have their own characteristic behaviours, locations and dangers.

#### *Ghosts*

Ghosts, or the spirits of the dead, play a prominent role in the consciousness of Aboriginal people especially from remote and rural areas. Numerous traditional ceremonies and practices are carried out in remote communities following a death to keep the dead person's spirit away from the living, including a taboo on the name of the deceased, the destruction of the deceased's possessions and 'fumigating' with smoke places where the deceased has lived. Clarke reports a similar function for post-death practices among Aboriginal people in southern South Australia.[17] The spirits of the dead are usually regarded as mischievous or dangerous, but in any case do not belong with the living, and should be helped along to their own proper permanent home, such as a waterhole on clan land. In some cases, ghosts are perceived as having good intent, such as when songmen receive songs through them.[18] Clarke adds that when ghosts appear in a dream, they may be understood as 'protectors' of their people.[19] Some Aboriginal Christians say that when Christians die, their spirit goes straight to be with Jesus, and so the various post-death practices are not relevant for them.

### Spirits of the land

A number of interviewees talked about spirits that belong to a certain terrain. They may become troublesome if people go on their land without acknowledging them. Some belong in sacred sites restricted to people of a particular age or sex or even to all humans, and violating this restriction may lead to sickness or even death. They do not seem to be perceived, however, in the way that 'territorial spirits' are described by writers such as Kraft.[20]

### Other spirits

Various other kinds of spirit beings are believed to exist, some overlapping with the previous two categories. These include beings that might be described as 'little people', which might lure children away at night time; spirits that appear as natural phenomena like a light shining (a 'min-min light'), which one interviewee

---

17. Clarke, 'Indigenous Spirit', 154.
18. Marett, Barwick and Ford, *Rak Badjalarr*; Garde, *Wurrurrumi Kun-Borrk*.
19. Clarke, 'Indigenous Spirit', 153.
20. Kraft, 'Christian Animism', 131.

had seen following him for 12 or 18 miles in western New South Wales; and named kinds of spirits that simply exist like flora or fauna as part of nature, but which might bring harm to people. Just as ghosts can deliver new songs to songmen, so can some of these other spirits.[21]

No interviewees mentioned Dreaming spirits, although these are significant in Aboriginal cosmogony. This may be because these spirits, who travelled across and shaped the land at the beginning of time, were understood to have been people or animals rather than spirits as such, although they were prototypical and ancestral beings rather than just the same as people or animals today. Further, these spirits are not still in the world as present entities that humans can be affected by – although their power is believed to be strongly present, especially at certain sites, such as where they went into the earth during their travels, or where they met other Dreamings in their travels. The power of these Dreamings will be discussed further later.

It is notable that the experience and concern of Aboriginal people relates to the interaction between humans and different kinds of spirits. This is very different from Hiebert's description of tribal religions, in which the world is seen as subject to the vagaries of interaction between different spirits, so that 'the gods, spirits, ancestors, and people of one village or tribe are in constant battle with those of surrounding villages and tribes'.[22]

*Omens*

There were a number of stories in the interviews that told of what might be called omens, which were regarded as part of Aboriginal spirituality, although not dealing with spirit beings as such. When people see a kind of animal or bird which may be specific to their own clan, perhaps behaving in an unusual kind of way, they believe it indicates that something has happened, often a death or some other bad news, or occasionally something good. Even when the person has not noticed or paid attention to the omen, he

---

21. Marett, Barwick and Ford, *Rak Badjalarr*; Garde, *Wurrurrumi Kun-Borrk*.
22. Hiebert, 'Spiritual Warfare', 170.

or she will often retrospectively be aware of it if bad news comes. 'When I heard that so-and-so had had an accident, I remembered the willy wagtail that I had seen hopping about, and I should have known that it was a message.'

### Power

Aboriginal people have well-developed ideas, not just of spirit beings but of spiritual power that is separate from beings. *Rainbow Spirit Theology* refers to 'life-forces' in the land.[23] Some of this power relates to Dreaming entities mentioned earlier, but is residual from them, rather than being exercised by them in the present. This power is particularly associated with sacred sites; hence some of the prohibitions against unauthorized access to them. Access may be gained to this power through ceremony, which, by recreating the actions of the Dreaming beings at the beginning of the world, draws on this power and uses it for various purposes, including the fruitfulness of the earth.

There is also spiritual power not specifically deriving from Dreaming ancestors, but able to be manipulated by certain people.

## Human interaction and response to spirits

### 'Everyday' interaction

While some people were regarded as having special power to control or deal with spirit beings or spiritual powers, interaction with spirits was not restricted to such people. They may have been specialists, but there was an everyday level of interaction that was appropriate for everybody. It was regarded as normal, for example, when going on a hunting or fishing expedition, or when travelling across land that was unfamiliar to the traveller, to call out to the spirits of that land to acknowledge them, and to indicate friendly intent. If this was not done, trouble could occur, such as no game or fish being caught, or losing one's way. If anybody got lost in unfamiliar country, they could call out to the spirits in the land to show them the way back to the beaten track.

---

23. Rainbow Spirit Elders, *Rainbow Spirit Theology*, 32, 39.

## Communal interaction

The kinds of ceremonies mentioned above that drew on, and brought into the present, the power of Dreamings, were essentially communal interaction with this power. Some ceremonies, and parts of other ceremonies were restricted to initiated males because initiation brought them into the realm of the sacred. Other ceremonies were open to women, and indeed there were women-only ceremonies that provided women access to power that they could use in their own domains, such as reproductive fertility and childbirth.

## Specialized personal interaction

Every Aboriginal society has people who are regarded as having a particular ability to relate to spiritual entities or manipulate spiritual power. In Aboriginal English they are often referred to as 'clever people'. People may come to consult them, and payment may be required for their services; or they may act independently. They may or may not be leaders of ceremony; in other words, their ability does not necessarily arise from ceremonial involvement. They often pass their power on within their family line, but if they deem their heir apparent to be unworthy, they may choose somebody else.

## For good

Such power is not necessarily regarded by the Aboriginal public as evil in itself, although 'clever people' are likely to be feared to some extent. 'Clever people' are consulted for healing, and may use a combination of 'natural' knowledge, such as the medicinal properties of plants, and 'supernatural' ability, pulling stones or bones out of sick people's bodies. Spiritual power can also be used for controlling the environment – including making rain or stopping strong wind; for love magic; for travelling 'in the spirit'; and for seeing into the future.

## For bad

More commonly, the ability to manipulate spiritual power is associated with sorcery, designed to harm people. In many remote Aboriginal communities, whenever an untimely death occurs (which these days is extremely frequently) it is almost invariably attributed to sorcery, and steps are taken to determine who is most likely to have committed such an act. The accusation of sorcery is not as frequent closer to 'mainstream' Australia, but some still believe in its effects.

### General characteristics of encounters with spirits

Many of the spirits, while not intrinsically malevolent, were described as potentially dangerous or tricky. Various actions were carried out in traditional practice to keep these trickster spirits at bay, such as those described earlier to segregate ghosts from the living. While this represents a reasonably negative relationship, it contrasts with Hiebert's description of the tribal world view in which he says that spirits 'help those who serve or placate them. They harm those who oppose their wishes or who neglect them. Humans must placate them to avoid terrible disasters.'[24] In Aboriginal culture the connection with the spirit world is not so highly charged – the spirits are not jealous of their own welfare or reputations, and do not seem to need appeasement. In some cases, such as spirits of the land, they mind their own business unless disturbed.

In the interviews the usual response to experience of spirits was one of fear or uneasiness, although not terror.

The attitude to spiritual power could perhaps be described as caution and awe – not unlike the attitude of Westerners to high voltage electricity. Initiates or ceremonial novices are encouraged to be fearful of the power that ceremonies can unleash, and indeed this respect or fear of power is what should motivate young men to conduct themselves in right ways within Aboriginal law. For this reason many of the most secret ceremonies, in Arnhem Land at least, are regarded as serving the primary purpose of 'discipline', although structurally; anthropologists might describe them as 'increase' or 'fertility' ceremonies. The sanctions for fighting against those who are closest to the spiritual world are high, including sickness or death for oneself or one's family.

There seems to be little evidence of what is described as 'spirit possession' in other contexts,[25] except in so far as ceremonies

---

24. Hiebert, 'Spiritual Warfare', 170.
25. E.g. Kraft, 'Christian Animism', 97, 104, 121.

re-enact the deeds of Dreaming ancestors, and in that sense, participants draw on the power of those beings.[26]


## Christ's victory and the powers in Christian Aboriginal Australia

### *The nature of the victory*

Aboriginal Christians express confidence that Jesus, in his death and resurrection, has defeated evil. The power of God demonstrated in those events is greater than any spiritual power, associated with either spirits or places, that can bring harm or trouble to people. The victory, however, is seen not as destroying this potentially harmful spiritual power, but protecting people from its dangers. How is God's power, manifest in Christ's victory, to be applied to situations of danger? One interviewee said it was simply a matter of claiming the name of Christ. This was put in a way that did not suggest a 'technique' or a magic word, but a recognition and acknowledgment that the power of Jesus was real and effective in dealing with the danger.

Most Aboriginal Christians we have listened to believe that Jesus' death and resurrection have defeated death and so the spirits of dead Christians are alive with Christ rather than waiting to be conducted to their permanent resting place on the land. Some Christians, however, speculate that being with Christ may not prescribe a geographical location, and that it may be possible for the spirits of dead Christians to be both with Christ and also in the geographical resting place of the spirits of the appropriate clan, waiting for the resurrection at the second coming of Christ and the renewal of all creation.

Finally, Christ's victory is seen by some as ordering the disordered spiritual realm. In this view not all spirits are evil, and so, as part of the final renewal of creation, they are brought into subjection to Christ. That is, they will not hurt people or lead them astray, but they may continue to exist in their location, or in conjunction

---

26. See e.g. Keen, *Knowledge and Secrecy*, 135–136.

with their natural phenomena, and be part of creation's praise of God as in Psalm 148.

### Consequences of Christ's victory

The most frequently reported result of belief that Christ is victorious over spiritual beings and powers is that there is no need to fear them any longer. As Peter Bolt puts it, 'the fear of the underworld that Jesus died to banish' is done away with.[27]

The interviewees expressed a range of opinions about the difference Christ made. Some people felt that continued involvement with the spirit world was incompatible with being a Christian. Although no biblical basis was expressed for this view, we may guess that it derives from (1) the law of Leviticus 19:31, 20:6, 27 and Deuteronomy 18:10–13, which outlaws contact with things that belong to the underworld, and people who seek to make contact with that world, and (2) the explanations given in 2 Kgs 17:17; 21:5–6 and 2 Chr. 33:5–6 of the downfall of the northern kingdom, and of King Manasseh of Judah.

We are aware of other views that contrast with this, and which seek a greater continuity between some aspects of traditional culture and the belief in Christ's victory and supremacy. It may be noted that fear does not seem to be a significant factor in these schemas.

Some Aboriginal Christians felt that Christ's victory was compatible with maintaining at least some traditional practices with regard to the spirit world. For example, Christ's victory over the powers means that he is ruler of all, but just as one would not enter somebody's house without knocking, so one would continue to acknowledge the presence of spirits of a hunting or fishing ground. Such people know their Bibles well enough to be aware of the prohibitions, but feel that to address spirits in this way is neither sorcery, which seeks to use spiritual power to harm others, nor divination, which seeks to know the future, nor to practise as a medium since they are not trying to get a message from the spirit beings.

Some Aboriginal Christians in remote areas value the forms of their traditional culture, while acknowledging that the meanings they express may not accord with their Christian beliefs. There

---

27. Bolt, *Living with the Underworld*, 143.

is some speculation, although it has not been put into action, about investing old forms with Christian meanings. Red ochre, for example, which is painted on bereaved relatives after death as a way of hiding them from the ghost of the deceased, could be reinterpreted as a sign of Christ's victory won by his red blood.

In a similar vein of speculation, although not exactly relating to deliverance from evil, Djiniyini Gondarra, a prominent Uniting Church minister from Arnhem Land, wonders if it is possible to salvage belief in the most significant Dreaming spirits of the Yolngu people, the Djang'kawu sisters, who were traditionally believed to have shaped and given social significance to much of the land. The power and supremacy of Christ would be seen in regarding him as the ultimate creator and owner of the land, while the Djang'kawu sisters would be seen as his workers.[28]

## Communicating Christ's victory

Speculation aside, we return to the main 'felt need' identified by Aboriginal Christians concerning spirits and spiritual power, namely their vulnerability and resulting fear.

In communicating the message of Christ's victory, two key concepts came through in interviews. First, that there is no uncertainty about the power of Christ – his victory is definite and complete. Secondly, having somebody pray in Christ's name for those suffering under some kind of spiritual affliction was one thing, but to have permanent protection from such attacks required a true relationship with Christ. This could be the basis of an evangelistic approach in Aboriginal communities.

## Conclusions

What are the implications of these findings for gospel work among Aboriginal people, not to mention people of other cultures where beliefs in the world of spirit beings and spiritual power are part of everyday life?

---

28. Bos, 'Dreaming', 430.

## When world views differ

If each Aboriginal church was separate unto itself, the picture might be a little sharper. Although the message to be communicated is clear (that Christ has won the victory, and there is no need to fear spiritual beings or powers), there is a lot of diversity among and within the groups that need to hear this message. We need to recognize the significance of the different world views that people come from. In Australia, because of the cultural dominance of the West, including the way that dominance is expressed in denominational structures and even funding issues, there is little likelihood that more than a few Aboriginal churches will be completely autonomous independent entities. That means that the world-view divide will continue to exist, not just between people, but between communities, institutions (such as denominational hierarchies or committees) and publications. We can read the Bible together, across our differences; and we need to be aware that in coming to the Bible from different backgrounds and world views we are likely to have different presuppositions and to ask different questions of the text.[29] Our reading will be more helpful if we can listen to one another, understand the language of one another (especially being aware that sometimes the same words are used with different meanings), acknowledge our different perspectives and, even when we do not agree, be willing to understand the other's viewpoint.

However, it is not that simple. What people believe or know is not completely separate from political realities.

## The politics of knowledge

The life situation of Australian Aboriginal Christians in Australia is that they are a marginalized minority. No matter how many apologies are made by various bodies, state and federal, about what has happened in the past, and whatever steps have been taken to improve conditions for indigenous Australians in education, health, housing, law, economics and governance, there is still a strong sense among many Aboriginal people, including the ones we have listened to, that European Australian people are a

---

29. Hwa, *Mangoes and Bananas*, 230.

powerful, colonizing force, viewed with at least some degree of suspicion. What implications does this have for interaction about the issue of Christ's victory over the powers?

Westerners are perceived by many Aboriginal people as being less 'spiritual', because they tend not to have spiritual entities apart from God in the forefront of their consciousness. White people are more likely to seek naturalistic explanations of unusual events, and tend to be dismissive of the possibility of causation that cannot be rationally explained. When it comes to the discussion of spiritual powers, then, Aboriginal Christians may feel that they are at an advantage, with first-hand knowledge that can stump the naturalistic accounts of white people. By the same token, Westerners are more likely to see Aboriginal people as superstitious or even in some cases 'influenced by Pentecostalism'. Because of the political power differential between them, however, differences can easily lead to the beliefs and practices of the weaker group being seen by the dominant partner as deficient or just plain wrong. This is likely to result in those beliefs and practices 'going underground', rather than being worked through and possibly (if necessary) even changed.

It is important to be aware also that knowledge is political in another sense. It is possible for people to comply with an external standard (e.g. how to deal with spiritual beings or powers) and to do this not because of their convictions, but to gain political or personal standing. This is more likely to be a problem where there is a significant power differential between groups, and it is the stronger or dominant side that must be more aware of it.

### Theology and colonization

When the belief systems are very closely tied to a person's identity, as they are in the case of Aboriginal beliefs in the spiritual world, then the political dimension of knowledge is an even more sensitive issue. As Doxtater says from a Native American perspective, 'Indigenous people contend that [. . .] their knowledge is the exercise of self-determination.'[30] In other words, what is presented as

---

30. Doxtater, 'Indigenous Knowledge', 625.

theology comes clothed in a political reality. In short, theology can be seen as an act of colonization. If there are differences about spiritual powers between Aboriginal Christians and non-Aboriginal Christians, it would not be surprising if some Aboriginal Christians preferred what they perceived as the most 'Aboriginal' opinion as an expression of resistance to the intellectual colonization of the Western outsider, although others would seek to avoid having their views shaped in this way.

As non-Aboriginal Christians seek to engage with Aboriginal Christians in this discussion, it is important to be aware of this dynamic, and to take steps to address it. This might be done first of all by explicitly acknowledging the dynamic and then developing appropriate ways of talking together, which will include factors of time, space and media.

If this is true of the Australian situation, it is true also of the relationship between the West and the Majority World, whether that interface is on the international level or within the borders of one country because of ethnic variety or immigration. It may also be true for different subgroups in a society divided by factors other than ethnicity. Because we believe that Christ's victory over the powers is real, we need to find ways of sharing this good news that acknowledge difference, while at the same time holding fast to the one truth.

## 8. DELIVER US FROM EVIL: PRAYER AND THE VICTORY OF CHRIST

**Donald S. West**

How do Christians appropriate the victory of Christ in the present time? Previous chapters have treated the historical, cultural, biblical and theological contexts of Christ's victory, but room has been left to consider the way by which Christians may avail themselves of the Father's conquest over evil and its agents in the death, resurrection and ascension of his Son. Answers to the above question have varied throughout the history of the church, and there is at the present time a great deal of interest in what is known as 'spiritual warfare' in some quarters, and virtually none in others. While criticisms may be levelled at recent forays into 'spiritual warfare', it is also worth asking whether more strident applications of spiritual warfare have arisen to fill the void left by a fairly general neglect of the teaching and examples of prayer found throughout the New Testament (NT).[1] In the light of this possibility, the present chapter will focus on what the NT says about prayer in the light of Christ's victory. It

---

1. This may be another example of filling the 'gap'; see Bolt's chapter (2) in this volume.

will, first, set out the theological context or framework into which the NT places all prayer. Only when this framework is grasped can the full range of NT prayer instructions and examples be employed in a balanced and profitable way. The next two sections follow trajectories that arise from this framework, namely that the victory of Christ provides a foundation for tremendous confidence in prayers being answered, and – somewhat to the opposite – also provides the catalyst for prayer in the midst of a constant battle with spiritual opposition. The chapter will finish with a few thoughts about how Christ's victory impacts prayers of thanksgiving and praise.

## The context of New Testament prayer: the 'already–not yet' era

### The other kingdom

Although the books of the Old Testament and the writings of Second Temple Judaism regularly portray God's people living in the midst of spiritual darkness and evil circumstances,[2] there is within them the fervent expectation of a future day of salvation in which the darkness will be suddenly dispelled and the present age will give way to the age to come. The NT writers, however, on the basis of the Christ event, claim that the age to come has already arrived (1 Cor. 10:11), even if its fullness is still awaited. In 2 Corinthians 5, for example, the apostle Paul says that if anyone is in Christ, a 'new creation' comes into being (2 Cor. 5:17). Yet he also says that this new work of God does not replace the old but is in the process of taking it over: 'So we do not lose heart. Though our outer self is wasting away, our inner self is being renewed day by day' (2 Cor. 4:16). Or, as 1 John 2:8 puts it, 'the darkness is passing away and the true light is already shining.'

According to the NT, then, the present age is mixed: old and new wineskins, good and bad fish, salvation and judgment. There is an 'Already' of the kingdom in which it is dynamically present in Jesus' ministry and in the proclamation of the gospel, but there

---

2. See Lövestam, *Spiritual Wakefulness*, 3–24, for details of OT and Second Temple references.

is also a 'Not Yet' in which this kingdom appears to be resisted by another kingdom, the kingdom of darkness.

But the resistance of the kingdom of darkness is not equal to the kingdom of God, nor should it be considered as a worthy opponent. This other kingdom is ultimately powerless, being ruled by deceitfulness, wickedness and murderous hatred (Mark 8:33; Acts 5:3; 1 Cor. 7:5; 2 Cor. 2:11; Eph. 6:11), and is incited by the desires of men and women to which they have given themselves over (Jas 1:13–15; 2 Cor. 4:4). In the opposition that ensues the devil is said to give particular attention to Christians, to the end that they might deny the Father and the Son (1 John 2:22; 4:2–3) or might break fellowship with one another over secondary matters. Much of his work is unnoticed and unpredictable. According to the parable of the sower, for example, Satan steals the Word as soon as it is preached (Mark 4:15; Luke 8:12). In another parable he sows weeds among the wheat (Matt. 13:39a). According to Paul, Satan masquerades in the church as an angel of light (2 Cor. 11:14) and may be behind over-zealous church discipline (2 Cor. 2:11) or even take advantage of prayer retreats (1 Cor. 7:5).

### 'Under God's mighty hand'

Although menacing, Satan's hand is not exercised independently of God. A number of biblical texts indicate that God may withdraw his protective hand and leave his people to face Satan alone – perhaps to test the genuineness of their faith, to prove their salvation or even to vindicate his righteousness (Job 1 – 2; cf. 1 Cor. 5:6; 1 Tim. 1:20). Paul, for example, says that his 'thorn in the flesh' was both 'given' to him [by God] *and* was also a 'messenger of Satan' (2 Cor. 12:7),[3] with the first attribute theologically prior.

God is frequently portrayed in Scripture as testing his people in severe circumstances – circumstances in which they may be inclined to disbelieve in his goodness or salvation purposes for them (e.g. Ps. 95). In the closing section of 1 Peter, for example, the writer exhorts his readers to be humbled 'under the mighty hand of God' (5:6). God's 'mighty hand' is most likely an allusion to the mighty

---

3. All emphasis in Bible quotations is added.

hand with which he redeemed Israel from Egypt (Septuagint Exod.
13:9; Deut. 3:24; 4:34; 5:15 etc.).[4] In the Exodus event God's hand
was under Israel as he lifted them as upon eagle's wings – but
what does it mean to be 'humbled *under* the mighty hand of God'?
Perhaps Peter is alluding to the period of the plagues (Exod. 7 –
11), in which the Israelites experienced a portion of the judgment
God delivered to the Egyptians.[5] Now, says Peter, in the present
age, the beneficiaries of the second exodus will continue to experience humiliation and suffering 'under' God's hand (1:6–9; 4:12–19)
as their salvation is being brought to them (1:13). The connection
between God's 'mighty hand' and the interference of the evil one is
made plain by the following verses (5:7–8).

Jesus also seems to sense the hand of God's judgment alongside
evil in the Garden of Gethsemane (Mark 14:36 // Matt. 26:39, 42;
Luke 22:42). There he speaks not only of a 'cup' (of judgment and
suffering), but also of a God-given 'hour' laid upon him, a defining
moment in the eschatological timetable (the Great Tribulation?)
that he prays will pass him by (Mark 14:35; *parelthē*). Indeed, Jesus
says that the cup is reserved not only for him but that the disciples
have their own hour when they will be 'handed over' (e.g. Mark
13:11) and receive a cup that they too must drink (Mark 10:38–39;
cf. Luke 12:50–51).

### Christ's own sufferings

The connection of Jesus and his disciples in Gethsemane points
to an underlying bond with Christ, to which the NT returns when
it speaks of the mixed nature of the present time. According
to Romans 8:17, it is our union with Christ that lies behind our
present distress: 'if [we are] children, then heirs – heirs of God and
fellow heirs with Christ – provided we suffer with him so that we
may also be glorified with him' (cf. Phil. 3:10).[6] To the Philippian
church Paul says it has been 'granted' (by God) not only to believe

---

4. Jobes, *1 Peter*, 311.

5. The plagues of blood, frogs, gnats, flies, boils (perhaps; see Exod. 9:11),
   hail and locusts are shared by both Egyptian and Israelite.

6. Allison, *End of the Ages*, 66.

in Christ but to 'suffer on his behalf' (Phil. 1:29).[7] 1 Peter strikes the same note when it says that Christians should not consider suffering for righteousness' sake something strange but should rejoice in so far as it is 'Christ's sufferings' they are enduring (1 Pet. 4:12–13). Dietrich Bonhoeffer, in his little book on temptation, reminds us of Jesus' words in Luke 22:28–29: 'You are those who have stood by me in *my* trials; and I confer on you a kingdom, just as my Father has conferred on me.'[8]

Bonhoeffer continues:

> It is not the temptations of the *disciples* which here receive the promise, but their participation in the life and the temptation of Jesus. The temptations of the disciples fall on *Jesus*, and the temptations of Jesus come upon the disciples.[9]

The present era, then, is mixed. It is a time of both immense opportunity and intense opposition in which God's 'new creation' in Christ is taking shape. It is a time of extremes – of plenty and of want. If Christians are to live in this age, they must learn to live with *both* extremes. To this point attention has been focused upon the nature of the present distress – the time of want. It is now time to consider prayer in the times of plenty.

## Confident prayer in the light of Jesus' victory

According to several writers of the NT, Christ's victory over Satan gives us tremendous confidence to approach God. At the end of the first chapter of 2 Corinthians Paul says:

> For the Son of God, Jesus Christ, whom we proclaimed among you [. . .] was not Yes and No, but in him it is always Yes. For all the promises of

---

7. Paul sees his own sufferings as the completion of the sufferings of the body of Christ (Col. 1:24; 2 Cor. 1:2–11; cf. Phil. 1:12–19).
8. New Revised Standard Version, with rearrangement.
9. Bonhoeffer, *Creation and Fall*, 123 (emphasis original).

> God find their Yes in him. That is why it is through him that we utter
> our Amen to God for his glory. (2 Cor. 1:19–20)

The Son of God, Jesus Christ – that is, the risen exalted Lord – has
both fulfilled the salvation plan of the Father and provided the
basis upon which confident requests can be made to the Father.
This is the era of the Father's generosity, an era reflected in the
prayer promises found throughout the NT.

### The prayer promises

The best-known of the prayer promises runs as follows: 'Ask, and
it will be given to you; seek, and you will find; knock, and it will be
opened to you' (Matt. 7:7 // Luke 11:9).

Jesus, who makes this promise, goes on to reason that if earthly
fathers know how to provide good gifts for their children – which
they do – how much more will the heavenly Father do so (cf. Luke
12:32). In Luke's version of this saying, Jesus says that the Father
will supply the *Holy Spirit* to those who pray (Luke 11:13). This
means that even the 'trivial' things of life – things that can take
up a surprising amount of our attention and energy – are being
gathered into God's plan of salvation by his Spirit as we pray. The
small things suddenly become big in God's hands.

The prayer promises express tremendous confidence. Note the
use of 'anything' in the following examples:

> Do not be anxious about anything, but in everything by prayer and
> supplication with thanksgiving let your requests be made known to God.
> (Phil. 4:6)

> And this is the confidence that we have toward him, that if we ask
> anything according to his will he hears us. (1 John 5:14)

What is it that gives these – and other prayer promises (e.g.
Mark 11:24; Heb. 4:16; Jas 1:5) – their openhearted certainty?[10]

---

10. The prayer-promise formula, which remains static in its many NT
    occurrences, is neither formulaic nor magical. Magical incantations and

The answer from the NT is that it is because the risen Jesus stands behind them. James 5:14–15 is a good illustration of this point:

> Is anyone among you sick? Let him call for the elders of the church, and let them pray over him, anointing him with oil in the *name of the Lord.* And the prayer of faith will save the one who is sick, and *the Lord* will raise him up. And if he has committed sins, he will be forgiven.

Just as Jesus acted as a mediator of God's power and promises in his earthly ministry, so now, in his exalted state, his healing power and generous forgiveness are being mediated through prayer. The key to these prayer promises – alluded to in the James passage above – is the power of Jesus' *name.* This name not only signals that Jesus has triumphed over all opposition in his death and resurrection, but that his power remains available for those who make requests in his name.

### *'In my name'*
Praying in Jesus' 'name' is more prominent in the Gospel of John than anywhere else in the NT – six out of the seven prayer

---

prayers in the surrounding context of the NT writings were markedly different from the prayer recommended by Jesus and the early Christians. The simplicity and directness of NT prayers and prayer instructions (and the free generosity of the Father assumed within them) are a refreshing change from the endless repetition of the vowels of the alphabet or of words made up from the combination of the names of various gods that dominate the long and confusing incantations of magic (cf. Matt. 6:7–8; Luke 11:5–8). See Aune, 'Prayer', 23–42; Betz, 'Introduction', xli–liii, for the function of prayer and magical incantations within the Greco-Roman context. Aune concludes, 'The whole spectrum of Greco-Roman prayer, however [. . .] has little in common with the Judeo-Christian prayer tradition [. . .]' (41). Betz's explanation of the popularity and endurance of magic is arresting in the light of the contemporary world: 'magic is nothing but the art of making people believe that something is being done about those things in life about which we all know that we ourselves can do nothing' (xlviii).

promises use this formula (John 14:13–14; 15:16; 16:23–24, 26; not 15:7).[11] The precise meaning of the phrase 'in my name' is debated, but on my reading it refers to making requests of the Father in the belief that he is fully revealed in Jesus of Nazareth. The parallel structure of the first prayer-promise cluster, John 14:12–14, makes this connection clear:

> [12]Truly, truly, I say to you,
> whoever *believes in me* (A1)
> will also do the works that I do; and greater works than these will he do (B1),
> because I am going to the Father (C1).
> [13]Whatever you ask in my name (A2),
> this I will do (B2),
> that the Father may be glorified in the Son (C2).
> [14]If you ask me anything in my name (A3),
> I will do it (B3).

Asking 'in my name' is parallel to 'believes in me'; that is, believing that he has come from the Father and is one with the Father (cf. 14:1–11; 'Believe me that I am in the Father and the Father is in me', 14:11).[12] Prayers in Jesus' name succeed because they acknowledge the unity of the Father and the Son in revelation and salvation. Jesus' ascension to the Father not only marks the completion of his 'work' of obedience to the Father (e.g. 4:34; 19:30), but also inaugurates a new era in the salvation plan of God. In John 14:12 Jesus ties the 'greater works' the disciples will do to his return to the Father. Based on the parallel structure of the unit we may expect that the prayer promises are also tied to the exaltation of the Son (B1, B2, B3).

---

11. Surprisingly, prayer in Jesus' 'name' is mentioned again only in Eph. 5:19–20, and there it is 'giving thanks for everything to God the Father in the name of our Lord Jesus' (cf. Matt. 18:19–20 and Jas 5:14, which come close to the phrase).

12. See supporting argument in West, 'Promises', ch. 6, §C.3.b.iii; West, 'Petionary Prayer', 235–240.

The first consequence of the victory of Christ upon petitionary prayer, then, is the tremendous confidence petitioners have before God as they ask in Jesus' name. In making our requests – no matter how insignificant they may seem – we are engaged in the forward movement of God's kingdom by his Spirit. There are conditions laid upon petitioners (sincere dependence upon God and heartfelt forgiveness of others), but these are small in comparison to the generosity of God who invites us to make our requests. Although we have called these texts 'promises', it also should be borne in mind that they mostly comprise commands to pray that are motivated by promises.[13] The question for us to answer is how we have dealt with these promises. Do we water them down, or soft-pedal them, perhaps afraid that some people might get the wrong idea and ask God for their football team to win on a Sunday? (Would that be so wrong in the first few days of being a Christian, especially at grand final time?) The frequency of these promises in the NT and their deep connection with the victorious rule of Christ cannot be overlooked in our ministries and lives. What of prayers unanswered, says a voice from within, how do we answer that? We will return to this question in a moment, but for now we must remember that ours is the age of extremes, where things that appear to be opposite occur at the same time. There are theological and exegetical questions around prayer, but we must appropriate the promises to prayer, fully expectant that the God who raised Jesus from the dead can do far more than we ask or think.

## Prayer in the face of the enemy and our distress

### The struggle for maturity

We have seen that in the present age God's salvation is mixed with his judgment and that Christians, even though they celebrate victory over their enemy, remain vulnerable (1 Pet. 5:9) and must continually draw upon this victory until the day of their salvation. Indeed, it is the nearness of the 'day' that leads to the frequent NT exhortations

---

13. K. Barth, *Prayer*, 9–21.

to 'watch', 'stay awake' (e.g. Mark 13:9, 23, 33, 35, 37; 14:34, 38), 'be strong', 'stand' (or 'stand firm', e.g. Eph. 6:10–11, 13), 'be sober' (e.g. 1 Pet. 5:8) and 'be humble' (e.g. Jas 4:6, 10; 1 Pet. 5:6).[14] Paul prays for the maturity of his churches in readiness for the day of Christ (Rom. 15:6[?]; 1 Cor. 1:8; Phil. 1:6, 10; 4:5–7[?]; 1 Thess. 3:13; 5:23),[15] mindful that it will require extreme effort. It is, as he says, a 'struggle' (*agōnizesthai, agōn*), both in his own ministry (1 Cor. 9:24–27; 1 Thess. 2:2) and for the maturity of the churches (Phil. 1:27–30; [3:12–14;] Col. 1:28 – 2:3; cf. 2 Cor. 11:28; Col. 4:12b).[16]

Perhaps the best known of Paul's 'struggle' texts is Ephesians 6:10–12:

> Be strong in the Lord and in the strength of his might. Put on the whole armour of God, that you may be able to stand against the schemes of the devil. For we do not wrestle against flesh and blood, but against the rulers, against the authorities, against the cosmic powers over this present darkness, against the spiritual forces of evil in the heavenly places.

These 'powers' seek to withstand the existence and advancement of the kingdom and people of God through deception (vv. 11, 13–14; on 'standing' in Paul, see Rom. 5:2; 14:4; 1 Cor. 15:1; 16:13; Gal. 5:1; Phil. 1:27; 4:1; Col. 4:12; 1 Thess. 3:8; 2 Thess. 2:15). It is, according to Paul, only through putting on the 'whole armour of God' (*panoplia tou theou*, Eph. 6:11, 13; cf. Isa. 59, esp. vv. 16–17; Wisdom 5.15–23; cf. 1 Thess. 5:8) and then 'wrestling' (*palē*) with the enemy at close quarters that we will overcome.[17] At one time, says Paul, we

---

14. The study of Lövestam, *Spiritual Wakefulness*, 25–143, remains a superb examination of a number of these themes in the Synoptic Gospels and the epistles of the NT. Prayer is particularly treated on pp. 64–77, but should not be lifted out from the complex of themes discussed there.

15. D. G. Peterson, 'Maturity', 185–204, reflects upon Paul's desire to bring about maturity among the churches.

16. To this may be added Paul's military language for his own ministry and that of his co-workers: 1 Cor. 15:32; 2 Cor. 6:5; 10:3–5; Phil. 2:25; Phlm. 2.

17. Although defined by Bauer, *Greek-English Lexicon*, 752, as 'engagement in a challenging contest', *palē* (Eph. 6:12) has implications of '"hand-to-

were all under the sway of these powers, being completely captive
to our own desires (Eph. 2:2–3; 4:17–19). But now, by faith in the
Christ who reigns over the powers (1:20–23; 2:1–6; 3:10; 4:7–10),
we have been given a new 'self', created in Christ Jesus to do good
works (2:10). This new self, like the pieces of armour of chapter
6, must be 'put on' through embracing truth, love and purity,
while the 'old self', corrupted by its desires for falsehood, hatred
and filthiness, must be 'put off' (4:21–24). Here Paul is concerned
not only for the final salvation of the individual Christian and the
church, but also for the health of marriages, families and even
the social structures in which believers are placed (5:20 – 6:9). If
Christians are to mature and reach the goal of salvation, they must
fight the good fight (cf. 2 Tim. 4:7; 1 Tim. 1:18–19; 6:12).

### 'Pray in the Spirit at all times'
At the close of this exhortation to 'stand', Paul issues a call for
prayer (6:18–20) that climaxes the second half of Ephesians.[18] It is
through prayer that the various items of armour are appropriated
into action and that the cosmic plan of God for his church is connected to the daily battle of the Christian soldier. Petition is not
an optional extra, but a vital part of succeeding in the struggle.[19]

---

hand" fighting [with] no means of inflicting wounds, pain, and death
[. . .] excluded' (M. Barth, *Ephesians*, 2: 763). See further discussion and
recent bibliography in O'Brien, *Ephesians*, 466–467, and esp. Gudorf, 'Use
of *palē*', 331–335), who concludes on p. 335 that the words *hēminhē palē*
should be translated as 'our wrestling'.

18. Arnold, *Ephesians*, 112, and Lincoln, *Ephesians*, 452, note that Eph.
6:18–20 brings to a climax the earlier prayers and prayer instructions of
Ephesians that have centred on the completion of God's great purposes
in his Son (1:15–23; 3:14–21; 5:18–20).

19. So e.g. Arnold, *Ephesians*, 112; Best, *Ephesians*, 604; and Lincoln, *Ephesians*,
451–452. Lövestam, *Spiritual Wakefulness*, 71, notes that *dia* in v. 18 is one
of the accompanying circumstances (citing Rom. 8:25; 14:20; 2 Cor. 2:4;
Blass and Debrunner, *Greek Grammar*, §223.3). Stanley, *Boasting*, 110–113,
questions whether prayer should be considered as a 'struggle' or not,
concluding that 'Paul does not conceive of prayer as a struggle, but as one

Such prayer, says Paul, must first of all be offered *continually* ('at all times', *en panti kairō*), not meaning incessantly, but in all seasons, since Satan's attacks are not predictable. Secondly, in times of spiritual threat, the kind of prayer offered must be 'in the Spirit' (*en pneumati*). The meaning of this phrase is debated, but I take it to be prayer in harmony with the Spirit's purpose in the mystery that has been revealed to Paul; that is, the unifying of all things under one head, even Christ (see esp. the final phrase of v. 18, 'on behalf of *all* the saints'; cf. 2:18; 5:18).[20] Finally, prayer that accompanies the 'armour of God' will not only be for our own needs, but for *others* who feel the heat of battle. Paul requests help in his current battle with the heavenly forces as he struggles to proclaim Christ boldly in his imprisonment (6:19–20).

### *'Keep alert in all perseverance'*

Paul adds another quality or attitude to prayer 'in the Spirit' in Ephesians 6:18. Together with prayer, he says believers must 'keep alert with all perseverance, making supplication for all the saints' (Eph. 6:18, *agrypnountes en pasē proskarterēsei kai deēsei peri pantōn tōn hagiōn*; cf. Luke 21:36; 1 Pet. 4:7). Prayer and keeping awake or

---

Footnote 19 (*cont.*)

means among others of taking part in the "contest" of the faith and the gospel' (113). Although this point may be granted generally, Paul appears to be saying that in certain circumstances prayer will be a struggle in the midst of *the* struggle.

20. Various options have been suggested for the phrase *en pneumati*. It is unlikely to refer to the spirit of the individual by which he or she prays (i.e. the 'heart'; e.g. Gal. 4:6) or to the gift of glossolalia (e.g. 1 Cor. 14:14–16) (Schnabel, *Korinther*, 808). Fee, *God's Empowering Presence*, 227, n. 29, argues that Paul refers to the Spirit of God praying through the spirit of the person (a view that fits neatly into his understanding of Rom. 8:26–27), as does Lövestam, *Spiritual Wakefulness*, 72, and O'Brien, *Ephesians*, 485. There is certainly a connection with the idea of 'weakness' in Rom. 8:26 if that word be understood to refer to the divinely imposed eschatological limitation (see West, 'Promises', ch. 8), but in Ephesians the Spirit is mentioned in terms of access (2:18) and thanksgiving (5:18–20) rather than frustration.

alert are frequently paired in NT exhortation.[21] The present world remains in darkness and its enticements and ease of life have an alcoholic affect that causes believers to forget that they belong to the day soon to dawn, and not to the night soon to pass away (1 Thess. 5:1–11).[22] Prayer is required in order to stay awake, alert and sober. But the reverse is also true: alertness is required to ensure that prayer continues. Paul wants the readers to 'pray in the Spirit on all occasions *to the end that (eis auto)* they might be alert in all perseverance' (Eph. 6:18, my tr.). 1 Peter 4:7 makes the same point: 'The end of all things is at hand; therefore be self-controlled and sober-minded for *the sake of your prayers.*' Prayer is a valuable weapon and accompaniment in the eschatological battle and must be kept sharp through sobriety and resistance to temptation.[23] The pleasantness of our surroundings and the comfort of our wealth – including the wealth of our Christian heritage – numb us to the reality of spiritual threat and danger. We must pray and stay awake, mindful that the battle in which we are engaged can turn on us at any moment.

To this point in this section we have been considering how prayer is portrayed within the 'battle zone' of spiritual conflict in a general fashion. It is time now to turn to some more specific ways in which the NT addresses or alludes to the battle in which we are engaged.

### Examples of praying in distress

Perhaps the most obvious instruction with respect to prayer in distress is found in James and 1 Peter, where we are told to 'resist

---

21. The combination of 'keeping alert' and praying is found throughout the NT (Col. 4:2–3; 1 Pet. 4:7; 5:6–10; Luke 21:36; Mark 14:38 // Matt. 26:38); it is frequently combined with the warning that the Lord's arrival is near; cf. Lövestam, *Spiritual Wakefulness*, 64–77.

22. See the summary of Lövestam, *Spiritual Wakefulness*, 133–143.

23. The need for vigilant prayer is reflected in Paul's injunctions to persevere in or be devoted to prayer (Rom. 12:12; Eph. 6:18–19; Col. 4:2–3; 1 Thess. 5:17; cf. 2 Thess. 3:1–2; Luke 18:1; Acts 1:14; 2:42; 6:4); Grundmann, '*kartereō*', 619. One also wonders whether Paul's own 'unceasing' prayers for his churches (Rom. 1:10; 1 Thess. 3:10; 2 Thess. 1:11) arise from his concern that believers remain alert as they await the parousia of Christ.

the devil' (Jas 4:7; 1 Pet. 5:9). Christians are to be alert to the evil one's meddling and influence (cf. 2 Cor. 2:11; 1 John 4:1–6) and are encouraged to resist it. In so doing they may be confident of success. Perhaps Paul's instructions to the Corinthians to 'flee from sexual immorality' (1 Cor. 6:18) and to 'flee from idolatry' (10:14) are related to this – both exhortations are connected with pagan sacrifices and the worship of the false gods and their demons rather than the true and living God (10:20). On these occasions we not only pray for God to deliver us from temptation, but also use our feet. May it help us sometimes to verbalize a 'No' to temptation or to our own desires – if this is accompanied with prayer for divine help? 'Resistance' requires a firm stand. We are, after all, putting 'to death the deeds of the body' (see Rom. 8:13).

A second example of prayer guidance in the present distress is relevant to preachers. Those of us involved in the ministry of the Word tend to pray for soft hearts or receptive ears so that our congregations may receive the Word. The parable of the sower would certainly direct us here, but from the same parable, should we not also ask for Satan to be kept at bay from the hearers, or for strength that they might endure the heat of persecution, or, again, for their determination in the pulling out of the weeds of the world (Mark 4:14–20 and pars.)?

For those in the midst of persecution, perhaps Peter's exhortation to cast 'all your anxieties on him, because he cares for you' (1 Pet. 5:7; cf. Phil. 4:6) needs to be recast into its original light. This verse is not primarily aimed at those who are troubled about falling share prices or the property-market slump, but who face extreme pressure upon their faith. Earlier Peter says, 'Do not fear their fear or be afraid, but instead sanctify Christ in your hearts, always being prepared to provide a defence to anyone who asks you for an accounting of the hope within you' (1 Pet. 3:14–15 my tr.). The 'heart' is where fear attaches itself and where anxiety sends down its roots.

From another angle of pastoral ministry, what does Scripture say for those tripped up or trapped by Satan's schemes? According to James, we should repent: 'Draw near to God [in prayer] . . . Cleanse your hands [. . . and] purify your hearts' (Jas 4:8, 10). We resist the devil as much through confession of sin as through running away from sin. We must be careful here not to give the impression that believers are immediately placed into Satan's realm the moment they sin or fail to confess a sin. James is addressing persistent sin and very hard hearts within the community – he equates their divisiveness and jealousy with 'murder' (4:2–3; cf. 3:13 – 4:10)! Hardness of heart before God and others about our sin contains within it a denial of the heart of the gospel: forgiveness. According to 1 John 1:8, 'If we say we have no sin, we deceive ourselves, and the truth is not in us.' This sounds like a statement of the obvious until we hear the echo in John 8:44, where Jesus says that a mark of the devil is that there is 'no truth in him'. There is no greater lie than that we can live in the light without forgiveness.

Satan's influence through temptation is real. The last petition of the Lord's Prayer assumes this truth when it says 'lead us not into temptation, but deliver us from evil [or the evil one]' (Matt. 6:13). Here 'temptation' should not be understood to refer to the 'time of trial' (perhaps the Great Tribulation, that moment of final horror unveiled immediately before the day of judgment).[24] Rather, Jesus refers to being led astray from God's Word and way by our own desires, being enticed by the false promise of life or freedom by the evil one. Jesus recommends that his disciples pray that the Father not expose them to the influence of the devil in their own strength. He elsewhere prays for their protection from the evil one (cf. John 17:11, 15); one expects we should do the same. However, if we are caught by our own desires and fall into sin, the final line of the Lord's Prayer instructs us to call out to God for help, since he alone has power to achieve our rescue.[25]

### Unanswered prayer

But what of those times when we are pressed all around and have prayed and there is no answer? Jesus' prayer in the Garden of Gethsemane – that the Father remove the 'cup' of his wrath – arises not out of disobedience, but out of a faith perhaps now illuminated by a more urgent understanding of the extremities he

---

24. This view is reflected in the recent translation of the verse found in some modern liturgies: 'Save us from the time of trial'; see McCaughey, 'Matthew 6.13a', 31–40, for a critique of this translation for liturgies.
25. For details, see West, 'Promises', ch. 2, §C.5.c.

now faces (cf. Mark 8:31; 9:12, 31; 10:33; 14:8, 21, 25).[26] Yet when Jesus has made his request three times, he stops, aware in a fresh way that drinking the 'cup' is necessary if the *Father's* salvation purposes are to be fulfilled (Mark 14:36).[27]

In Mel Gibson's interpretation of Christ's passion, the tempter is portrayed as a shadowy figure behind the scenes. While not specifically mentioned in the Gethsemane episode, there is evidence that Jesus is aware of Satan's presence. For example, he tells the disciples to 'watch and pray that you may not enter into temptation' (Mark 14:38). In Mark's narrative, Satan has already attempted to divert Jesus in the wilderness (under the Spirit's leading, Mark 1:12–13; Matt. 4:1–11 // Luke 4:1–13) and later through his disciple Peter (Mark 8:32–33 // Matt. 16:22–23; cf. Luke 22:31–32), so his activity is more than conceivable in the Garden of Gethsemane. If this is the case, we can conclude that Jesus' prayer in the garden enabled Satan to be resisted, and permitted Jesus a fresh understanding of and commitment to God's mission, even though his original request was not granted.

A second example of unanswered prayer is the episode of Paul's 'thorn in the flesh' from 2 Corinthians 12:7–10. Paul says he had been struck down with a 'thorn in the flesh, a messenger of Satan,

---

26. The Gethsemane petition is conditioned by Jesus' request that what God wills might be the thing that occurs and not what he wants. In this second part of the petition he uses the present tense of the verb 'to will' (*thelō*), signalling his deeper commitment and orientation. Throughout Mark's Gospel Jesus is presented as someone who puts God's will above his own (Mark 3:35; 10:29–30) and who calls his disciples to put their desires beneath those of God (8:34–38; 9:35; 10:35, 42–45). They are to think upon the things of God and not the things of men (8:33; cf. 10:45). Matthew's version of the Gethsemane prayer echoes the third petition of the Lord's Prayer ('your will be done, on earth as it is in heaven', Matt. 6:10; cf. 26:42).

27. Mark mentions two occasions when Jesus prays (14:35–36, 39), and a third may be presumed from 14:41. Matthew is more specific, 26:39, 42, 44. Luke mentions only one prayer session (22:42). To pray three times about something is to be assured of a final decision in the heavenly court; so Delling, '*treis, tris, tritos*', 216–225; cf. Furnish, *2 Corinthians*, 529.

to pummel me' (v. 7 my tr.). The identity of this thorn has perplexed many, but Paul alludes to both its physical and devilish aspects: it is both a thorn in the *flesh* and a messenger of *Satan*.[28] These aspects had a combined effect – Paul sensed that his chronic ailment threatened his ministry.[29] In his distress Paul says that he 'pleaded with the Lord' about this 'three times' that he 'might remove [it] from me' (12:8 my tr.; *hyper toutou tris ton kyrion parekalesa hina apostē ap' emou*).[30] 'Three times', as in the Gethsemane scene, is a sufficient number to be assured of a final decision in the heavenly courtroom. The word Paul uses for 'pleaded', in the aorist tense (*parekalesa*), amplifies the finality of Paul's prayer. His thorn was there to stay; he concluded that his ministry would be less effective from now on.[31]

At that time, Paul says, he received a revelation from the Lord (12:9a): 'My grace is sufficient for you, for my power is made perfect in weakness.'[32] The Lord who said 'No' to Paul's request

28. Most scholars consider the thorn to be some kind of chronic physical ailment (in the 'flesh'); others consider the phrase a metaphor for Paul's opponents (see 11:14–15, where Paul implies his opponents are 'ministers [*of Satan*]'). The secondary literature is substantial, but a good review of opinions is found in an excursus in Thrall, *Second Epistle to the Corinthians*, 2: 809–818. More recent investigations, e.g. J. E. Powers, 'Thorn in the Flesh', 85–99, do not offer further insight.

29. Stanley, *Boasting*, 55.

30. A choice as to whether it is the thorn or the angel of Satan that Paul wishes removed is difficult. Two arguments have been put forward for it to be Satan: (1) if Satan is seen as the enemy of Paul (e.g. 2 Cor. 2:11), then his angel could be the unnamed object of the verb *apostē*; and (2) the verb *aphistanai* usually takes a personal object in Paul's writings. However, the two elements (the thorn and the pummelling) are in apposition in v. 7, with *skolops* in the leading role. The physical nature of the thorn (and pummelling) fits better with the *Peristasenkataloge* found throughout the book; these refer not to Satan or his minions as intermediate causes of anguish, but to concrete expressions of suffering.

31. So Allo, *Saint Paul*, 312, cited in Martin, *2 Corinthians*, 6, 418.

32. Barnett, *Second Epistle to the Corinthians*, 572, notes that this revelation forms the climax of Paul's defence of his ministry in 2 Corinthians.

for the removal of his thorn in the flesh now says 'Yes' to his future ministry *and to his thorn!* The Lord's promise of his grace is not aimed at the prayer referred to in verse 8 but at the presupposition underneath it: that without the removal of the 'thorn' Paul's ministry would not succeed. The Lord could remove the thorn, but instead wants Paul to continue on with it in his grace. Once again, prayer in the midst of distress and satanic trial is not answered according to its intent, and yet the request is placed into the wider work of God's salvation purposes. Both Jesus and Paul were confronted with opportunities to doubt the goodness or care of God, and yet both petitioners, through prayer, were given deeper insight into the circumstances that had come upon them.

### God's protective presence

But does the teaching of the NT allow us to expect 'insight' into God's purposes only when we pray in the midst of distress? According to three passages from Paul, those who pray in such circumstances may be assured of the very presence of God. The first example occurs in the situation just examined. Following his revelation from the Lord in 2 Corinthians 12, Paul says he boasts all the more gladly of his weaknesses 'so that the power of Christ might *dwell upon me*' (2 Cor. 12:9b my tr.). A second hint is found in Romans 8:26–27. This is a key text about the Spirit's role in prayer that cannot be dealt with in detail here, but in which Paul says that the Spirit *intercedes within the heart* of the saints who groan inwardly as they long for redemption in the midst of a divinely imposed limitation at the present time.[33] Finally, in his prayer promise of Philippians 4:6–7, Paul says that by casting anxiety aside and making every request known to God, 'the peace of God, which surpasses all understanding, will guard your

---

Footnote 32 *(cont.)*

    The tone of the Lord's revelation contrasts strongly with Paul's resignation in his prayer. The use of the perfect tense of the verb 'to say' (*eirēken*, 'he said – and is saying') and the present tenses of the promise ('is sufficient', *arkei*; 'is made perfect', *teleitai*) oppose the finality of the aorist tense of Paul's thrice-uttered plea in v. 8.

33. See West, 'Promises', ch. 9, for argument.

hearts and your minds in Christ Jesus'. The Father, the Son and the Spirit are all mentioned by Paul as closely protecting the petitioners, who, in the struggle that now exists, cast their confusion, frustration and even their daily anxieties upon God. This protective presence ties in to the need to pray for divine protection in the midst of the testing and temptation noted earlier.

In this longer section of the chapter we have first explored the nature of prayer in the midst of distress. In this context Christians may assume the meddling hand of the evil one and are called upon to pray for alertness, forgiveness and protection, and to continue to endure in the knowledge that God is present with them and working his salvation purposes out in ways invisible to human eyes. Two responses are often made to this kind of prayer. For some, there is the danger of over-emphasizing the presence of Satan and discerning spirits under every rock. This danger often has another attached that hides underneath: to press on in our own strength and never really depend upon God in prayer. The other danger – often felt in the midst of overwhelming circumstances – is to give the devil too much 'room', making him our focus rather than God. Open-hearted prayer in Christ's name counters both these tendencies and leads us back to the safe harbour of God's love and protection (Phil. 4:7; Ps. 145:17–20).

## Thanksgiving and praise in the light of Christ's victory

This chapter has concentrated upon petitionary prayer – that is, prayer that makes requests of God, either for ourselves (supplication and confession) or for others (intercession). But the victory of Christ has not only impacted petitionary prayer, but *all* prayer, including thanksgiving and praise. Note Paul's link in the following two verses:

> Wretched man that I am! Who will deliver me from this body of death? Thanks be to God through Jesus Christ our Lord! (Rom. 7:24–25a)

> The sting of death is sin, and the power of sin is the law. But thanks be to God, who gives us the victory through our Lord Jesus Christ. (1 Cor. 15:56–57)

Here Paul exults in thanksgiving to God because of the 'victory' of Christ. But to what victory does he refer? These prayers not only look back at the cross and resurrection, but forward to the climax of Christ's work, when the body of death is finally delivered and death is wiped away. This means that thanksgiving is offered in the here and now *in spite of* all the possible contingencies we face. Because of Christ's work – which is certain of completion – we always have a reason for giving thanks to God (2 Cor. 6:2).

Thanksgiving for Paul is not something he keeps separate from the rest of his prayer life, like a pick-me-up when things are down. Rather, the Christ event for which he constantly gives thanks also gives him the confidence to go into the spiritual battlefield with his petitions. As Gordon Wiles states, Paul lives in a situation where 'victories are continually associated with new occasions of need'.[34] These new situations anticipate further thanksgiving to God (cf. 2 Cor. 1:8–11; 4:7–15). Underneath this prayer 'two-step' of petition and thanksgiving is Paul's desire that Jesus' lordship regulate all things (Col. 2:6–7).[35] Because Jesus reigns in the present, Christians are called to rejoice (or give thanks) in any and every circumstance (2 Cor. 1:10–11; 2:14; 4:15; 9:11–15; Phil. 1:18; 2:17–18; 3:1; 4:4, 10; 1 Thess. 5:18) and end every prayer with the 'Amen' that anticipates God's provision and renders the glory to him (cf. 2 Cor. 1:20).[36]

A final word on praise: our joy and praise should be found not only in material and spiritual benefits supplied by God's hand, not only in our families and churches, and not only in the conversion of men and women to God through the work of the Spirit and the Word, but also in God who made everything and who, through his Son, victoriously ransomed a people for himself. The book of Revelation supplies hymn after hymn – with increasing length and intensity as it reaches its climax – that tells forth the victory God has won over Satan and his agents by a conqueror it calls 'King of kings and Lord of lords' (19:16). True, many of the hymns of the Apocalypse are situated *after* the final judgment has taken place

---

34. Wiles, *Paul's Intercessory Prayers*, 166–167.

35. Pao, *Thanksgiving*, 106–107.

36. Wiles, *Paul's Intercessory Prayers*, 170.

(e.g. 11:17–18; 15:3b–4; 19:1–10), but not all of them. All of them, however, remind us that we must now declare the worthiness, power, salvation, holiness and justice of our Lord and God and of his Christ. Although we have an 'Already' for which we give thanks, we praise God here and now for his 'Not Yet' as well.

## Conclusions

Prayer in the light of the victory of Christ is offered in the midst of the tension between the astonishing generosity of the Father and the continued, thorny opposition of the world, the flesh and the devil. Because of the Son's ascension to the Father, believers may be enthusiastically confident that their needs will be supplied by one who can do more than they can ask or think (Eph. 3:20). At the same time, however, they are commanded to be 'strong in the Lord and in the strength of his might' and to 'stand' against the evil powers that wage war against the saints, being vigilant in petition and intercession to render effective the armour that God supplies for the struggle. Prayer in the present time will not always be experienced with release from distress. Jesus' prayer in Gethsemane and Paul's 'thorn in the flesh' provide sobering examples of a 'No' to petitionary prayer. And yet, even at these times, Christ's victory is experienced through the protective presence of God and the anticipation of Christ's final triumph over his enemies. There is, therefore, always reason to render thanks to God, even though the victory is yet to be seen. Moreover, every circumstance provides new opportunities to don the weaponry that God supplies and to plead with God for our own needs and for the needs of our 'brotherhood throughout the world' (1 Pet. 5:9), who, in Christ, endure the same kinds of suffering we do.

> Rejoice always,
> pray without ceasing,
> give thanks in all circumstances,
> for this is the will of God *in Christ Jesus* for you. (1 Thess. 5:16–18)

## 9. CHRIST'S VICTORY OVER THE POWERS AND PASTORAL PRACTICE

### Peter G. Bolt and Donald S. West

This chapter aims to draw out some of the pastoral and practical implications of the previous chapters, especially in relation to real concerns about the continued influence of evil powers in and over the lives of ordinary human beings. This aim is impossible to achieve in any complete sense, for these concerns are many, and, although common to humanity, will take different forms – from an apparent indifference found among Western secular culture to an apparent obsession found among more animistic cultures. Nevertheless, in the light of the preceding chapters the present chapter attempts to lay down some core principles of biblical thinking and practice concerning evil powers and Christian ministry.

### The essentials of Christian ministry are culture-independent

It is important not to be so overwhelmed or confused by the variety of human responses to evil powers that we forget the source from which the principles of ministry must always be derived. A great deal of confusion has been introduced in the wake of discussions about 'contextualization'. Now it is certainly a biblical ministry principle to be 'all things to all people' (1 Cor. 9:22; i.e. 'I try to please everyone in everything I do'). That is, to adapt our approach in all the things that do not matter, so that we might reach people for Christ with the unchanging gospel that really does matter. There is no doubt that, when informed by considerations of this biblical flexibility, genuine insights have emerged from missiological discussions of 'contextualization'. On the other hand, the New Testament (NT) gives us absolutely no reason to think that our basic ministry principles or practices should be *derived from* human culture(s). The essentials of ministry, in relation to both principle and practice, arise, not from the target culture, but from the gospel of Jesus Christ. Rather than being shaped by the culture in front of them, Christian ministers, therefore, ought to be pushed from behind by the gospel.[1]

There is a commonality about human beings in their lostness. The various forms of life we know as 'culture' should not be so exalted as to blur or mask the fact (reported clearly in the Scriptures) that human beings have rebelled against their Creator and continue to do so; that they are therefore given over to the consequences of their sin, which is the expression of God's present wrath (Rom. 1:18–32), and they will face God's future wrath at the last day (Rom. 2:5). Until then, unless they turn to Christ, human beings are lost (Luke 19:10), and can be described as 'having no hope and [being] without God in this world' (Eph. 2:12), being 'darkened in their understanding, alienated from the life of God' (Eph. 4:18). Because of the lack of connection with the sovereign Creator, who has human welfare in mind, human life is felt to be chaotic and apparently random, subject to the whims

---

1. The oft-made dichotomy in missiological discussions between 'sender culture' and 'receptor culture' is misguided, since there is actually a 'gospel culture' that places every human culture under scrutiny. If the error of a previous missionary age was to regard Western culture imperialistically as always right, many contemporary discussions of contextualization are prone to the same erroneous imperialistic assumption in reverse by saying the target culture is always right. The gospel critiques all cultures at all times.

of the vague forces beyond ourselves. In an endeavour to provide some protection and security against such forces, human beings have become enslaved to all kinds of human practices, rules and regulations (Col. 2:20–23). It is among these things that we find what we call 'culture'.[2] It is important to notice that, in the NT, we learn about human culture and its enslaving tendencies at exactly the moment we are told that Christ has liberated us from it.

Because it is the gospel that ought to shape Christian ministry, it is therefore possible to articulate a basic approach to Christian ministry that is the same, whatever cultural forms the Christian minister might operate within. It is equally possible to articulate a basic approach to Christian ministry that is properly alert to concerns about evil powers, no matter whether it is exercised in the face of secularism, animism or any combination or variation in between. This chapter therefore also aims to provide some assistance for a practical approach to Christian ministry, which operates from the assumption that 'we know that we are from God, and the whole world lies in the power of the evil one' (1 John 5:19).

## The gospel does not exploit, but soothes, human weakness

### *The cry for deliverance and the weakness of the flesh*
Within this world, lying under the power of the evil one, human beings often cry out for deliverance of various kinds. The pain, grief and difficulty of living in this fallen world need no lengthy exposition here. Every human suffers under his or her own sinfulness, vulnerabilities, weaknesses and fears, as well as the sinfulness, vulnerabilities, weaknesses and fears of others. This creates a world that is groaning, for, as the 'present form of this world is passing away' (1 Cor. 7:31), the very fabric of God's creation longs for the great day of deliverance, the resurrection of the body (see Rom. 8:18–23)!

---

2. Cf. Tacitus' words about the Britons' adopting Roman practices, 'the simple natives gave the name "culture" to this factor of their slavery' (Tacitus, *Agricola* 21.2). For a further exploration of the above approach to 'contextualizing' issues, see Bolt, 'Interpreting Australian Society'.

Becoming a Christian does not remove people from the suffering that clings to this fallen, groaning world, but, in fact, the Spirit
of God increases our groaning towards that final day, generating a
deeply felt hope within us (Rom. 8:23–27). Even if there is no res-
olution of the problems of our mortal body in this life, our bodies
will certainly be renewed on that great day. In the meantime, as
Christ's people continue to suffer along with the world, the gospel
works in them to bring about the new life that springs from the
hope of resurrection. The Spirit of God is given to every person
who puts his or her faith in Christ, and, because the Spirit is the
Spirit of resurrection (Rom. 8:11), he begins to draw and drag us
towards the day when death (our last and greatest enemy) will be
removed for ever.

Until that day we live in the 'overlap of the ages'. We are human,
and thus live as mortal human beings, destined for the grave. At
a deep level this brings a terrible anxiety to life: it creates long-
ings and desires for things that promise security for our existence,
answering the desires of our mortal bodies (Rom. 6:12: 'mortal
body [. . .] passions'). But, on the other hand, the Spirit of God is
drawing us towards the day of Christ, helping us to fix our hearts
on the security found in the kingdom of God, and transforming us
from the heart outwards (2 Cor. 3:17–18; 4:16–18). As we undergo
this transformation the Spirit is recreating the image of God in us
as we begin to see the life of the Spirit manifest in and among the
various relationships of human life (Col. 3:10, then 3:5 – 4:6; or
Eph. 4:23–24, then 4:25 – 6:9).

But this is not a tension that is easy to live with, since it exerts a
pressure on us at the profoundest levels of our being. The struggle
between the 'flesh' and the 'spirit' will be a constant part of Christian
existence until the Lord comes again, bringing our new resurrection
bodies. That will be the day of ultimate deliverance for the children of
God (Rom. 8:21). The freedom we experience now is 'by faith'; that
is, it comes as the gospel promises us an assured future, based upon
the already finished work of Christ. However, faith needs to have
constant recourse to those promises. For, right back to the time of
Abraham, God's people have experienced a tension between believing the promises of God and believing the evidence of our painful
experience – for the two often appear to conflict with each other.

### The exploitation of our weakness by promises of 'deliverance'

With profound weakness at the core of the human being, it is no surprise that this opens us up to exploitation by false teachers, who promise deliverance from evil and suffering before the future resurrection day, and by the evil powers that work behind the scenes for the same destructive cause. Deep questions arising from human experience (Are we good enough? Strong enough? Sanctified enough? Faithful enough?) make people vulnerable to empty promises. These human questions are intensified and deepened all the more by the realization that they are part of the 'eschatological weakness' to which God has subjected us, so that through our sense of frustration and incompletion we might groan towards the deliverance he has promised us in his glorious new creation. This deeper sense of weakness – almost hopelessness – can make people even more vulnerable to the false promises that seem always to be a part of 'this present evil age'.

An important strand within its piety has made evangelicalism particularly vulnerable in this regard. The struggle portrayed in Romans 7 between the flesh and the spirit, issuing in the cry for deliverance, has had a long-standing influence upon evangelical descriptions of the Christian life. Within the piety with roots in Methodist discussions about entire sanctification, but particularly associated with the influential Keswick movement, this description took on a particularly important role. However, when expositors found the answer to the cry for deliverance (7:24) in the 'life of the Spirit', as portrayed in the first half of Romans 8, this produced a particularly volatile mixture. On this reading, living by the Spirit would bring – even in the midst of this present life – deliverance from the struggle portrayed in Romans 7, which Christian people experience in their own lives. And so the promise of the 'Victorious Christian Life' was born.

This exposition, however, misses several key items in the apostle's argument: Paul cries out for deliverance from 'this body of death' (7:24). This cry is answered by the promise of 'the redemption of our bodies' (8:23), and the life of the Spirit is a life of groaning towards this day (8:23), which generates hope, not 'sight' (i.e. experience). In turn, this hope issues in character-building patience as we wait for that day of deliverance (cf. Rom. 5:3–4).

The Spirit works towards that day (8:11), and begins the process of our renovation by renewing the mind, but any 'victorious Christian life' will be experienced only on the resurrection day.

Because of its long and powerful influence, Keswick piety has become very deeply embedded in contemporary evangelicalism. As Tony Payne's chapter has shown, the stream of evangelicalism represented by Keswick moved from promising entire sanctification to promising healing, and then, after the 'expansive charismatics' began to focus upon demons, to promising deliverance from evil powers. Correspondingly, the understanding of the Christian life within this stream makes people vulnerable to these demonological views. When people are struggling to overcome some oft-experienced weakness, they are open to the suggestion that they are lacking in victory because of a demonic influence from which they need to be delivered. In a day when ministers are also craving 'ministry success' – defined in terms of thriving, well-attended congregations (as if that is somehow an endorsement of *their* ministry!)[3] – they, too, if they are struggling in ministry, are susceptible to the suggestion that they might be experiencing some demonic oppression from which they must be delivered if they wish to experience the 'success' they properly deserve.

### The language of power and the promise of deliverance

It is a feature of this long stream within the evangelical tradition to speak of 'power'; that is, the power to have a more victorious, more successful or more liberated Christian life and ministry. This is a subtle declension from the biblical use of the language of power, where the gospel is the power of God for salvation (1 Cor. 1:18, 24; 2:4–5), people are given the power to believe (Eph. 3:16–19) and believing brings the Spirit who is powerful enough to raise the dead (Rom. 8:11; 1 Cor. 6:14), and where the Spirit gives believers the power to persevere patiently (Col. 1:11) in the midst of weakness,

---

3. Such an environment also leaves Christian churches prey to attracting the wrong kinds of people into the ministry, such as those with narcissistic personality disorders – with all the terrible fallout they bring to such positions. See e.g. Sperry, *Ministry and Community*, ch. 2.

suffering and difficulty (2 Cor. 12:9; Phil. 3:10), and fills them with hope (Rom. 15:13) so that they will eventually arrive at the glorious day of resurrection. This is the power to endure through, or in, the struggle, not to get rid of it.

Although this strand of evangelical piety sincerely desires to take sin seriously, it can be asked whether it takes sin seriously enough. The picture painted by Romans 8 shows that human sin has deeply distorted the entire cosmos, which now groans towards the day of resurrection. We are so deeply affected by sin that, if it will ever be overcome, it will require nothing short of a resurrection. That will be the great day of power, when, in a twinkling of an eye, those in Christ will rise and be transformed into the persons God always intended them to be. This is the moment when we will finally enter into the fullness of Christ's victory (1 Cor. 15:55–57).

### *The power of the gospel to work this great deliverance*

But Christ has already been victorious over the devil, and deliverance has already been won for us. This is the good news of the gospel, which tells us that 'the reason the Son of God appeared was to destroy the works of the devil' (1 John 3:8) and that

> since therefore the children share in flesh and blood, [the Son] himself
> likewise partook of the same things, that through death he might destroy
> the one who has the power of death, that is, the devil, and deliver
> all those who through fear of death were subject to lifelong slavery.
> (Heb. 2:14–15)

How did this come about? Christ died to save sinners. He died for our sins and, by dealing with sin, rescued us from sin's penalty: death. Thus he neutralized the power of the devil to accuse and to wield the power of death over us. The Son of God defeated the devil *indirectly*, by dealing with our sin on the cross.

This is the good news the gospel announces and, because of the work of Christ on our behalf, the gospel is the power of God for salvation: the power of God for deliverance. The gospel speaks of Christ's victorious work on the cross, and, by speaking of it, mediates that work to those who believe, so that the gospel does its saving work in them. They are transferred from death to life

(John 5:24). This is the miracle that is even greater than the physical miracles Jesus did when he walked the earth (John 14:12; cf. 5:21–22), since it depends upon his epoch-turning resurrection and ascension. The word of the gospel looks weak and insignificant (1 Cor. 1:18 – 2:5), and yet is powerful enough to transfer people from the domain of darkness into the kingdom of the beloved Son (Col. 1:13). It is no surprise that the devil seeks to snatch this word away from people just as soon as they hear it (Mark 4:15), for it spells out his defeat. It is also clear, once again, that the word of the gospel delivers people from the devil's clutches *indirectly*, by removing their blindness and so bringing them to faith in Jesus Christ (2 Cor. 4:4–6).

The power of the gospel does not stop at conversion. The gospel continues to bring its soothing word to those struggling with their human weakness. The gospel works its power to transform lives by bringing the comfort and assurance of sins forgiven. There is no need to fear any more, because perfect love casts out fear (1 John 4:18), and we are no longer slaves, but sons (see Rom. 8:15). Any strategy or ministry or temptation or experience that reintroduces fear is not preaching the gospel. This can become a key 'test' of ministry: are we bringing the soothing balm of the gospel of sins forgiven? In the end, the gospel – and the comfort and the freedom it brings – is the only way towards human transformation (see 2 Cor. 3:17–18).

The key question that continues to face the believer throughout life in this suffering world therefore remains: in spite of what we see and in spite of what we might be experiencing, will we put our faith in Christ and believe that his gospel word will do its powerful work in our own lives and in the lives of others? This question becomes especially important when faced by the threat of the evil powers.

## Ministry in the midst of the powers of evil

### *Ministry basics: the Word of God and prayer*

The basics of Christian ministry are quite simple: the proclamation of the powerful Word of God, and prayer to God that he will continue to save people through it. Not only are people initially converted through the Word of God and prayer, but these are also the two instruments by which Christian congregations are brought to maturity.

### The methods of the devil are confronted in the whole of life

The writers of the NT were certainly well aware that 'the whole world lies in the power of the evil one' (1 John 5:19), and yet references to the evil powers lay mainly in the 'past' from their perspective since Jesus had dealt with the principalities and powers. The devil is defeated, even if still operating in the period of his blind rage before the end (cf. Rev. 12:12). The epistles, written in the light of Jesus' defeat of the powers found in the Gospels, contain no encouragement to engage with the devil directly. 'Spiritual Warfare' (Eph. 6:10–19; 1 Pet. 5:8–9 etc.) is a metaphor for the entire Christian life, rather than some narrowly conceived exorcistic practice. To hijack the biblical language of spiritual warfare into such a narrow application runs the danger of regarding evil as only present in 'dramatic' encounters, and of trivializing 'deliverance' by making it an event in which the baneful presence of evil powers is supposedly removed in an equally dramatic encounter. But what seems fairly clear in the NT is that the 'dramatic' encounters belong to the ministry of the Messiah and his immediate followers.

There is a more 'normal' or everyday way in which the devil operates, which is clearly indicated in the Gospels and Acts, but, unlike the 'dramatic' encounters, is also present in those documents that more directly address the continuing situation in which Christians live, this side of the resurrection day; that is, the epistles. Even though God always remains in charge and this world is his world, there is a sense in which it has been delivered over to Satan: 'the whole world lies in the power of the evil one' (1 John 5:19); 'to you I will give all this authority and their glory, for it has been delivered to me, and I give it to whom I will' (Luke 4:6); 'the ruler of this world' (John 12:31). The devil is not only in the 'dramatic', but also operates in the humdrum, mundane, routine features of ordinary life – including the things we know as 'culture'. What are the things that take people from God and distract them from his Word (cf. Mark 4:15)? Do these not include such things as wealth, marriage and family, business, concerns about status in society, pleasure-seeking, education and human wisdom, friends and other social relations, being busy with what to eat, drink and wear, attractive but false teaching that meets our own needs, and the like? If so, then here are Satan's 'methods' and 'schemes' (cf. 2 Cor. 2:11; Eph. 6:11) – easy to miss because they are all around us and so much a part of our lives.

### The whole Christian life is 'spiritual warfare'

With this backdrop, it is clear that when Ephesians talks about a 'spiritual warfare', it is referring to the Spirit-given ability to 'stand'; that is, to continue to live in Christ's new way, in the midst of the ordinary relationships of life. Living in the world that lies in the power of the evil one, people, until they come to Christ, cannot live properly (as God intended them to live). But once Christ brings his true deliverance, ordinary life becomes the sphere of sanctification, and 'spiritual warfare' means taking hold of the strength he supplies, in order to live for Christ. Given the context of this saying in Ephesians (the only explicit mention of 'spiritual warfare' in the NT), surely this phrase is speaking about the ongoing struggle to live Christ's 'spiritual life' in the midst of the ordinary, daily life of the Christian (see Eph. 4 – 6). This will therefore continue to rub the devil's nose in his own defeat.

The 'battle' that Christians find themselves caught up in, according to the same passage, is therefore, just like Christ's victorious battle beforehand, *indirect.* As Christians take hold of the wonderful provisions of God in the work of Jesus Christ, this is exactly the way they will defend themselves against the devil's methods. This is not a call to turn and face the devil in some fevered last-ditch battle; it is a call to live for Christ, believing the gospel word that the devil has been defeated, being constantly soothed by it, and entering into the new life for which Christ has already delivered us.

By finishing his letter with the dramatic image of a soldier preparing for battle, Paul is able to remind his readers of the apocalyptic perspective that the gospel brings to life. When Peter used his human wisdom to rebuke Jesus in that famous encounter on the road near Caesarea Philippi, he learned from Jesus' stinging counter-rebuke that such human thinking set him firmly on the side of Satan (Mark 8:33). Paul's 'spiritual warfare' passage emerges from the context of a long discussion about the new life given to believers in Christ, and reminds them that there is more to life than what simply meets the eye. There may be all kinds of human reasons for why life is difficult, and why it is so hard to get rid of sin and to transform relationships positively, but the battle does not stop there. It is essential to be 'strong in the Lord and in the strength of his might' because this world lies under the power of the evil one. There is another battle going on as we seek to live for Jesus: 'For we do not wrestle against flesh and blood, but against the rulers, against the authorities, against the cosmic powers over this present darkness, against the spiritual forces of evil in the heavenly places' (Eph. 6:12).

### This is a battle already won

In these last days Satan has been defeated and now turns against God's people in a blind rage, knowing his time is short (Rev. 12:12). There is no need to translate this battle into the kinds of encounters with unclean spirits that confronted Jesus from time to time in the Synoptic Gospels. Even there, we should notice that Jesus did not take the initiative, but the unclean spirits rose up against him. Certainly, when this happened, he swiftly and decisively dealt with them, but his focus even from the beginning of the Gospels was on the major battle he had come to fight upon the cross. This ultimate battle was also an indirect battle, for by paying for our sin and so removing the grounds of accusation that could legitimately be used against us by the devil (John 14:30), Jesus neutralized the devil's power. When the Son of God died on the cross, it was time for 'the ruler of this world' to be 'cast out' (John 12:31), and this spelled the defeat of the principalities and powers in the heavenly places as well (Col. 2:15).

If the Son of God defeated the devil *indirectly*, then it is no real surprise that our spiritual battle will also be fought *indirectly*. With Christ's victory behind us, the 'wrestling' that Paul encourages in Ephesians 6:12 does not involve a direct encounter with the devil – as if we are supposed to turn to face him, look him in the eye, directly address him by name, and call him out for a fight.

The only one we are to have direct and personal dealings with is the Lord Jesus Christ, as we take hold of his strength, and put on his armour, and stand with our eyes firmly fixed upon him. In this way, our battle with the forces of evil is *indirect*, since the major battle has already been fought on our behalf by the Lord Jesus Christ. And, as we continue to struggle with the 'world, the flesh and the devil', we do so by continuing to fix our eyes upon Jesus and taking hold of the various spiritual resources pictured in Ephesians 6:14–17 as the soldier's weaponry. This passage is not encouraging anyone to engage in the kinds of dramatic encounters with evil spirits that are found among the exorcists.[4] In fact, it is encouraging a far more powerful engagement with the evil powers, for as we speak the word of God, it is the very sword of the Spirit that is being wielded; and as we speak a word of prayer, we speak to the Lord of the entire universe and call him 'Father'. And, as we clothe ourselves with truth, righteousness, the gospel of peace, faith and salvation, this ministry of the Word of God and prayer will ensure that we stand, even against whatever flaming darts and evil methods the devil might throw at us. By taking hold of Christ's resources, the life of the Spirit will continue to be manifest in us (Eph. 4:17 – 6:9, esp. 5:18).

## Ministry as helping people see things God's way

### *The exposing of superstition*
Because it is shaped and directed by the one gospel, the basics of Christian ministry ought to be the same in any culture, whether it is exercised among people for whom the evil powers are an ever-present, consciously remembered reality, or among people who have drunk deeply from the wells of Western secularism. The Word of God and prayer are the essentials of Christian ministry at both ends of the spectrum, and at every point along it.

Both contexts are susceptible to different forms of the devil's methods. But whether at the 'obsessed with fear' end of the spectrum,

---

4. See e.g. the botched attempt in Acts 19:13–17.

or at the 'totally indifferent' end, a person needs to hear the word about Jesus and put his trust in him – for the first time and in an ongoing way. Those at one end need to hear that there is no reason to fear, for Christ has the victory already over the evil powers; those at the other end need to hear that there is a devil, who has held them in unwitting slavery, but, even if that is news to them, there is no need to fear, because Christ already has him defeated. The significance of his defeat for all people everywhere is that the devil no longer wields the power of death, but Christ has him neutralized. Those in Christ will one day finally be delivered from 'this body of death', and this hope of resurrection transforms life in the here and now.

It is easy for the Western secularist to declare animism to be 'superstition'. There is also a strong tradition within Protestantism that deals with the 'creepy spiritual side' (for want of a better term) of the world by declaring it to be superstitious, and/or denying that such things as ghosts (e.g.) exist, and denying that such things as necromancy (e.g.) actually work. This denial, however, is not a biblical one. Within the Scriptures ghosts and necromancy are not denied; they are simply warned against. God's people are not to engage the spirits of the dead, the underworld or even the devil, because God has spoken his word and it is sufficient to give guidance for all that we need to live for him in this world.

But the answer is not for Western secularists to become animists again – which is an implication that could be drawn, for example, from Paul Hiebert's influential essay 'The Flaw of the Excluded Middle'.[5] Instead, we need to realize that each end of the spectrum is actually a version of 'superstition'. The one sees an evil spirit in or under every stone, so to speak, and the secularist finds spiritual evil nowhere. Both are 'superstition', since both positions are not true to the reality of this world as explained by the word of God. There is no need for the 'secularist' to become an 'animist', just as there is no need for the 'animist' to become a 'secularist'. Both need to become Christians; both need to see the world God's way (cf. Mark 8:33).

Christian ministry should deal with people's perceptions of reality, even if those perceptions may not conform to reality, as

---

5. Hiebert, 'Flaw'.

described by God's Word. If people are afraid of the evil powers, then the gospel ministers to that fear. If people are deluded into thinking that there are no spiritual realities, then they do not need to learn about evil powers as the first step; they need to hear about Jesus Christ and respond to him. It is the news of his death and resurrection that shatters any confident dismissal of spiritual realities, and, in time, a proper understanding of those two great events will also bring an understanding of the evil powers defeated in them.

### Moving beyond 'weird experiences'

In a more animistic culture, people will already have their stories of encounters with evil powers, as well as their stories of how the local diviners and 'witch doctors' have been able to help those in distress in fairly dramatic ways. As Western culture retreats further from its Christian roots, it is becoming increasingly common to encounter those in Western society who have had all kinds of 'weird experiences', which they attribute to unseen spiritual forces. As the impact of the 'deliverance ministries' of the expansive charismatics is felt more within congregations of Christ's people, similar accounts of dramatic encounters with evil and equally dramatic 'rescues' from it are increasingly being spoken about. Such accounts become part of the repertoire of 'ministry experience' from which demonological information is then derived, so that further deliverance ministries can be encouraged.

Dramatic experiences are always gripping, and, certainly in the post-Enlightenment world of the West, there is a drive to domesticate such experiences by asking for an explanation. Those who have been involved themselves might well ask, 'How do you explain what happened to me?' For those who promote 'deliverance ministries' this becomes an endorsement of their approach. 'It is obviously from God, because look what happened here. How do you explain that?' This endorsement of certain practices by their dramatic results is, of course, the same kind of endorsement that a village witch doctor uses to give credibility to his own practices, as Hiebert himself noted during his time as a missionary.[6] In other

---

6. See ibid., 189–190.

words, this sounds very much like fighting the devil on his own terms, whereas, according to the apostle Paul, our weapons ought to be different – even though they appear 'weak' by comparison (2 Cor. 10:1–12; cf. 1 Cor. 1:18–25)!

Paul himself had a 'weird experience' in which he 'was caught up to the third heaven' (2 Cor. 12:2), but rather than using this experience to endorse his ministry by a recourse to 'power', he preferred to boast about nothing 'except of my weaknesses' (v. 5), for it is there that the grace of God is truly displayed. The only reason he mentioned his experience at all was because he was forced to enter such a foolish discussion by the foolishness of the 'super apostles' troubling the Corinthians! His preference, therefore, would have been to keep it to himself.

So, what do we do with the 'dramatic experiences' that have happened to us, by us or around us? And, if we remember the post-Enlightenment *rationalistic* drive to have intellectual satisfaction (or the *empirical-pragmatic* drive towards this being some kind of endorsement of certain practices), how are we going to explain this, or what are we going to do with it?

There is really no reason to deny weird experiences, nor is there reason to affirm them, or to explain them, or to give them any value as endorsements of anything. This is not the blasé attitude of a sceptic; it is the proper attitude of a believer. The Scriptures have no problems acknowledging that 'weird things' happen, and, as said above, they do not take the approach of denying the existence of unseen forces and beings. Instead, the biblical portrayal shows us how to live in a world with this kind of reality. The Scriptures are also clear that miracles, signs and other kinds of 'weird things' (e.g. the chirping and muttering of a medium in contact with the dead; see Isa. 8) are not to be taken as evidence or endorsement for anything, because these things can actually lead people astray (Deut. 13). The key questions at all times for the believer (whether in the face of secularism, animism or any variant along the spectrum) are, 'What does the Word of God say? What is it that I need to believe? What comfort do I find there? How can I live it out?'

The experience itself establishes nothing. What is important is how people respond to it. Does it fill them with fear? Does the mystery of being unable to explain it give them anxiety? Ministers of the gospel may not be able to explain the experience, but they do know the answer to the real pastoral issue: there is no need to fear. Jesus is in charge. He already has the victory. In Christ nothing can ever separate us from the love of God – nothing in this world, nothing in the next, and no evil power. We are secure. We need to take our eyes off this weird experience, and keep turning our eyes to Jesus.

### What about New Testament instructions on dealing with the devil?

Proper consideration of a biblical theme, such as the relationship of Christian ministry and evil powers, must consider texts that appear to address it directly. When the NT is surveyed, there are surprisingly few direct instructions in regard to dealing with the devil – seven only in fact: (1) married couples are warned against abstaining from sex, lest the devil takes opportunity of their lack of connection[7] to tempt them (1 Cor. 7:5); (2) the Ephesians are instructed not to sin in their anger, and so (presumably) not to give a place for the devil in the midst of their congregation (Eph. 4:27, 'opportunity'); (3) they are instructed to put on the whole armour of God, so that they might stand firm against the methods of the devil (Eph. 6:11); (4) they are instructed to take up 'the shield of faith', which will enable the extinguishing of the evil one's darts (Eph. 6:16; cf. Ps. 91:5); (5) James calls upon his readers to submit to God, and to resist the devil, with the promise that he will flee (Jas 4:7); (6) Peter urges watchfulness, because of the devil's penchant to wander around like a lion seeking some prey (1 Pet. 5:8); and (7) John warns his readers to love and not to be like Cain, who belonged to the evil one (1 John 3:12).[8]

---

7. Despite the English translations, rather than 'lack of self-control' (which would be *akrateia*), the word Paul uses here (*akrasia*, 'bad mixture') denotes the lack of being joined. In other words, the source of temptation comes from the objective circumstances of the couples' lack of sexual coupling, rather than some weakness within them as individuals.

8. These imperatives are not intended to promote any kind of direct encounter with Satan, but encourage dealing with the temptation that

In addition to those promises in regard to the devil attached to the imperatives alluded to above (that, 'armoured up', we will stand against his methods, that he will flee as we resist and that faith will extinguish his darts), there are two more: Paul tells the Romans that God will soon crush Satan under their feet (Rom. 16:20; cf. Ps. 91:13), and the Thessalonians learn that, because the Lord is faithful, he will both establish and guard them from the evil one (2 Thess. 3:3; cf. John 17:15 and 1 John 5:18).

### Do not address the devil: talk to your own Father!

In all of the above instructions about the devil, it is notable that there is no call to confront the devil, to conduct exorcisms, to be exorcised or for any direct dealings with the devil at all. It is particularly noteworthy that there is no call to address the devil directly, and, in fact, to do so runs counter to Jesus' (and Paul's) silencing of the demons.[9] This means that there is no biblical justification at all for the practice in some 'deliverance ministries' of directly conversing with evil spirits. The few occasions when Jesus addressed spirits directly (Mark 1:25; 3:12; 5:7–13; 9:25) – and it is also worth remembering that he had no need to do so at all (see Mark 7:29) – do not provide a precedent for Christian practice, since this was part of the 'works of the Messiah' (Matt. 11:2 my tr.), and Christians are not the Messiah.[10] As noted above,

---

Footnote 8 (*cont.*)

   comes about by our own desires, because of believing the lie. See West's
   chapter (8) in this volume.

9. See the discussion in Bolt's chapter (2) in this volume.

10. The same may also be said about the references in the book of Acts to evil
    spirits being cast out. Acts has only five accounts involving evil spirits (5:15–
    16; 8:6–7; 16:16–18; 19:11–12, 13–17). The only instance of the casting out
    of an evil spirit is when Paul reluctantly dealt with an annoying spirit in Acts
    16:16–18. Comparison of Paul's words in Acts 16:18 with those of Jesus in
    Luke 4:33–34 and 8:28–29 (and others) indicates a parallel is being drawn,
    perhaps validating Paul's apostolic ministry alongside that of the Twelve. In
    any case, from Acts and from Paul's own letters, casting out spirits is clearly
    not a feature of Paul's ministry. This instance represents the last reference to

the instructions about dealing with the devil that are found in the
epistles (i.e. in the parts of the Scriptures most directly addressed
to ordinary Christian people) give no warrant at all for addressing
demons.

This also rules out the new perspective of charismatic prayer
language referred to by Nigel Wright, for example, that

> is now to be addressed not only *to God* but *against* those forces which are
> ranged against him, limiting and annulling their power and influence.
> Prayer involves identifying and binding the enemy. It is a form of warfare.
> Intercession becomes a specialist ministry in which the intercessor acts as a
> warrior on the front-line, doing battle with evil powers in Christ's name.[11]

We have been granted, as the children of God, the magnificent
privilege of calling the God of the universe 'Abba! Father!' (Rom.
8:15; Gal. 4:6; cf. Mark 14:36), so why would we not step firmly
'into this grace in which we stand' (Rom. 5:2)?[12] We should always
address God, never the devil, his minions or anyone else. This is
condemned indirectly in the OT prohibitions against divination and
necromancy, and perhaps best summarized by Isaiah's question

> And when they say to you, 'Inquire of the mediums and the
> necromancers who chirp and mutter,' should not a people inquire of
> their God? Should they inquire of the dead on behalf of the living? To
> the teaching and to the testimony! If they will not speak according to this
> word, it is because they have no dawn. (Isa. 8:19–20)

The only spirit being who is to be addressed by God's people is
God himself. Prayer is to the one who invites us into his presence
and promises answers. The language of 'praying against' may have
once been an example of dramatic rhetoric, but it should now be

---

> such practice in the book of Acts, apart from the botched exorcism attempt
> in Acts 19, which, being based around ancient exorcism, does not provide
> any precedent or analogy for Christian ministry.

11. Wright, 'Charismatic Interpretations', 160 (emphasis added).

12. See West's chapter (8) in this volume.

dispensed with altogether, because the rhetoric has taken over and become reality for many.

## Not intellectual satisfaction, but existential assurance: some case studies

Given the Scriptures do not give us sufficient information about the devil to get a clear picture, there will always be questions that we would like to have a more satisfactory answer to, intellectually. But we must not allow such questions to sidetrack us into wrong practice. Even if the Scriptures do not answer all of our *intellectual questions* about the devil, what is revealed about Jesus Christ is more than enough to answer our *existential situation* of living in a world given over to the power of the evil one.

In fact, it is essential to get used to living with the tension of not enough information, and to forget some of the questions that keep on doing the rounds. Such questions will take us nowhere (because the Scriptures are not clear enough to answer them). We must also continue to recognize that the Scriptures have their own questions to answer, and we must be prepared to sit under the scriptural lead. It is possible to get sidetracked by our own intellectual questions and so to miss the existential questions and answers given by Christ in his gospel. The gospel tells of our bondage to sin, of Christ's victory, and of the security we have in Christ. The gospel removes us from fear and brings us the assurance of God's love.

Thus we have derived a key ministry strategy when faced with serious questions about demons and the devil: the gospel may not answer our intellectual questions, but it addresses our existential need for removal of fear and establishment of security. Some examples may help us to see what this kind of principle looks like in practice.

### Avoiding the side-track, and embracing assurance
First, to illustrate how the need for intellectually satisfying answers can hijack proper Christian ministry, we can cite the oft-asked question 'Can a Christian be demon-possessed?' This is a question that holds much fascination for many, and the answers bounce

backwards and forwards and (at least as it seems from watching this ball being batted around for over thirty years) not much progress has been made with answers, and even the question seems to have been modified ('perhaps not possessed, but what about *demonized?*').

It is a principle drawn from the Enlightenment that we are able to think all things out with the pure light of reason. It is rather strange, therefore, to so often encounter the post-Enlightenment drive towards 'intellectually satisfying answers' when it comes to spiritual – or demonic, as the case may be – issues. Now it certainly seems *logical*, and even biblical and *theological*, that 'the Lord is the Spirit, and where the Spirit of the Lord is, there is freedom' (2 Cor. 3:17) – so how could a Christian ever be possessed, or even *demonized* (however that might be defined)? But, in the current climate created by the expansive charismatics, this *logical* (theological/biblical) answer will immediately be countered with an *experiential* answer, whether from the 'ministry experience' of those in 'deliverance ministries', or (and far more tragically) from those who have been their victims. ('But, what happened to me? A demon was cast out of me? How do you explain that?')

It is a principle drawn from the fact that Christian faith arises only from God's revelation that we can only *say* clearly what has been *revealed* clearly. Where there is a silence in the revelation, or where information is only partially given, then we cannot say much. There are two kinds of things in the universe, the 'secret things' that 'belong to the LORD our God', and the 'things that are revealed', which 'belong to us and to our children for ever' (Deut. 29:29). Not everything has been revealed, so no matter how hard we think about these things, they may remain inaccessible to us. On the other hand, the things that are revealed belong to us and – as the verse goes on to say – they have a very practical orientation: 'that we might do them'. This, too, gives us a great deal of guidance for pastoral practice.

If God's Word does *not* answer our questions, then the believer should realize that this matter is not something we need to know in order to live for God in this world. The next (and more important) question therefore becomes 'What is the practical issue behind the supposedly "intellectual" question?' To return to our example,

when people ask about Christians being possessed (either aca-
demically or for the purpose of explaining their own experience),
the underlying issue is most likely anxiety or fear at the terrible
prospect of becoming, or being, one of Satan's victims. Now, once
the fear behind the question is exposed, we can ask the pastoral
question 'How does the gospel minister to this person who has
this fear?' As we ask the question, we realize it is easy to answer.
The gospel proclaims that the devil is defeated, that the devil's
power has been neutralized, that Christ is installed (for our sake!)
high above any powers, that nothing can separate us from the love
of God in Christ, and no one can snatch us out of the Father's
hand, and more and more and more! We also realize that 'perfect
love casts out fear' (1 John 4:18) and we have been made children
of God and therefore that 'you did not receive the spirit of slavery
to fall back into fear, but you have received the Spirit of adoption
as sons, by whom we cry, "Abba! Father!"' (Rom. 8:15). Profound
comfort is found in the victory of Christ, and this is what needs
to be applied to this situation, and, along with the Word of God
should go a prayer or two, thanking the heavenly Father for our
security, and praying that he will continue to keep us in his hand.

### Avoiding the quick fix, and heading for the resurrection day

As a second example, we can return to the struggle with which
this chapter opened. Until Jesus comes again, Christian people will
continue to experience a struggle between the old and the new;
the flesh and the spirit; the desires of the body and the prompt-
ings of the Spirit; the ever-present reality of this world, and the
promise of the next; the sufferings of this age, and the hint of the
glories to come. This is a daily experience and the gospel needs to
be firmly inserted into this daily struggle, with the gentle reminder
to keep on believing it, and plenty of prayer that God will supply
the strength required to persevere until the end. Pastors need to be
alert to the 'quick fix' alternatives, and eschew them; teach against
them; not get caught up in them themselves. In the present climate
there is a special danger as people are being told that the struggle is
a sign of demonic oppression, or demonization, or certain kinds of
demons clinging to them for various reasons. The only thing such
suggestions achieve is to generate further fear; and if that is the

outcome, then this is not the gospel of Christ at work. The gospel banishes fear and brings comfort based upon the victory of Christ. The struggle is always there, but it does not mean the devil has got you: Christ has defeated the devil! In fact, in a strange turnaround that pastors should constantly remind their people about, as the struggle intensifies, it is probably the work of the Spirit himself, convicting of sin, moving towards sanctification, causing the Christian heart to long for the day of resurrection. Once again the pastoral strategy is clear: the comforting Word of God, which tells of Christ's victory; the comforting experience of prayer, as we make our requests known to our loving heavenly Father. And then, more of the same tomorrow!

### *Do not fear a godlike devil, but fix your eyes on Jesus, and rejoice in the absence of fear!*

For the third example, we can consider the element of demonic distraction, which is even reported by those encouraging 'deliverance ministry'.

It is the task of the Christian life to 'lay aside every weight, and sin which clings so closely, and let us run with endurance the race that is set before us, looking to Jesus, the founder and perfecter of our faith' (Heb. 12:1–2). It is the task of the Christian minister to keep directing people to Jesus, and encouraging them to fix their eyes on him.

Not much is said in Scripture about the various methods by which the devil seeks to influence people, but it seems clear from Jesus' own temptation (Matt. 4:9) and from the way the beasts work in Revelation 13, that one of his major moves is to draw people to worship him, rather than the Father. As one who can disguise himself as 'an angel of light' (2 Cor. 11:14), who owns 'all the kingdoms of the world and their glory' (Matt. 4:8) and one who appeals to what is 'a delight to the eyes' (Gen. 3:6), he can certainly be attractive. It is interesting to notice how quickly people can become absorbed by such a 'fascinating topic' as the devil or demons. And if there are some spectacular occurrences thrown in, or if something inexplicable actually happens to you, then it is easy to get hooked. The eyes are taken off Jesus and placed upon the devil and his works.

This is the effect of having the kind of dualistic or semi-dualistic views of the devil that are all too common in charismatic discussions and approaches. It certainly adds apocalyptic drama to speak of the great 'battle' between God and the devil, but it is unscriptural to depict this battle as if the contestants are evenly pitched, or as if its outcome is unknown, or as if the battle has not already been won by Jesus on the cross.

It is also easy to lapse into what might be called 'de facto dualism'. Because we were made to live in God's world, our minds readily bend towards the way that God's world works, and so it is all too easy to speak of the devil in the same categories as we do God – with the only difference being that we place him on the 'bad' side, whereas God is placed on the side of the 'good'. But just because God works with order and arrangement, why do we think the devil should be orderly, with a hierarchical kingdom? Just because God has plans and purposes, why do we think that the devil works to a plan in the same way? God has traditionally been described as all powerful, all knowing and present in all places, but why should we think the devil also possesses those attributes?

The minimal information given in the Scriptures about the devil and demons is instructive at this point. We are not told about him, because we do not need to know much about him. He is a defeated enemy. In the Son of God we have a champion who not only *has* dealt with him, but who will continue to deal with him on our behalf. Our eyes need to be fixed upon Jesus, not looking at the devil. Our words need to be directed to the heavenly Father in prayer, not spoken to a demon whom we think is troubling us. We must not be distracted, for to wallow in the mud only leaves us in the mud. We have a Saviour, and are firmly placed in the Father's hand. That is where our eyes, our ears, our attentions need to be constantly fixed – and the devil will fall into his own place. There is no need to fear the evil powers any more. Not ever. The victory already belongs to Jesus Christ.

# BIBLIOGRAPHY

Adams, E. (2000), *Constructing the World: A Study in Paul's Cosmological Language*, Studies of the New Testament and its World (Edinburgh: T. & T. Clark).

Alexander, D., and D. W. Baker (eds.) (2003), *Dictionary of the Old Testament Pentateuch* (Downers Grove and Leicester: IVP).

Allison, D. C., Jr. (1985), *The End of the Ages Has Come: An Early Interpretation of the Passion and Resurrection of Jesus*, Studies of the New Testament and its World (Edinburgh: T. & T. Clark).

Allo, P. E. B. (1956), *Saint Paul: Seconde épître aux Corinthiens*, Études bibliques (Paris: Beauchesne).

Anderson, N. T. (2000), *The Bondage Breaker*, 2nd ed. (Eugene, Oreg.: Harvest House).

Anderson, N. T., and T. M. Warner (2000), *The Beginner's Guide To Spiritual Warfare: Using Your Spiritual Weapons, Defending Your Family, Recognizing Satan's Lies* (Ann Arbor: Servant).

Anderson, P. (2007), 'Why This Study Is Needed and Why It Is Needed Now', in P. N. Anderson, F. Just, S. J. Thatcher and T. Thatcher (eds.), *Jesus, John, and History*. Vol. 1: *Critical Appraisals Of Critical Views* (Atlanta: Society of Biblical Literature), 13–67.

Arnold, C. E. (1992), *Ephesians, Power and Magic: The Concept of Power in Ephesians in Light of its Historical Setting* (Grand Rapids: Baker).

Athanasius (1971), *De Gentes* and *De Incarnatione*, ed. R. W. Thomson, Oxford Early Christian Texts (Oxford: Clarendon).

Aune, D. E. (1999), 'Archai', in Van der Toorn, Becking and Van der Horst, *Dictionary of Deities and Demons*, 77–80.

— (2001), 'Prayer in the Greco-Roman World', in R. N. Longenecker (ed.), *Into God's Presence: Prayer in the New Testament* (Grand Rapids: Eerdmans), 23–42.

Bailey, C. (n.d.), *Some Greek and Roman Ideas of a Future Life*, Occasional Papers of Classical Association 3 (Cambridge: Cambridge University Press, publication of 1915 lecture).

Barnett, P. W. (1997), *The Second Epistle to the Corinthians*, New International Commentary on the New Testament (Grand Rapids: Eerdmans).

Barrett, C. K. (1978), *The Gospel according to John: An Introduction with Commentary and Notes on the Greek Text* (London: SPCK).

Barth, K. (1941), *A Letter to Great Britain from Switzerland* (London: Sheldon).

— (1956), *Church Dogmatics* IV.1: *The Doctrine of Reconciliation*, tr. G. W. Bromiley, ed. G. W. Bromiley and T. F. Torrance (Edinburgh: T. & T. Clark).

— (1958), *Church Dogmatics* IV.2 *The Doctrine of Reconciliation*, tr. G. W. Bromiley, ed. G. W. Bromiley and T. F. Torrance (Edinburgh: T. & T. Clark).

— (1976), *Church Dogmatics* III.3: *The Doctrine of Creation*, tr. G. W. Bromiley and R. J. Ehrlich (Edinburgh: T. & T. Clark).

— (2002), *Prayer*, ed. D. E. Saliers, tr. S. F. Terrien (Louisville: Westminster John Knox).

— (2004), *Church Dogmatics* IV.4: *The Christian Life. Lecture Fragments*, tr. G. W. Bromiley (London: T. & T. Clark International).

Barth, M. (1974), *Ephesians: A New Translation with Introduction and Commentary*, Anchor Bible 34, 34A (Garden City, N.Y.: Doubleday).

Basham, D. (1972), *Deliver Us From Evil* (Old Tappan: Fleming H. Revell).

Bauckham, R. (1998), 'For Whom Were the Gospels Written?', in R. Bauckham (ed.), *The Gospels for All Christians: Rethinking the Gospel Audiences* (Edinburgh: T. & T. Clark), 9–48.

Bauer, W. (2000), *A Greek-English Lexicon of the New Testament and Other Early Christian Literature*, rev. and ed. F. W. Danker, 3rd ed. (Chicago: University of Chicago Press).

Beasley-Murray, G. R. (1987), *John*, Word Biblical Commentary 36 (Dallas: Word).

Belle, G. van (1994), *The Signs Source in the Fourth Gospel: Historical Survey and Critical Evaluation of the Semeia Hypothesis*, Bibliotheca ephemeridum theologicarum lovaniensium 116 (Leuven: Leuven University Press).

Benedict, H. (2002), *St. John Chrysostom: The Devil and Magic*, tr. C. Hatzidimitriou, 2nd ed. (New Skiti, Greece: Attendants of Hiermonk Spyridon).

Berkhof, H. (1977), *Christ and the Powers*, 2nd ed. (Scottdale, Pa.: Herald).

Best, E. (1998), *A Critical and Exegetical Commentary on Ephesians*, International Critical Commentary (Edinburgh: T. & T. Clark).

Betz, H. D. (1992), 'Introduction to the Greek Magical Papyri', in *The Greek Magical Papyri in Translation Including the Demotic Spells*, 2nd ed. (Chicago: University of Chicago Press), xli–liii.

— (ed.) (1992), *The Greek Magical Papyri in Translation, Including the Demotic Spells*, 2nd ed. (Chicago: Chicago University Press).

Blass, F., and A. Debrunner (1961), *A Greek Grammar of the New Testament and Other Early Christian Literature*, tr. R. W. Funk (Chicago: University of Chicago Press).

Blocher, H. A. G. (2000), 'Evil', in T. D. Alexander and B. S. Rosner (eds.), *New Dictionary of Biblical Theology* (Leicester: IVP), 465–467.

— (2002), 'Agnus Victor: The Atonement as Victory and Vicarious Punishment', in J. G. Stackhouse (ed.), *What Does It Mean to Be Saved? Broadening Evangelical Horizons of Salvation* (Grand Rapids: Baker), 67–91.

— (2004), 'Justification of the Ungodly (*Sola Fide*): Theological Reflections', in Carson, O'Brien and Seifrid, *Justification and Variegated Nomism*, 2: 465–500.

Boardman, W. (1857), *The Higher Christian Life* (New York: Garland, repr. 1984).

Bolt, P. G. (1996), 'Jesus, Daimons and the Dead', in A. N. S. Lane (ed.), *The Unseen World: Christian Reflections on Angels, Demons and the Heavenly Realm* (Carlisle: Paternoster; Grand Rapids: Baker), 75–102.

— (1998), '"With a View to the Forgiveness of Sins": Jesus and Forgiveness in Mark's Gospel', *Reformed Theological Review* 57.2: 53–69.

— (2003), *Jesus' Defeat of Death. Persuading Mark's Early Readers*, Society for New Testament Studies Monograph Series 125 (Cambridge: Cambridge University Press).

— (2006), 'Interpreting Australian Society for Christian Mission', in B. L. Kaye (ed.), *'Wonderful and Confessedly Strange': Australian Essays in Anglican Ecclesiology* (Adelaide, SA: ATF), 293–313.

— (2007), *Living with the Underworld* (Kingsford, NSW: Matthias Media).

Bonhoeffer, D. (1997), *Creation and Fall; Temptation: Two Biblical Studies*, tr. J. C. Fletcher and K. Downham (New York: Touchstone).

Bos, R. (1988), 'The Dreaming and Social Change in Arnhem Land', in T. Swain and D. Bird Rose (eds.), *Aboriginal Australians and Christian Mission* (Bedford Park, SA: Australian Association for the Study of Religions), 422–437.

Boyce, M. (ed. and trans.) (1984), *Textual Sources for the Study of Zoroastrianism* (Manchester: Manchester University Press).

Brown, D. (1978), *Understanding Pietism* (Grand Rapids: Eerdmans).

Brown, R. E. (1966, 1970), *The Gospel according to John: A New Translation with Text and Commentary*, Anchor Bible 29, 29A (Garden City, N.Y.: Doubleday).

— (1982), *The Epistles of John: Translated with Introduction, Notes, and Commentary*, Anchor Bible 30 (Garden City, N.Y.: Doubleday).

Brunon, J.-B., and P. Grelot (1973), 'Evil Spirits', in Léon-Dufour, *Dictionary of Biblical Theology*, 149–150.

Caird, G. B. (1956), *Principalities and Powers: A Study in Pauline Theology* (Oxford: Clarendon).

Calvin, J. (1960), *Institutes of the Christian Religion*, tr. F. L. Battles, ed. J. T. McNeill (Philadelphia: Westminster).

— (1965), *The Epistles of Paul the Apostle to the Galatians, Ephesians, Philippians and Colossians*, Calvin's New Testament Commentaries 11, tr. T. H. L. Parker, ed. D. W. Torrance and T. F. Torrance (Grand Rapids: Eerdmans).

Carson, D. A. (1991), *The Gospel according to John* (Grand Rapids: Eerdmans).

— (2004), 'The Vindication of Imputation: On Fields of Discourse and Semantic Fields', in M. Husbands and D. J. Trier (eds.), *What's at Stake in the Current Debates* (Downers Grove: IVP), 46–78.

Carson, D. A., P. T. O'Brien and M. A. Seifrid (eds.) (2004), *Justification and Variegated Nomism*. Vol. 2: *The Paradoxes of Paul*, Wissenschaftliche Untersuchungen zum Neuen Testament 2.181 (Tübingen: Mohr Siebeck).

Catholic Church (1994), *Catechism of the Catholic Church* (Homebush, NSW: St Pauls).

Chajes, J. H. (2003), *Between Worlds: Dybbuks, Exorcists, and Early Modern Judaism* (Philadelphia: University of Pennsylvania).

Charles, R. H. (1913), *The Apocrypha and Pseudepigrapha of the Old Testament in English*, 2 vols. (Oxford: Clarendon).

Chavalas, M. W. (1996), 'Magic', in Elwell, *Evangelical Dictionary of Biblical Theology*, 502–503.

Clarke, P. A. (2007), 'Indigenous Spirit and Ghost Folklore of "Settled" Australia', *Folklore* 118: 141–161.

Clifford, R. J. (1972), *The Cosmic Mountain in Canaan and the Old Testament*, Harvard Semitic monographs 4 (Cambridge, Mass.: Harvard University Press).

Clines, D. J. A. (1979), 'The Significance of the "Sons of God" Episode', *Journal for the Study of the Old Testament* 4: 1333–1346.

Coetzee, J. C. (1968), 'Christ and the Prince of This World in the Gospel and the Epistles of St. John', *Neotestamentica* 2: 104–121.

Cornford, F. M. (1924), 'Greek Views of Immortality', in J. Marchant (ed.), *Immortality* (London: Putnam), 15–38.

Cox, R. L. (1969), *The Four-Square Gospel* (Los Angeles: Foursquare).

Cunningham, L. (1994), 'Satan: A Theological Meditation', *Theology Today* 51: 3359–3366.

Daly, G. (1994), 'Creation and Original Sin (paragraphs 268–421)', in M. J. Walsh (ed.), *Commentary on the Catechism of the Catholic Church* (St Paul, Minn.: Liturgical), 82–111.

Dawson, J. (1991), *Taking our Cities for God: How to Break Spiritual Strongholds* (Milton Keynes: Word).

— (1994), *Healing America's Wounds* (Ventura: Regal).

Day, P. L. (1999), 'Satan, I–III', in Van der Toorn, Becking and Van der Horst, *Dictionary of Deities and Demons*, 726–732.

Dayton, D. (1987), *Theological Roots of Pentecostalism* (Metuchen: Scarecrow).

Delling, G. (1972), '*treis, tris, tritos*', in Kittel and Friedrich, *Theological Dictionary of the New Testament*, 8: 216–225.

Dieter, M. E. (1987), 'The Wesleyan Perspective', in M. E. Dieter (ed.), *Five Views on Sanctification* (Grand Rapids: Zondervan), 11–46.

Dio Cassius (1925), *Roman Histories*, vol. 8, Loeb Classical Library, tr. E. Cary (London: W. Heinemann; Cambridge, Mass.: Harvard University Press, repr. 1968).

Diogenes Laertius (1931), *Lives of Eminent Philosophers*, vol. 2, Loeb Classical Library, rev. ed.; tr. R. D. Hicks (Cambridge, Mass.: Harvard University Press, repr. 1991).

Doxtater, M. G. (2004), 'Indigenous Knowledge in the Decolonial Era', *American Indian Quarterly* 28.3: 4618–4633.

Doyle, R. C. (1999), *Eschatology and the Shape of Christian Belief* (Carlisle: Paternoster, repr. 2000).

Duling, D. C. (1975), 'Solomon, Exorcism, and the Son of David', *Harvard Theological Review* 68.3–4: 235–253.

Dunnett, W. M. (1996), 'Powers', in Elwell, *Evangelical Dictionary of Biblical Theology*, 619–620.

Dunnett, W. M. (1996), 'Satan', in Elwell, *Evangelical Dictionary of Biblical Theology*, 714–715.

Eckhardt, A. R. (1994), 'Between the Angelic and the Diabolic', *Theology Today* 51.3: 405–415.

Elgvin, T. (2000), 'Belial, Beliar, Devil, Satan', in Evans and Porter, *Dictionary of New Testament Background*, 153–157.

Ellingworth, P. (1993), *The Epistle to the Hebrews: A Commentary on the Greek Text* (Grand Rapids: Eerdmans).

Elwell, W. A. (ed.) (1996), *Evangelical Dictionary of Biblical Theology* (Grand Rapids: Baker).

Engelsviken, T. (2008), 'Spiritual Conflict: A Challenge for the Church in the West with a View to the Future', in Van Engen, Whiteman and Woodberry, *Paradigm Shifts in Christian Witness*, 116–125.

Engen, C. E. van, D. Whiteman and J. D. Woodberry (eds.) (2008), *Paradigm Shifts in Christian Witness: Insights from Anthropology, Communication, and Spiritual Power. Essays in Honor of Charles H. Kraft* (Maryknoll: Orbis).

Eslinger, L. (1979), 'A Contextual Identification of the *bene ha'elohim* and *benoth ha'adam* in Genesis 6:1–4', *Journal for the Study of the Old Testament* 13: 65–73.

Evans, C. A., and S. E. Porter (eds.) (2000), *Dictionary of New Testament Background* (Downers Grove and Leicester: IVP).

Fee, G. D. (1994), *God's Empowering Presence: The Holy Spirit in the Letters of Paul* (Peabody, Mass.: Hendrickson).

Ferdinando, K. (1999), *The Triumph of Christ in African Perspective. A Study of Demonology and Redemption in the African Context* (Exeter: Paternoster).

Ferguson, E. (1984), *Demonology of the Early Christian World*, Symposium Series 12 (New York: Edward Mellen).

Fletcher, J. (1876), *Five Checks to Antinomianism*, vol. 5 (London: Wesleyan Conference Office).

Forsyth, N. (1987), *The Old Enemy: Satan and the Combat Myth* (Princeton: Princeton University Press).

Fossum, J. (1999), 'Simon Magus', in Van der Toorn, Becking and Van der Horst, *Dictionary of Deities and Demons*, 779–781.

Francke, A. M. (1909), *Faith in Christ, Inconsistent with a Solicitous Concern about the Things of This World*, tr. Joseph Downing (London: Downing).

Freedman, D. N. (ed.) (1992), *Anchor Bible Dictionary*, 6 vols. (Garden City, N.Y.: Doubleday).

Furnish, V. P. (1984), *2 Corinthians: A New Translation with Introduction and Commentary*, Anchor Bible 32A (Garden City, N.Y.: Doubleday).

Gaffin, R. B. (2008), 'Justification and Union with Christ: *Institutes* 3.11–18', in D. W. Hall and P. A. Lillback (eds.), *Theological Guide to Calvin's Institutes: Essays and Analysis* (Phillipsburg: Presbyterian & Reformed), 248–269.

Garcia, M. A. (2008), *Life in Christ: Union with Christ and Twofold Grace in Calvin's Theology* (Carlisle: Paternoster).

Garde, M. (2007), CD notes to *Wurrurrumi Kun-Borrk: Songs from Western Arnhem Land by Kevin Djimarr. The Indigenous Music of Australia CD 1* (Sydney: Sydney University Press).

Gaston, L. (1962), 'Beelzeboul', *Theologische Zeitschrift* 18: 247–255.

Gnanakan, C. (2007), 'The Manthiravadi: A South Indian Wounded Warrior-Healer', in Riddell and Riddell, *Angels and Demons*, 140–157.

Goldsworthy, G. L. (1991), *According to Plan* (Leicester: IVP).

Green, L. C. (1980), *How Melanchthon Helped Luther Discover the Gospel: The Doctrine of Justification in the Reformation* (Fallbrook, Calif.: Verdict).

Grundmann, W. (1965), '*kartereō, proskartereō, proskarterēsis*', in Kittel and Friedrich, *Theological Dictionary of the New Testament*, 3: 617–620.

Gudorf, M. E. (1998), 'The Use of *palē* in Ephesians 6:12', *Journal of Biblical Literature* 114: 331–335.

Gundry, R. H. (2002), *Jesus the Word according to John the Sectarian: a Palaeofundamentalist Manifesto for Contemporary Evangelicalism, Especially Its Elites in North America* (Grand Rapids: Eerdmans).

— (2004), 'The Nonimputation of Christ's Righteousness', in M. Husbands and D. J. Trier (eds.), *What's at Stake in the Current Debates* (Downers Grove: IVP), 17–45.

Hagan, G. M. (1996), 'Divination', in Elwell, *Evangelical Dictionary of Biblical Theology*, 182–183.

Hammond, F. (1973), *Pigs in the Parlor: A Practical Guide to Deliverance* (Kirkwood: Impact).

Hardesty, N. (2003), *Faith Cure: Divine Healing in the Holiness and Pentecostal Movements* (Peabody: Hendricksen).

Harford, C. (1907), *The Keswick Convention: Its Message, Its Method and Its Men* (London: Marshall).

Harink, D. (2003), *Paul Among the Postliberals: Pauline Theology Beyond Christendom and Modernity* (Grand Rapids: Brazos).

Helm, P. (2004), *Calvin's Ideas* (Oxford: Oxford University Press).

Henten, J. W. van (1999), 'Mastema', in Van der Toorn, Becking and Van der Horst, *Dictionary of Deities and Demons*, 553–554.

Herrmann, W. (1999), 'Baal-Zebub', in Van der Toorn, Becking and Van der Horst, *Dictionary of Deities and Demons*, 154–156.

Heuvel, A. H. van den (1966), *These Rebellious Powers* (London: SCM).

Hiebert, P. G. (1994), 'The Flaw of the Excluded Middle', in *Anthropological Perspectives on Missiological Issues* (Grand Rapids: Baker), 189–201 (originally published in *Missiology* 10.1 [1982]: 35–47).

— (2000), 'Spiritual Warfare and Worldview', in W. D. Taylor (ed.), *Global Missiology for the 21st Century: The Iguassu Dialogue* (Grand Rapids: Baker), 163–178.

Holl, K. (1927), 'Luthers Bedeutung für den Fortschritt der Auslegungskunst', in *Gesammelte Aufsätze zur Kirchengeschichte*. Vol. 1: *Luther* (Tübingen: Mohr Siebeck), 544–582.

Hooker, M. D. (1973), 'Were There False Teachers in Colossae?', in B. Lindars and S. S. Smalley (eds.), *Christ and Spirit in the New Testament*, Festschrift for C. F. D. Moule (Cambridge: Cambridge University Press). 315–331.

Horrobin, P. (1991–5), *Healing through Deliverance*. Vol. 1: *The Foundation of Deliverance Ministry*; Vol. 2: *The Practice of Deliverance Ministry* (Chichester: Sovereign World).

Horton, M. S. (2007), *Covenant and Salvation: Union with Christ* (Louisville: Westminster John Knox).

Hutter, M. (1999), 'Asmodeus', in Van der Toorn, Becking and Van der Horst, *Dictionary of Deities and Demons*, 106–108.

Hwa, Y. (1997), *Mangoes and Bananas: The Quest for an Authentic Asian Christian Theology*, Regnum Studies in Mission (Oxford: Regnum).

Jenkins, P. (2002), *The Next Christendom: The Coming of Global Christianity* (New York: Oxford University Press).

Jobes, K. H. (2005), *1 Peter*, Baker Exegetical Commentary on the New Testament (Grand Rapids: Baker).

Judd, C. (1880), *The Prayer of Faith* (Buffalo: H. H. Otis).

Jüngel, E. (2001), *Justification: The Heart of the Christian Faith*, tr. J. F. Cayzer (Edinburgh: T. & T. Clark).

Kay, W. K. (2007), 'Pentecostals and Angels', in Riddell and Riddell, *Angels and Demons*, 63–83.

Keen, I. (1994), *Knowledge and Secrecy in Aboriginal Religion* (Melbourne: Oxford University Press).

Kittel, G., and G. Friedrich (eds.) (1964–76), *Theological Dictionary of the New Testament*, tr. G. W. Bromiley, 10 vols. (Grand Rapids: Eerdmans).

Knight, J. A. (1978), 'John Fletcher's Influence on the Development of Wesleyan Theology in America', *Wesleyan Theological Journal* 13 (spring): 13–33.

Koehler, L. (1957), *Old Testament Theology*, tr. A. S. Todd, 3rd ed. (London: Lutterworth).

Kooten, G. H. van (2003), *Cosmic Christology in Paul and the Pauline School: Colossians and Ephesians in the Context of Graeco-Roman Cosmology, with a New*

*Synopsis of the Greek Texts*, Wissenschaftliche Untersuchungen zum Neuen Testament 2.171 (Tübingen: Mohr Siebeck).

Köstenberger, A. J. (1998), *The Missions of Jesus and the Disciples according to the Fourth Gospel: With Implications for the Fourth Gospel's Purpose and the Mission of the Contemporary Church* (Grand Rapids: Eerdmans).

— (2004), *John*, Baker Exegetical Commentary on the New Testament (Grand Rapids: Baker Academic).

Kotansky, R. (2000), 'Demonology', in Evans and Porter, *Dictionary of New Testament Background*, 269–273.

Kovacs, J. L. (1995), '"Now Shall the Ruler of This World Be Driven Out": Jesus' Death as Cosmic Battle in John 12:20–36', *Journal of Biblical Literature* 114.2: 227–247.

Kraft, C. H. (1995), '"Christian Animism" or God-Given Authority?', in Rommen, *Spiritual Power and Missions*, 88–136.

Kruse, C. G. (2000), *The Letters of John* (Grand Rapids: Eerdmans).

Kuemmerlin-McLean, J. K. (1992), 'Demons: Old Testament', in Freedman, *Anchor Bible Dictionary*, 2: 138–140.

— (1992), 'Magic – Old Testament', in Freedman, *Anchor Bible Dictionary*, 4: 468–471.

Lausanne Movement, 'Deliver us from Evil – Consultation Statement, 2000'; Nairobi Consultation, <http://www.lausanne.org/nairobi-2000/consultation-statement.html>, accessed 30 July 2008.

Léon-Dufour, X. (1973), 'Magic', in Léon-Dufour, *Dictionary of Biblical Theology*, 327–328.

— (ed.) (1973), *Dictionary of Biblical Theology*, 2nd ed. (Boston: St Paul's Books, repr. 1995).

Lincoln, A. T. (1990), *Ephesians*, Word Biblical Commentary 42 (Dallas: Word).

— (2000), *Truth on Trial* (Peabody: Hendrickson).

Lindstrom, H. (1980), *Wesley and Sanctification: A Study in the Doctrine of Salvation* (Grand Rapids: Francis Asbury).

Lovejoy, A. O. (1933), *The Great Chain of Being: A Study of the History of an Idea* (New York: Harper, repr. 1965).

Lövestam, E. (1963), *Spiritual Wakefulness in the New Testament*, Lunds universitets årsskrift (Lund: Gleerup).

Luther, M. (1883–1983), *D. Martin Luthers Werke: Kritische Gesamtausgabe, Schriften*, ed. J. K. F. Knaake, G. Kawerau et al., 61 vols. plus indexes (Weimar: Hermann Böhlaus Nachfolger).

— (1955–86), *Luther's Works*, ed. J. Pelikan and H. T. Lehman, 55 vols. (Philadelphia: Fortress).

— (1957), 'Sermon on the Twofold Righteousness', in *Luther's Works*. Vol. 31: *Career of the Reformer I*, tr. L. J. Satre (Philadelphia: Fortress), 297–306.

Lyonnet, S. (1973), 'Satan', in Léon-Dufour, *Dictionary of Biblical Theology*, 522–523.

McCaughey, D. (1985), 'Matthew 6.13a. The Sixth Petition in the Lord's Prayer', *Australian Biblical Review* 33: 31–40.

McCormack, B. L. (2006), '*Justitia aliena*: Karl Barth in Conversation with the Evangelical Doctrine of Imputed Righteousness', in B. L. McCormack (ed.), *Justification in Perspective: Historical Developments and Contemporary Challenges* (Grand Rapids: Baker), 167–196.

McGrath, A. E. (2005), *Iustitia Dei: A History of the Christian Doctrine of Justification*, 3rd ed. (Cambridge: Cambridge University Press).

MacGregor, G. H. C. (1954–5), 'Principalities and Powers: The Cosmic Background of Paul's Thought', *New Testament Studies* 1: 17–28.

Maltby, H. S. (1913), *The Reasonableness of Hell* (Santa Cruz: n.p.).

Marett, A., L. Barwick and L. Ford (2001), Booklet accompanying Bobby Lane, *Rak Badjalarr: Wangga Songs from North Peron Island* (Canberra: Aboriginal Studies).

Marshall, I. H. (1978), *The Epistles of St John* (Grand Rapids: Eerdmans).

Martin, R. P. (1986), *2 Corinthians*, Word Biblical Commentary 40 (Waco: Word).

Michaels, J. R. (1989), *John*, New International Biblical Commentary (Peabody: Hendrickson).

Moberly, R. W. L. (1988), 'Did the Serpent Get it Right?', *Journal of Theological Studies* 39.1: 1–27.

Moloney, F. J. (1998), *The Gospel of John*, Sacra pagina (Collegeville, Minn.: Liturgical).

Moreau, A. S. (1996), 'Demon', in Elwell, *Evangelical Dictionary of Biblical Theology*, 163–165.

Murphy, E. F. (2003), *The Handbook for Spiritual Warfare*, rev. ed. (Nashville: T. Nelson).

Myland, D. W. (1985), 'The Latter Rain Covenant', in D. Dayton (ed.), *Three Early Pentecostal Tracts* (New York: Garland), 1–222.

Noll, S. (1998), *Angels of Light: Powers of Darkness* (Leicester: IVP).

O'Brien, P. T. (1982), *Colossians, Philemon*, Word Biblical Commentary 44 (Nashville: T. Nelson).

— (1984), 'Principalities and Powers: Opponents of the Church', in D. A. Carson (ed.), *Biblical Interpretation and the Church: Text and Context* (Exeter: Paternoster), 110–150.

— (1999), *The Letter to the Ephesians*, Pillar New Testament Commentary (Grand Rapids: Eerdmans; Leicester: Apollos).

O'Mathúna, D. P. (2003), 'Divination, Magic', in Alexander and Baker, *Dictionary of the Old Testament Pentateuch*, 193–197.

Ott, C., and H. A. Netland (eds.) (2006), *Globalizing Theology: Belief and Practice in an Era of World Christianity* (Grand Rapids: Baker).

Painter, J. (2007), 'Memory Holds the Key: The Transformation of Memory in the Interface of History and Theology in John', in P. N. Anderson, F. Just, S. J. Thatcher and T. Thatcher (eds.), *Jesus, John, and History*. Vol. 1: *Critical Appraisals of Critical Views* (Atlanta: Society of Biblical Literature), 229–245.

Palmer, P. (1856), *The Way of Holiness* (London: Heylin).

Pao, D. W. (2002), *Thanksgiving: An Investigation of a Pauline Theme*, New Studies in Biblical Theology 13 (Leicester: Apollos).

Parker, S. B. (1999), 'Council', in Van der Toorn, Becking and Van der Horst, *Dictionary of Deities and Demons*, 204–208.

Parsons, M. (2007), 'Binding the Strong Man: The Flaw of the Excluded Middle', in Riddell and Riddell, *Angels and Demons*, 106–125.

Pausanias (1935), *Description of Greece*, vol. 4. *Books VIII (22)–X*, tr. W. H. S. Jones, Loeb Classical Library (Cambridge, Mass.: Harvard University Press; London: W. H. Heinemann, repr. 1979).

Penney, D. L., and M. O. Wise (1994), 'By the Power of Beelzebub: An Aramaic Incantation Formula from Qumran (4Q560)', *Journal of Biblical Literature* 113: 627–650.

Penn-Lewis, J. (1912), *War on the Saints: A Text Book for Believers on the Work of Deceiving Spirits among the Children of God* (London: Overcomers Book Room).

Peretti, F. (1986), *This Present Darkness* (Westchester, Ill.: Crossway).

— (1989), *Piercing the Darkness* (Westchester, Ill.: Crossway).

— (1992), *Prophet* (Wheaton, Ill.: Crossway).

Peters, T. (1994), 'Satanism: Bunk or Blasphemy?', *Theology Today* 51.3: 381–393.

Peterson, D. G. (2000), 'Maturity: The Goal of Mission', in P. G. Bolt and M. D. Thompson (eds.), *The Gospel to the Nations: Perspectives on Paul's Mission* (Leicester: Apollos), 185–204.

Peterson, D. L. (1979), 'Genesis 6:1–4, Yahweh and the Organization of the Cosmos', *Journal for the Study of the Old Testament* 13: 47–64.

Piper, J. (2002), *Counted Righteous in Christ: Should We Abandon the Imputation of Christ's Righteousness?* (Wheaton: Crossway; Leicester: IVP).

Piper, R. (2000), 'Satan, Demons and the Absence of Exorcisms in the Fourth Gospel', in D. G. Horrell and C. M. Tuckett (eds.), *Christology, Controversy and Community: New Testament Essays in Honour of David R. Catchpole* (Leiden: Brill), 253–278.

Plumer, E. (1997), 'The Absence of Exorcisms in the Fourth Gospel', *Biblica* 78: 350–368.

Plutarch (1936), *Plutarch's Moralia*. Vol. 5: *De defectu oraculorum*, tr. F. C. Babbitt, Loeb Classical Library (Cambridge, Mass.: Harvard University Press; London: W. Heinemann, repr. 1969).

— (1959), *Plutarch's Moralia*. Vol. 7: *De genio Socratis*, tr. P. H. de Lacy and B. Einarson, Loeb Classical Library (Cambridge, Mass.: Harvard University Press; London: W. Heinemann, repr. 1968).

Powers, D. G. (2001), *Salvation through Participation: An Examination of the Notion of the Believers' Corporate Unity with Christ in Early Christian Soteriology* (Leuven: Peeters).

Powers, J. E. (2001), 'A "Thorn in the Flesh": The Appropriation of Textual Meaning', *Journal of Pentecostal Theology* 18: 85–99.

Preisendanz, K., and A. Henrichs (eds.) (1973–4), *Papyri Graecae Magicae: Die griechischen Zauberpapyri*, 2 vols. (Stuttgart: Teubner).

Priest, R. J., T. Campbell and B. A. Mullan (1995), 'Missiological Syncretism', in Rommen, *Spiritual Power and Missions*, 9–87.

Prince, D. (n.d.), *Expelling Demons: An Introduction into Practical Demonology* (no publication details given).

— (2001), *Complete Salvation and How to Receive It* (n.p.: DPM-International).

Rad, G. von (1975), *Old Testament Theology*, tr. D. M. G. Stalker (London: SCM).

Rainbow Spirit Elders (2007), *Rainbow Spirit Theology*, 2nd ed. (Adelaide: Australian Theological Forum).

Reinhard, D. R. (2005), 'Ephesians 6:10–18: A Call to Personal Piety or Another Way of Describing Union with Christ?', *Journal of the Evangelical Theological Society* 48: 521–532.

Riddell, P. G., and B. S. Riddell (eds.) (2007), *Angels and Demons: Perspectives and Practice in Diverse Religious Traditions* (Leicester: Apollos).

Ridderbos, H. (1997), *The Gospel of John: A Theological Commentary*, tr. J. Vriend (Grand Rapids: Eerdmans).

Riley, G. J. (1999), 'Devil', in Van der Toorn, Becking and Van der Horst, *Dictionary of Deities and Demons*, 244–249.

Robinson, D. W. B. (1997), 'Origins and Unresolved Tensions', in R. J. Gibson, (ed.), *Interpreting God's Plan: Biblical Theology and the Pastor* (Carlisle: Paternoster; Adelaide: Openbook), 1–17.

— (2008), 'The Gospel and the Kingdom of God', in P. G. Bolt and M. D. Thompson (eds.), *Donald Robinson: Selected Works*. Vol. 1: *Assembling God's People* (Camperdown, NSW: Australian Church Record/Moore College), 388–408.

Rommen, E. (ed.) (1995), *Spiritual Power and Missions: Raising the Issues*, Evangelical Missiological Society Series 3 (Pasadena: William Carey Library).

Rosner, B. S. (1998), 'The Progress of the Word', in I. H. Marshall and D. G. Peterson (eds.), *Witness to the Gospel: Theology of Acts* (Grand Rapids: Eerdmans), 216–233.

Russell, J. B. (1981), *Satan: The Early Christian Tradition* (Ithaca: Cornell University Press).

Ryle, J. C. (1879), *Holiness* (London: Hunt).

Salier, B. (1997), 'What's in a World? κόσμος in the Prologue of John's Gospel', *Reformed Theological Review* 56.3: 105–117.

— (2008), 'The Obedient Son: The "Faithfulness" of Christ in the Fourth Gospel', in M. Bird and P. Sprinkle (eds.), *The Faith of Jesus Christ: Exegetical, Biblical, and Theological Studies* (Carlisle: Paternoster), 267–285.

Sandford, J., and M. Sandford (1992), *A Comprehensive Guide to Deliverance and Inner Healing* (Grand Rapids: Chosen).

Schnabel, E. J. (2006), *Die erste Brief des Paulus an die Korinther*, Historisch Theologische Auslegung. Neues Testament (Wuppertal: Brockhaus; Giessen: Brunnen).

Schnackenburg, R. (1968, 1980, 1982), *The Gospel according to John*, tr. K. Smyth, 3 vols. (London: Burns & Oates).

Schweitzer, A. (1998), *The Mysticism of Paul the Apostle*, tr. W. Montgomery (Baltimore: Johns Hopkins University Press).

Schweizer, E. (1982), *The Letter to the Colossians: A Commentary*, tr. A. Chester (Minneapolis: Augsburg).

Scotland, N. (2007), 'The Charismatic Devil: Demonology in Charismatic Christianity', in Riddell and Riddell, *Angels and Demons*, 84–105.

Scurlock, J. A. (1992), 'Magic – Ancient Near East', in Freedman, *Anchor Bible Dictionary*, 4: 464–468.

Seifrid, M. A. (2004), 'Paul's Use of Righteousness Language against its Hellenistic Background', in Carson, O'Brien and Seifrid, *Justification and Variegated Nomism*, 2: 39–74.

Silvoso, E. (1994), *That None Should Perish: How to Reach Entire Cities for Christ Through Prayer Evangelism* (Ventura: Regal).

Spender, R. D. (1996), 'Idol, Idolatry', in Elwell, *Evangelical Dictionary of Biblical Theology*, 363–365.

Sperling, S. D. (1999), 'Belial', in Van der Toorn, Becking and Van der Horst, *Dictionary of Deities and Demons*, 169–171.

Sperry, L. (2000), *Ministry and Community: Recognizing Healing and Preventing Ministry Impairment* (Collegeville, Minn.: Liturgical).

Stanley, D. M. (1973), *Boasting in the Lord: The Phenomenon of Prayer in Saint Paul* (New York: Paulist).

Stendahl, K. (1963), 'The Apostle Paul and the Introspective Conscience of the West', *Harvard Theological Review* 56: 199–215.

Stoops, R. F., Jr. (1992), 'Simon [Magus]', in Freedman, *Anchor Bible Dictionary*, 6: 29–31.

Stuhlmacher, P. (1995), *How to Do Biblical Theology*, Pittsburgh Theological Monograph Series 38 (Allison Park, Pa.: Pickwick).

Tacitus (1970), *Agricola. Germania. Dialogues*, tr. W. Peterson, rev. M. Winterbottom, Loeb Classical Library (London: W. Heinemann; Cambridge, Mass.: Harvard University Press).

Tannehill, R. C. (2006), *Dying and Rising with Christ: A Study in Pauline Theology* (Eugene, Oreg.: Wipf & Stock).

Thiselton, A. C. (2007), *The Hermeneutics of Doctrine* (Grand Rapids: Eerdmans).

Thompson, M. M. (2005), *Colossians and Philemon*, The Two Horizons New Testament Commentary (Grand Rapids: Eerdmans).

Thrall, M. E. (1994, 2000), *A Critical and Exegetical Commentary on the Second Epistle to the Corinthians*, International Critical Commentary, 2 vols. (Edinburgh: T. & T. Clark).

Tiénou, T. (2006), 'Christian Theology in an Era of World Christianity', in C. Ott and H. A. Netland (eds.), *Globalizing Theology: Belief and Practice in an Era of World Christianity* (Grand Rapids: Baker), 37–51.

Tinker, M. (2000), 'The Phantom Menace, Territorial Spirits and SLSW', *Churchman* 114: 71–81.

Tonstad, S. K. (2008), '"The Father of Lies," "The Mother of lies," and the Death of Jesus (John 12:20–33)', in R. Bauckham and C. Mosser (eds.), *The Gospel of John and Christian Theology* (Grand Rapids: Eerdmans), 193–208.

Toorn, K. van der, B. Becking and P. W. van der Horst (eds.) (1999), *Dictionary of Deities and Demons in the Bible*, 2nd ed. (Leiden: Brill; Grand Rapids: Eerdmans).

Torijano, P. A. (2002), *Solomon, the Esoteric King: From King to Magus, Development of a Tradition* (Leiden: Brill).

Torrance, T. F. (1965), 'Justification: Its Radical Nature and Place in Reformed Doctrine and Life', in *Theology in Reconstruction* (London: SCM), 150–168.

Travis, J., and A. Travis (2008), 'Deep-Level Healing Prayer in Cross-Cultural Ministry', in Van Engen, Whiteman and Woodberry, *Paradigm Shifts in Christian Witness*, 106–115.

Turretin, F. (1994), *Institutes of Elenctic Theology*. Vol. 2: *Eleventh Through Seventeenth Topics*, tr. G. M. Giger, ed. J. T. Dennison (Phillipsburg: Presbyterian & Reformed).

Twelftree, G. H. (1993), *Jesus the Exorcist: A Contribution to the Study of the Historical Jesus* (Peabody, Mass.; Hendrickson).

— (2007), *In the Name of Jesus: Exorcism Among Early Christians* (Grand Rapids: Baker Academic).

Unger, M. F. (1952), *Biblical Demonology: A Study of the Spiritual Forces Behind the Present World Unrest* (Wheaton, Ill.: Scripture Press).

Vanhoozer, K. J. (2006), '"One Rule to Rule Them All?": Theological Method in an Era of World Christianity', in C. Ott and H. A. Netland (eds.), *Globalizing Theology: Belief and Practice in an Era of World Christianity* (Grand Rapids: Baker), 85–126.

Vos, G. (1975), *Biblical Theology: Old and New Testaments* (Edinburgh: Banner of Truth).

Vriezen, T. C. (1958), *An Outline of Old Testament Theology* (Oxford: Blackwell).

Wagner, C. P. (1991), *Engaging the Enemy: How to Fight and Defeat Territorial Spirits* (Ventura, Calif.: Regal).

— (1992), *Prayer Shield: How to Intercede for Pastors, Christian Leaders, and Others on the Spiritual Frontlines* (Ventura, Calif.: Regal).

— (1996), *Confronting the Powers: How the New Testament Church Experienced the Power of Strategic-Level Spiritual Warfare* (Ventura, Calif.: Regal).

— (ed.) (1991), *Territorial Spirits: Insights on Strategic-Level Spiritual Warfare from Nineteen Christian Leaders* (Chichester: Sovereign World).

— (ed.) (1993), *Breaking Strongholds in Your City: How to Use Spiritual Mapping to Make Your Prayers More Strategic, Effective and Targeted* (Ventura, Calif.: Regal).

Wahlde, U. von (1982), 'The Johannine "Jews": A Critical Survey', *New Testament Studies* 28: 33–60.

Wallace, D. B. (1996), *Greek Grammar Beyond the Basics* (Grand Rapids: Zondervan).

Walker, A. (1995), 'The Devil you Think you Know', in T. Smail, A. Walker and N. Wright (eds.), *Charismatic Renewal: The Search for a Theology* (London: SPCK), 86–108.

Walton, F. R. (1970), 'After-Life', in N. G. L. Hammond and H. H. Scullard (eds.), *Oxford Classical Dictionary*, 2nd ed. (Oxford: Clarendon, repr. 1991), 23–24.

Walton, J. H. (2003), 'Serpent', in Alexander and Baker, *Dictionary of the Old Testament Pentateuch*, 736–739.

Watson, W. G. E. (1999), 'Helel', in Van der Toorn, Becking and Van der Horst, *Dictionary of Deities and Demons*, 392–394.

Wesley, J. (1952), *Plain Account of Christian Perfection* (London: Epworth).

West, D. S. (2008), 'Petitionary Prayer in the "Now" and "Not Yet"', in P. G. Bolt and M. D. Thompson (eds.), *Donald Robinson – Selected Works: Appreciation* (Camperdown, NSW: Australian Church Record/Moore College), 235–240.

— (2008), 'Promises to and Limitations upon Prayer in the New Testament: A Study of Their Relationship' (PhD diss., Edith Cowan University).

Wiéner, C. (1973), 'Idols', in Léon-Dufour, *Dictionary of Biblical Theology*, 251–252.

Wiles, G. P. (1974), *Paul's Intercessory Prayers: The Significance of the Intercessory Prayer Passages in the Letters of Paul*, Society for New Testament Studies Monograph Series 24 (Cambridge: Cambridge University Press).

Woodberry, J. D. (2008), 'Power and Blessing', in Van Engen, Whiteman and Woodberry, *Paradigm Shifts in Christian Witness*, 98–105.

Woodhouse, J. W. (2008), *1 Samuel: Looking for a Leader*, Preaching the Word (Wheaton: Crossway).

Wright, N. G. (1996), 'Charismatic Interpretations of the Demonic', in A. N. S. Lane (ed.), *The Spiritual Word* (Carlisle: Paternoster; Grand Rapids: Baker), 149–163.

— (2003), *A Theology of the Dark Side* (Carlisle: Paternoster).

Yarborough, R. W. (1996), 'Biblical Theology', in Elwell, *Evangelical Dictionary of Biblical Theology*, 61–66.

# INDEX OF SCRIPTURE REFERENCES AND OTHER ANCIENT SOURCES

# Exploring EXODUS

Exploring EXODUS
Literary, theological and contemporary approaches

Edited by Brian S. Rosner and Paul R. Williamson

This volume, based on the 2007 Moore College School of Theology, acknowledges that reading Exodus for all its worth, as a witness to the gospel and as wisdom for Christian living, is an enormous challenge. The book's appeal for today is unmistakable, in terms of its epic scope and moral complexity.

The opening chapter surveys the 'uses, re-uses and misuses' of Exodus in contemporary culture, and exhorts us to feel the book's raw power,

by facing squarely its moral challenges and being shaped by its sometimes bewildering theology.

In response, subsequent chapters explore major units of the text and the main theological and ethical issues that they raise. Topics covered are the exodus event itself; its significance in contemporary theologies of liberation; Moses at Sinai; the Law in Exodus; the tabernacle; and how we should preach Exodus.

ISBN:
978-1-84474-313-1

Available from your local Christian bookshop or via our website at **www.ivpbooks.com**

NEW STUDIES IN BIBLICAL THEOLOGY

# The Cross
# from a Distance

## Atonement in Mark's Gospel

Peter G. Bolt

Series Editor: D. A. Carson

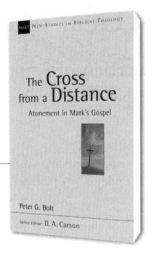

At the climax of Mark's Gospel, Jesus of Nazareth is put to death on a Roman cross. The text tells us that, in that lonely hour, a group of women were watching the crucifixion 'from a distance'. In a sense, they are given a stance towards the cross that we can share. It is an event that occurred so long ago, in a world that in many ways seems so foreign to our own.

In this exploration of Mark's Gospel, Peter Bolt looks at why the cross is so prominent in the narrative; asks what contribution Mark's teaching can make to our understanding of the atonement; and shows how this teaching can inform, correct and enrich our own preaching of the gospel in the contemporary world. He helps us to stand in wonder before the God who has come close to us in the cross of Jesus Christ, and to live in hope of the better things to come.

ISBN:
978-1-84474-049-9

Available from your local Christian bookshop or via our website at www.ivpbooks.com

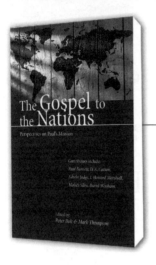

# The **Gospel** to the **Nations**

*Edited by Peter Bolt &
Mark Thompson*

The mission of the apostle Paul, to proclaim the gospel to the nations, continues to be of vital relevance for the Christian church at the beginning of the twenty-first century. By Paul's own testimony, the gospel he was set apart to preach focused on Jesus Christ, crucified and risen, as the fulfilment of God's promises (Romans 1:1–13). Hence if we are to be true to the apostle, we must seek to understand his mission and message from the perspective of biblical theology.

This impressive collection explores facets of such a perspective, under four broad headings: the Old Testament background to Paul's mission; New Testament studies; the wider context of the world in which Paul's message was proclaimed; and the use of that message in history and contemporary thought. These essays offer fresh and important contributions to Pauline studies, and were commissioned in honour of Peter T. O'Brien (Moore College, Sydney), who has made Paul's concerns his own through distinguished scholarship and personal ministry.

ISBN:
978-0-85111-468-2

Available from your local Christian bookshop
or via our website at **www.ivpbooks.com**

**BST** The Bible Speaks Today

## THE MESSAGE OF
# EVIL AND SUFFERING

Evil and suffering may be a mystery to us, but they are not a mystery to God. The Bible writers have no time for an unreal idealism, in which the life of faith is free from anguish, pain and perplexity. They are confident that God's power and wisdom are great enough not just to cope with the realities of suffering and evil, but to overcome and transform them, and to enable us to be 'more than conquerors' in a broken and hurting world.

With warmth and clarity, Peter Hicks expounds a range of relevant biblical texts that enable us to set the issue of evil and suffering firmly in the context of the nature and purposes of God. Central to his approach is the conviction that the key lies in the cross and resurrection of Jesus Christ, the suffering and triumph of God himself. In valuable practical sections he explores the Bible's teaching on how we are to live in a world of evil and suffering.

ISBN:
978-1-84474-148-9

Available from your local Christian bookshop or via our website at www.ivpbooks.com

www.ivpbooks.com

For more details of books published by IVP, visit our website where you will find all the latest information, including:

Book extracts          Downloads
Author interviews      Online bookshop
Reviews                Christian bookshop finder

You can also sign up for our regular email newsletters, which are tailored to your particular interests, and tell others what you think about this book by posting a review.

We publish a wide range of books on various subjects including:

Christian living          Small-group resources
Key reference works       Topical issues
Bible commentary series   Theological studies